Theater and Crisis

Theater and Crisis

MYTH, MEMORY, AND RACIAL RECKONING IN AMERICA, 1964–2020

Patrice D. Rankine

LEVER
PRESS

Copyright © 2024 by Patrice D. Rankine

Lever Press (leverpress.org) is a publisher of pathbreaking scholarship. Supported by a consortium of higher education institutions focused on, and renowned for, excellence in both research and teaching, our press is grounded on three essential commitments: to be a digitally native press, to be a peer-reviewed, open access press that charges no fees to either authors or their institutions, and to be a press aligned with the liberal arts ethos.

This work is licensed under the Creative Commons Attribution-NonCommercial 4.0 International License. To view a copy of this license, visit http://creativecommons.org/licenses/by-nc/4.0/ or send a letter to Creative Commons, PO Box 1866, Mountain View, CA 94042, USA.

The complete manuscript of this work was subjected to a closed ("double-blind") review process. For more information, please see our Peer Review Commitments and Guidelines at https://www.leverpress.org/peerreview

DOI: https://doi.org/10.3998/mpub.14330085
Print ISBN: 978-1-64315-059-8
Open access ISBN: 978-1-64315-060-4

Library of Congress Control Number: 2024930517

Published in the United States of America by Lever Press, in partnership with Michigan Publishing.

To the children breaking glass. Theirs is still the Kingdom of Heaven.

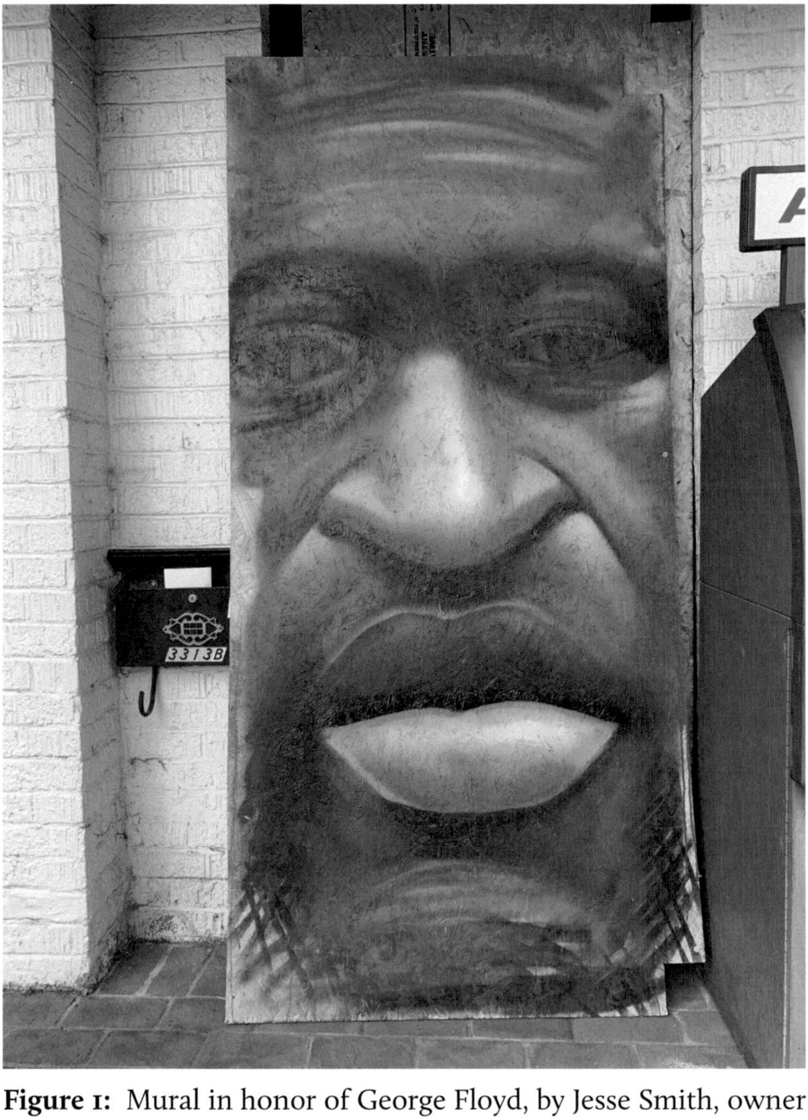

Figure 1: Mural in honor of George Floyd, by Jesse Smith, owner of Loose Screw Tattoo, Richmond, VA.

Contents

Member Institution Acknowledgments

Lever Press is a joint venture. This work was made possible by the generous support of Lever Press member libraries from the following institutions:

Amherst College
Berea College
Bowdoin College
Carleton College
Central Washington University
Claremont Graduate University
Claremont McKenna College
Clark Atlanta University
College of Saint Benedict & Saint John's University
The College of Wooster
Davidson College
Denison University
DePauw University
Grinnell College
Hamilton College
Hampshire College
Harvey Mudd College
Hollins University
Iowa State University
Keck Graduate Institute
Knox College
Lafayette College
Macalester College
Middlebury College
Morehouse College
Norwich University
Occidental College
Penn State University
Pitzer College
Pomona College
Randolph-Macon College
Rollins College
Santa Clara University
Scripps College

Skidmore College
Smith College
Spelman College
Susquehanna University
Swarthmore College
Trinity University
UCLA Library
Union College
University of Idaho
University of Northern Colorado
University of Puget Sound
University of Rhode Island
University of San Francisco
University of Vermont
Ursinus College
Vassar College
Washington and Lee University
Whitman College
Whittier College
Willamette University
Williams College

Acknowledgments

I am certain that there will be many pandemic-born books emerging out of the watershed that was 2020. I am hopeful that by extending back in time over half a century, *Theater and Crisis* does more than reflect on 2020. For what the book is and offers, I have many people and institutions to thank.

Lectures and roundtable discussions by videoconferencing proliferated during the pandemic, and I was fortunate to have been invited to lead many of them, which served both to spark my intellectual curiosity beyond the administrative work I had been doing, and also to develop and hone my initial reactions to the events of the day. I thank Ellen O'Gorman, Director for the Institute for Greece, Rome, and the Classical Tradition, and the colleagues at the University of Bristol for the invitation to deliver the 2021 Morse Lecture, where I presented an earlier version of my work on the relationship between James Baldwin's *Blues for Mister Charlie* and Aeschylus' *Oresteia*. The conversation helped me to develop the connection further while allowing the space between the two authors to breathe. The City University Core Books workshop provided a similar opportunity to explore how we might teach these authors, which had been my initial intention when I began writing in March 2020. I thank Andrea Fabrizio and

Gregory Marks for that invitation. Sarah Olsen at Williams College invited me to speak in her class on tragedy during that first year of the pandemic. Having delivered that Zoom presentation under the haze of a COVID vaccine, my hope is that the chapter on the Tectonic Theater Project's *Laramie Cycle Plays* is more coherent than what I said to Professor Olsen's students on that evening. Dorothy Kim invited me to take part in the September 2020 Race Before Race symposium hosted by Brandeis University but taking place on Zoom. I presented a small portion of my work on the relationship between Jean-Jacques Rousseau, August Wilson, and Alan Bloom at that symposium. I would also like to thank Lillian Doherty for inviting me to be part of the conference on Oedipus in honor of Gregory A. Staley, where I began to work out questions that have become central to this book.

As we returned to normalcy (or our new norm) in the fall of 2022, I presented aspects of the chapter on Oedipus and Black youth in the 1980s and 1990s online for the Dartmouth University Zarbin Lecture in Classics. I thank Roberta L. Stewart for the invitation and the colleagues and students for attending and raising stimulating questions—and especially one student who sensed the anti-Oedipus strand without my even saying it. Julie Hejduk, Ken Jones, and the colleagues at Baylor University were among my first in-person lectures in the fall of 2022. I thank them for the invitation to their conference, "Classics and Classical Education in the Black Community." They and my fellow panelists indulged the radicalism of my ideas on Euripides' *Bacchae*, Wole Soyinka, and Amiri Baraka's Dionysiac destructiveness. Although I'm sure a Black radical strand was not the intention of the organizers, I thank them for their engagement, and Alden Smith raised a compelling connection to Euripides' *Cyclops* that I had not considered and am still interested in pursuing. Last but not least, in the category of lectures and invitations, I thank Jacquelyn Fetrow, President at Albright College, for inviting me to be part of the 2022 Empowering Albright Voices, where I had the opportunity to test the central idea of this book: that narratives, classical and otherwise, are encoded in memory, visually and narratively, as epiphanic.

I have been fortunate to be affiliated with several outstanding institutions across my career as an educator. I am grateful to the provost's office at University of Richmond for recognizing my need to conduct scholarship even while serving as Dean for the School of Arts & Sciences and for providing ongoing research funds to travel, do research, and for other forms of professional development. During that period, Dawn Barrett served not only as an outstanding professional coach, but she also introduced me to research on group psychodynamics, which subsequently influenced both how I approached my role as Dean and how I was conceiving of race and other political or collective phenomena. At the University of Chicago, I arrived at an institution where I have been able to stretch and become comfortable with the interdisciplinary, field-expanding approaches that I had always taken, but with which I never quite felt completely at ease. I am grateful for the colleagues in the Department of Classics; those in the Division of Humanities, and in particular Dean Anne Robertson. The Franke Institute and the Institute on the Formation of Knowledge have each provided a storybook intellectual environment, as have the workshops in classics. Outside of the university, I am grateful to Brandon Carter, artistic director of the American Shakespeare Center for producing Antoinette Nwandu's *Pass Over* and for indulging me in a conversation about this unorthodox choice for the little hamlet in Staunton, Virginia.

From Lever Press, Beth Bouloukos kindly ran what was an annual publishing forum that I offered the faculty at the University of Richmond in the School of Arts & Sciences. Not only was I eager to invite Richmond into a consortium of colleges supporting open access (a goal I did not accomplish), but I also began to think about the kind of work I might like to produce on such a platform. Once I proposed a topic, Hannah Brooks-Motl shepherded the project along through peer review. I thank the two anonymous reviewers for their kindness on what was a very undercooked offering, but I am also indebted to Hannah for her close reading, diplomacy, and generosity of time and spirit. Although Beth and Hannah are now involved in other projects at Amherst College Press, Sean Guynes has stepping in without missing a beat. I am grateful to the University of Michigan for his time, commitment, and responsiveness. He made the journey home easy and safe.

I return, in this dedication and as a constant of my life, to my wonderful, loving family, and to the mythic ties that provided my first images and stories. These include the experiences and memories of my steadfast mother and father, Patricia and George Rankine; my beautiful and brilliant sister, Clarel Rankine Shaw and her husband Phillip; my nephew Donovan (Donte) Shaw; and all of the Rankines, Crooks, and Farquharsons who have always been there, no matter what. My partner Rania Sweis believed in this project even when it was unfathomable. To her, for her patience and constancy, I owe more than she can ever fathom. During the pandemic, Jordan became my Zion, as Lauren Hill might put it, the joy of our lives. And thanks go even to Julien, who has now made his way home.

Preface

Theater and Crisis considers race and American drama from 1964–2020 in light of the retrospective illumination that the global pandemic provided. Although I draw from events that occurred in 2020 to revisit the recent past, I propose an understanding of image, myth, and memory that transcends the historical and local particularities. I argue that the happenings in the United States leading to talk of "racial reckoning" mask a deeper anxiety of identity that is mythic and psychological, requiring the tools of dramatic, literary, and psychoanalytic analysis, which provide a complementary accounting to history, political philosophy and sociology, or scientific study.[1] The collective projections onto recent American figure like George Floyd or Kyle Rittenhouse are manifestations of these anxieties. As media generated and produced icons with accompanying stories that resonate with broader publics, I name these manifestations "epiphanic encoding," a term that encapsulates both the visual and narrative aspects of their significance, the quasi-religious following that the figures have engendered, their role in triggering longstanding individual and collective memories, and in producing new ones.

Throughout *Theater and Crisis*, I use the terms "America" and "American" to designate the U.S. and its broader cultures.

I recognize that the term "America" also applies to Canada, and Central and South America. For the purposes of *Theater and Crisis*, I focus on the U.S., the fifty states but also the imagined continuity across these localities that any nation presumes of itself.[2] As *Theater and Crisis* is concerned with the idea of racial reckoning in the U.S., I refer throughout to categories of white and Black Americans. I recognize these antiphonal categories do not comprise the fullness of identities across the country, which include Native, Asian, Hispanic and Latino populations. "BIPOC" is a relatively recent category that has come to comprise Black, Indigenous, and People of Color, but BIPOC is not immune from criticism. After a spate of violence against Asian people in the U.S. during the pandemic, "AAPI," Asian American and Pacific Islanders, came into more popular usage. Notwithstanding the urgency of claims in the public domain from each of these groups, the divide between Black and white Americans continues to shape broader conversations about diversity and racial reconciliation across the country. As such, the antiphonal categories are the focal point of *Theater and Crisis*. Although I use Black to refer to people of African descent, the focus on the ocular or visual register suggests that recent immigrants to the U.S. from countries across Africa or the Caribbean are read into existing perceptions of long-standing descendants of enslaved Africans brought to the continent beginning in the sixteenth century.[3] In the expanded nomenclature that became popular during the pandemic, the throwback "people of color" expanded a racial calling to all nonwhite people. Whiteness is a normative category that will be further clarified throughout the book.

As it pertains to 2020, to overstate the disruption in the U.S., indeed to world events, even history, of the novel coronavirus, or COVID-19, would be impossible. The World Health Organization (WHO) declared COVID-19 a global pandemic on March 11, 2020. Anticipating impending shifts, leaders across businesses, educational institutions, and workplaces in every industry made the move, sometimes sudden, to shut down in-person operations.

In addition to private decisions, the municipal "lockdown" (or "stay-at-home," or "shelter-in-place") orders circumscribed alternatives to physically attending schools or going to the office. From the beginning, people and communities would experience disparate impacts, as the designation of "essential workers" came to signal. As two examples, delivery personnel and factory workers in meat-processing facilities across industries reported high incidences of illness (see, e.g., Reuben 2020). The resurgence of workplace unions at such businesses as Amazon, Starbucks, and Apple has a direct correlation to the disruption that happened in 2020 and the subsequent return to work, even if there had already been unease beneath the surface prior to this.[4]

For many across the planet, COVID-19 forced unanticipated choices. Most individuals could, perhaps for the first time in their lives, determine from where they would remotely report to their places of work or schools. A spate of new decisions emerged. It will take some time to assess the staggering effects of these unprecedented circumstances, but in the immediate days, weeks, and months after March 11, 2020, families decamped from large cities like New York City, which was—immediately and directly—an "epicenter" for the virus.[5] Why keep the family in a cold climate when you might teleconference from the beach? Why go to work at all when retirement could be so proximate an option? The long-term consequences of this exodus on the City's economy, indeed that of world financial markets, had yet to be fully assessed more than two years after the initial event, notwithstanding the return of many individuals, families, and businesses to urban centers by July 2022.[6] Thus, the initial fork in the road that led to subsequent redirections, the "crisis" of this book's title, was COVID-19 and its effects on every sector of life, from the arts and education to business and commerce, the planning of families, and individual decisions about how best to live one's life. The image of a fork in the road, or a crossroad, well characterizes the choices that people and communities faced at the dawn of the pandemic.[7]

At the level of the individual, the turning point, the crisis, might not have begun on March 11, 2020, but the pandemic forced an unexpected urgency, an intensification of living and dying, which the news conferences, daily death-toll tallies, and reports of corpses on ice, piling up in trucks outside of NYC hospitals and funeral homes, reified.[8]

As it pertains to the arts, the theater industry would be among the most visible and symbolic in its initial reaction to the pandemic, although its complete shutdown would not prove to be permanent or fatal. On March 12, 2020, Broadway theaters in NYC closed their doors, a move that would "inevitably cost tens of millions of dollars for investors and artists and associated businesses."[9] The decision to stop productions was inevitable, given the disease's contagiousness and the gubernatorial and mayoral restrictions on mass gatherings. Along with other municipalities, NYC was in a state of emergency. Like concerts and festivals, live theater requires living human beings breathing the same air and responding to the same stimuli, a dangerous proposition during a pandemic. Along with other workers, some theater personnel channeled their energies into new avenues of expression, testing the drama's resilience and ability to adapt. On April 29, 2020, NYC's Public Theater broadcast the first new play during COVID-19 written and performed exclusively on a videoconferencing platform: *What Do We Need to Talk About?* The performance presented Richard Nelson's Apple family, not seen for a decade since the 2010 production of *That Hopey Changey Thing*, responding to the lockdown and various aspects of this new normal. The family's situation reflected what many people experienced during the pandemic's first month. Co-workers, schoolmates, families, and friends were gathering on Zoom not only in virtual meetings, but also at happy hours and dinners; stockpiling cleaning supplies and toilet paper, contributing to the supply chain issues that continued well into 2020, and altering their plans toward radical life changes. *What Do We Need to Talk About?* presented life as it was being lived by many, though in fictional, dramatized form. What the lasting impact of these new conditions for theater would be was a matter of ongoing speculation.

THEATERS OF AMERICAN CRISES

As I will discuss at the end of *Theater and Crisis*, Nelson's first pandemic play raised the prospect that the narrative and visual dimensions of drama could override, if even temporarily, its ritual aspects, by which I mean patrons traveling to the theater, interacting with other guests, being ushered to seats, silencing cellphones, and so on.[10] The Zoom experience, however, lacked bidirectionality; shared collective reactions were lacking. As can happen in crisis, moreover, the situation was evolving rapidly, and this first Apple Family Zoom play would be quickly dated, whether as an instant classic, or as passée. Real-life drama was upstaging crafted ones, which were likely too slow to hold the attention events themselves commanded. Notwithstanding the lockdowns, groups continued to gather across the globe, in some cases in direct protest of the local mandates that ostensibly restricted crowds. A drama of another order was being performed in the streets. People were gathering in demonstrations that surged across the globe, and these had ritual overtones as well. It will be some time before the immediate surge in demonstrations is fully studied,[11] but within the U.S., the unforeseen shifts surfaced existing tensions along the lines of state and federal authority, racial identity, and class. These demonstrations further evidenced the entangled, intertwined nature of many of the issues that protestors were raising. As early as April 15, 2020, there were signs of activity among U.S. conservative groups, members of which felt the pandemic mandates violated their constitutional rights.[12] Consistent with the impact of Zoom on workplace activity, technology and media were sites of promulgation, whether the May 7th protests in Indianapolis, Indiana, stemming from three deaths at the hands of police officers, or the May 8th murder of Ahmaud Arbery, which was captured on videotape.

When cellphone videos were posted to YouTube and other social media outlets after a Black man's life expired on May 25, 2020 under the suffocating pressure of a white police officer's knee, for some a watershed moment had occurred.[13] The story of George Floyd became global news. His death intensified movements that were building up during the first few months of the pandemic.

By early July 2020, Nelson broadcast his second lockdown edition of the Apple Family plays, *And So We Come Forth*. As I will discuss, the play was tentative on discussions of race, memory, and racial reconciliation, although it countenanced the protests. Theater is an active site for the performance of individual and collective identities, and Nelson's Apple Family plays presented some public hope that dramatic recitation would continue holding to form. Within a short time of the first play's broadcast in April, a document titled "BIPOC Demands for White American Theatre" (2020) appeared online, the work of several theater practitioners who saw the protests as an analytic tool for American theater. The document, which I discuss further in Chapter 1, will be a subtext throughout the book as a kind of therapeutic intervention that has recurred in theater in the U.S. since at least 1964. *And So We Come Forth*, despite the exacerbation with the toppling of monuments expressed in the play, makes no mention of the document or of George Floyd. The omissions belied the subtext of protest—and awareness of protest—throughout the broadcast.

Nelson's approach to current events was akin to not talking about the terminal illness of a family member, a metaphor from which he directly draws in *What Do We Need to Talk About?* For others living through the crisis, immediate and direct discussion was a more fitting approach. Responding to the murder of George Floyd, on May 28, 2020, Minneapolis City Council Vice President Andrea Jenkins asked that racism be declared a public health emergency:

> Until we name this virus, this disease that has infected America for the past 400 years, we will never, ever resolve this issue. To those who say bringing up racism is racist in and of itself, I say to you, if you don't call cancer what it is, you can never cure that disease. And so in an effort to try and cure this disease, I am stating exactly what everyone else has witnessed, and that is racism.[14]

By pointing to "the past 400 years," Jenkins traced the epidemiology of race in America to slavery and the mass trafficking of African people to the U.S., a blight that even the most intransigent American forebears recognized. In his 1781 *Notes on the State of Virginia* (Jefferson 2011), writing from the same Commonwealth where in 1619 enslaved Africans were first transported to Williamsburg to work the land, Thomas Jefferson warned that this scourge resulting from white people's treatment of the Black enslaved would not disappear without incident, speculating that the removal of Black people from the country was the only real remedy. Echoing Jefferson's diagnosis but diverging from his prescription, Jenkins asks that the country not hide from the issue but rather treat the scourge with the same vigor reserved for COVID-19, cancer, and other deadly diseases. To her, Floyd's murder was only the most recent evidence of recurring flare-ups of an insidious sickness across America.

Jenkins' broader point, her originalist analysis of American history, would come under scrutiny by the fall of 2021. Those resisting the analysis disagreed with the characterization of America as somehow inherently racist, nor did they condone the teaching of this idea to their children.[15] By this time, many schools across the U.S. were reopening their doors, and elected officials and prospective candidates running for elected office rejected the reading of a "cancer[ous]" society in need of remediation. They resisted the idea of deeper education around race, or the "defund[ing]" of the police departments at the center of national controversy for their treatment of Black people, who are also citizens. For the time being, however, the dire diagnosis of race in America would persist. Although Jenkins' was among the most notable uses of the language of disease and crisis for American life publicly, others followed suit. Responding to many days and nights of protest in Richmond, Virginia, the city's mayor Lavar Stoney told reporters at a press conference on June 4, regarding the removal of confederate statues: "We have two pandemics in this country, COVID-19 and racism."[16]

THE MAKING OF MYTH

As a scholar trained in classical languages and literatures, I was interested in how interlocutors on various sides of the arguments about America's racial reckoning were bound up in deeper symbolism. All parties were performing identities centuries in the making, whether they called on classical tropes, Christian ones, or others at the foundation of the country. During the January 6, 2021 events at the Capitol, some groups involved in protest would draw from a Greek slogan attributed to Spartans defending Thermopylae from the Persian invasion in 480 BCE, *molon labe* ("come and take it"), to assert their rejection of the authority of the federal government.[17] On the other side of the political divide, others draw the idea of slavery as an "original sin" from Christian language and imagery.[18] In other words, all parties act out scripts already present in a broader drama, each playing a part inflected from preexisting characters, roles, and settings. This is not to say that the drama does not change over time. In fact, the reality of time shapes the chronological approach of *Theater and Crisis*. But myth shifts the perspective and problematizes chronology. Rather than a metaphor of a terminal illness, like cancer, the psychoanalytic therapy that an individual person might experience is a more fitting analogy to the work of myth and memory in society.

As I will demonstrate throughout *Theater and Crisis*, even in the postmodern age of the twenty-first century, the U.S. remains a purveyor of Western traditions, which Judeo-Islamo-Christian and

Greco-Roman narratives primarily comprise. Myth is a category of experience that binds together the images and stories with which I am concerned. The story of Dionysus' birth by Zeus, expulsion from Thebes, and fateful return belongs in the category of myth, and for the purpose of this book, so does Moses' birth, his rearing in Egypt, the revelation that he is to be a leader of the Jewish people (in his encounter with God as a burning bush), and his exodus from Egypt along with the Hebrew people, whom the Pharaoh held in captivity.

Although the mythological quality of the Greco-Roman register might seem to be a given, to say that Judeo-Islamo-Christian narratives are myths is not to opine on their role in active belief systems, as Ciara Bottici affirms in *A Philosophy of Political Myth* (2007). In her discussion of Baruch Spinoza's treatment of the Biblical stories, we find that these stories, first,

> transmitted a moral message. Second, the story of their [the Jewish people's] chosenness, by addressing their particular needs, contributed to grounding – again in the sense of *begründen* – the specificity of their polity: theocracy. The biblical prophecy, by recalling the covenant with God to the Jews, made respecting the law appear as necessary.
>
> (Botticci 2007: 173)

Both as it pertains to their moral message and to this issue of grounding, the Biblical stories, as myths addressing "particular needs" through a "moral message," run parallel to classical ones in ways that professional classicists have by and large neglected because of the professional field's at-times artificial separation of Judeo-Islamo-Christian and Greco-Roman traditions. The merger of these registers in my treatment is unusual but elementary, once we identify what myth is and how it functions in the contemporary world. I will return to the issue of how these narratives serve in grounding, pivotal to Bottici's analysis, momentarily. First, to a definition.

If we accept the deep scholarship on the meaning of myth across time, of which Bottici is among the most relevant for my purposes in *Theater and Crisis*, we read the real-life George Floyd as a figure of political myth, owing to the distillation his life and death, its moral message and grounding within a particular social context, a broader public. To say that the narrative became myth is not to detract from the horrific events leading to Floyd's death or the fervent response to those events among various groups in the U.S. The analysis along the lines of myth strengthens our understanding of the images, narrative, and their meaning. The story of Kyle Rittenhouse, the Illinois resident who traveled to Kenosha, Wisconsin to protect businesses during social unrest and on August 25, 2020, killed two men and wounded another with an assault rifle, works in a similar way, as I will show by way of conclusion. It can be said that the ancient and contemporary figures, from Moses to Dionysus, Floyd to Rittenhouse, are imagined as embodiments of a narrative grounded in the present but calling upon ideas from the past. I am referring not to their lives as lived but rather to the symbols they became for a broader public, their spectacular, imaginary projections onto the world stage.[19] What matters in this latter context is the event's symbolic, or mythic (larger-than-life) significance, not what we might call its factual or historical truths, which, as we will see, is a false distinction. Although contemporary discourse retains the contrast between truth and falsehood when considering reality, or history, and fiction, the study of myth reveals that the categories works in culture in much more complex ways than the designation of falsehood, or lie, can account. It is also not sufficient to say that myth speaks to deeper truths about psychology, storytelling, cultural experience, and processes of history and memory, although this would be a necessary starting point.[20]

Bottici lays out a genealogy of myth that coincides with the work of Bruce Lincoln (see, e.g., Lincoln 2000). Their framework is worth a brief overview. Until the Platonic dialogues, the word "myth" (Greek *mythos*) is often parallel with—though not identical to—Greek *logos*, the latter coming to be associated with Christian doctrine, such as in its deployment in the Biblical book of John: "In the beginning was the Word (*logos*), and the *logos* was with God. And the *logos* was God" (John 1:1). Any contention in ancient Greek literature about myth (as *mythos*) is really a debate about authority, that is, who gets to influence people within the society. Traditional centers of authority include the poet (or artist), whose means of communication with the public is storytelling, for example, Aeschylus, Sophocles, or Euripides. The priest is another, whose line of authority for the message leads directly to the divine, and thus myth (*mythos*), as it were, is a kind of authoritative truth. In Plato's *Republic*, the ruler is to replace the old myths, those the poets and priests used to tell, with ones that better serve the community. Such useful myth is the work of a "noble lie" (*gennaion ti hen*, Plato, *Republic* 3, 414b–c), which Socrates conveys in the *Republic* through such examples as the allegory of the cave, a way of explaining the process that individuals and communities undertake toward discovering the truth. The poet, the priest, and the politician are all makers of myth.

As Bottici argues, until the Enlightenment, the necessity of myth was not in question. Church fathers, such as Origen, saw in myths allegories of ontology, or forms of knowledge. Christianity subsumed this epistemology. The story of Christ was the one true mystery to be unveiled, the revelation of *logos* as independent from myth, in Platonic fashion—not the noble lie, but the Forms, truth itself. In the triumph of Christianity was also the clarification of truth and reality, independent of the falsehoods that myth purportedly conveys. The Enlightenment was the apogee of this revelation of truth. Reality was objective and constant and could be measured. The individual was rational—enlightened—and could discover this reality through reason (*cogito ergo sum*, as Descartes had it). Even Christian revelation was subsumed within this process of Enlightenment.

Myth experiences a resurgence under Romanticism. Poets and storytellers were again holders of a deeper truth—a *truer* truth, the reality beyond scientific reasoning. Myth among the Romantics is mystical. It is not a ubiquitous cultural form but one reserved for artists and savants, poets, and creators of comics, which can be for popular consumption but still not deemed a form of knowledge or politics. Citing Johann Georg Hamann, "a forerunner of romanticism and implacable opponent of the Enlightenment's core values" (2000: 51), Lincoln characterizes the conflict well:

> Where Enlightenment philosophies construed reason as abstract and universal, he [Hamann] insisted that language was concrete, specific, and particular: there could no more be a universal reason than there could be a universal language. Where they championed reason as the highest of human accomplishments, he characterized language as a gift of God and therefore its superior.
>
> (Lincoln 2000: 52)

In Lincoln's description, we see again the contrast between reason (abstract, universal) and myth, storytelling, or "language" (concrete, specific, particular). Language, manifested in a "primordial past" through stories such as those in the "Hebrew bible," was superior to the abstractions of the Enlightenment.

The Enlightenment distinction between reason and religion remains in contemporary discourses around science and the imagination. As Bottici sees, a stalemate present in Hamann's distinction between reason and language was the notion of separate spheres of experience: aesthetic, moral, and intellectual (Bottici 2007: 74). Each sphere was autonomous to the others. We will see in Chapter 4 how Rousseau applies the idea of autonomy to his analysis of theater. Bottici is unsatisfied even with the Romantic restoration of myth as a "totality" of these spheres because "Romanticism simply reproduced the Enlightenment's view of myth" (76). Within Romanticism, myth becomes another form of religion, "restor[ing] the heteronomy of a divine revelation against which Enlightenment had developed its project for individual autonomy" (76). In contrast to this distinction between individual autonomy, where reason is supreme (again, *cogito ergo sum*), and divine revelation, Bottici offers *political* myth.

As will become evident throughout *Theater and Crisis*, a category (or definition) of political myth will help us to understand the mythologization of George Floyd, a phenomenon not unlike the role of a figure like Moses in African American social practice. Such a category of myth will illuminate modern performances of Euripides' *Bacchae*, as political, and the stagings of a Black Oedipus in *The Gospel at Colonus* as ostensibly—though not truly—apolitical. Throughout the book, we range from Baldwin calling upon myth to reveal ancient truths present in American racial categories, to Wole Soyinka recalling childhood memories in mythic form. Myth can highlight disjuncture (a fault line, or breach in a narrative)—Oedipus cannot be Black, but can one be Moses and queer?—and ideal representations, as we will see in *Theater and Crisis*' culminating representation of Moses in Antoinette Nwandu's play, *Pass Over*. When I say these iterations of myth are political, I concur with Bottici, rejecting the Enlightenment distinction between intellect and the imagination, that "a purely rational model of society risks being a model for a world that does not exist" (Bottici 2007: 1). In her book *Reimagining Greek Tragedy on the American Stage*, Helene P. Foley (2012), often asserts that reproductions of Greek drama in the U.S. were not political matters until the "identity politics" of the 1960s.[21] During this period, the plays began to grapple with immediate, contemporary issues in the public sphere—the Vietnam War, Women's Rights, and later, HIV/AIDS—in ways heretofore imperceptible. In Foley's analysis, the category of the political has a distinct inflection, something akin to what is commonly referred to as politicization.

The idea of politicizing Greek drama presumes an autonomous, aesthetic sphere, independent of politics, that is then influenced, or contaminated, by contemporary concerns, perhaps even contentious ones. The treatment of myth throughout *Theater and Crisis* presumes no such autonomy.[22] The ways that stagecraft, costuming, and gesture contemporize and localize ancient characters and storylines render the question of politics in Foley's analysis a begged one that would cause us to miss the politics implicit in an adaptation like Ellen McLaughlin's *Helen*, which I discuss in Chapter 5. In *The Oxford Handbook of Greek Drama in the Americas* (2015), Robert Davis, Edith Hall, and Niall W. Slater all point to a politics of representation, in late nineteenth- and early twentieth-century productions of classical plays, well before Foley's watershed 1960s.

Coming, at last, to a workable definition of myth that resonates throughout *Theater and Crisis*: myth is a narrative (needless to say, in language) that "answers a need for significance" (Bottici 2007: 178), beyond simple *meaning* in the world, through grounding, "in the sense of *begründen*" (178), a concept she uses throughout *A Philosophy of Political Myth*.[23] By significance, Bottici asserts that "something that is significant is something that situates itself between the two extremes of a simple meaning and the meaning of life and death" (178). Myth "is not only the product, but also the producer of common identities" (15). As we have seen, myth demonstrates that grounding "is not only achieved by a pure reason calculating abstract consequences, but also by inserting the advent of civil society into a narrative that coagulates significance" (143). The working definition of myth as narrative that provides significance through grounding in certain images and events helps us to understand why George Floyd would be akin to a sacrificial victim to so many people, a martyr like Christ, but not to others. Political myth is "the work on a common narrative" by which "the members of a social group (or society) provide significance to their political experience and deeds" (15). Meaning is generated by the group; it does not exist as a truth outside of the collective, or the body politic. The group can be a subaltern, like Black Americans, as well as the nation at large.

Throughout *Theater and Crisis*, I highlight the iconic or spectacular dimension of myth, an undercurrent that Bottici foregrounds in her later work (Bottici 2014), although in *A Philosophy of Political Myth* she is already well-attuned to "the forms that political myth could assume under the contemporary conditions of a global society of spectacle" (2007: 15). Iconicity—what Bottici will come to call the "imaginal"—conveys not just what political myth is but also how it is produced, which is to say through images and performance. In *A Philosophy of Political Myth*, Bottici first broaches the idea of icon, or the image, through the idea of prophecy, which she asserts, citing Spinoza, "is a creation of the imagination understood as an idea produced on the basis of present or past bodily impressions" (14). In Chapter 1, I begin to discuss image production as "present or past bodily impressions" through the idea of hauntings, a recurrent trope throughout *Theater and Crisis*. Haunting generally points to the past, whereas prophecy is future-oriented—for example, Emmett Till as a figure that would return as George Floyd, who warns us of the repeatable future. As I will begin to lay out in the chapter, haunting has an ethics, a call to action, and this too is prophetic. Mamie Till unveils the martyrdom of Emmett through the haunting image of her son's mangled body, the lynched victim displayed in an open casket. Through the image she indicates the mythic Emmett Till, not one of the many nameless children randomly killed in segregated America, but a haunting prophecy for all to heed. George Floyd becomes a contemporary conjuring of the same specter, a revisitation that suggests something unresolved in the culture. (See Figure 1.)

As potentially epiphanic, the specter, the image, calls on memory to (re)encode aspects of political life that lay dormant or forgotten. Myth as first icon, or image, "a creation of the imagination," hearkens back to Plato (Bottici 2007: 14). Early Christian intellectuals understood myths as allegories, or *figurae*, literal forms with symbolic importance (56).[24] Such figures are constitutive of reality. Even in an age of science and decisions driven by empirical data, Bottici reminds her reader, through the Greek philosopher Cornelius Castoriadis, that it is only "through the internalisation of the worlds and the imaginary significations created by society that an 'individual', properly speaking, is created out of a 'screaming monster'" (222). The Enlightenment sensibility relegated the imagination to the realm of the *imaginary*.[25] As a result of this demotion of myth, the "importance of images and imagination in social life" would have to be "rediscovered" (223).[26] My deployment of the idea of epiphanic encoding, which I discuss more fully in the next chapter, draws from Bottici's work to address the crisis of racial reckoning in the U.S. that spectacularly haunted 2020. The haunt happens both as story and as image, *figura*, or *phantasia*.

Throughout *Theater and Crisis*, I alternate between the term "fantasy" and "phantasia" to denote the image production that precedes narrative in the mythmaking process.[27] As Bottici notes, *phantasia* is "the Aristotelian term for imagination," which, given the emergent distinction between reason and the imaginary, continuing into the Enlightenment, had been "moved to the realm of the unreal" (2007: 72). In psychoanalytic terms, the fantasy or phantasy is a projection of individual neurosis or psychosis, but narrative and action in the real world evolve from this very neurosis and psychosis. Some of these narratives and images engender collective action. In fact, their significance, the very "determination to act," is precisely what makes them myth, as opposed to history, if we follow Bottici's analysis.

As the description of fantasy or phantasy shows, the language of psychoanalysis underlies the work of myth in social and political realms. Freudian psychology built on the symbolic significance of stories and images. As a part of the representational world, psychoanalysis is important throughout *Theater and Crisis*. The encoding of myth is psychological, that is, a memory process, but not merely in the way that Freud understood. Freud and the other founding psychoanalysts like Carl Jung subscribed to a scientific process based in the Enlightenment. For them, myth would conform to scientific reason. The Oedipus complex, for example, is discernible in individuals and indicative of a repeatable, measurable phenomenon, or, as Jung had it, an archetype. There is a collective function of myth that this scientific reduction misses. Myth does work in society, serving a political function, but it is not a complex to be applied from abstraction to individual. Rather, myth is a process that is best discerned and uncovered. The process functions through memory, which is encoded. For this reason, events such watching a play can trigger memory in ways that are more effective than the average political speech.

Although historical periodization can reveal how myth has been understood, myth (as the process I have described) flattens past, present, and future in its functioning as a recurrent process of memory. The chronological framework of *Theater and Crisis* provides the book its structure, but it is also a baseline against which riffs on a particular story or phantasy will recur. Experiencing the murder of George Floyd, some people will offer that nothing has changed. The differences between Floyd and Emmett Till, however, are notable, even if both come to be represented as figures for Christ. As cyclical, myth is timeless or outside of time. Myth is ancient, conveying death and life; phantasy, metaphor, and figure (or allegory); but it is also embodiment, process, and flesh-and-blood reality. Moses and Dionysus are as available for political signification as Emmett Till and George Floyd, and even when these figures are not being politicized, they are political. As August Wilson argued, the choice to stage Shakespeare, whether through colorblind casting or otherwise, is as political as telling stories of the Great Migration of Black people from the South to northern American cities. Wilson's therapeutic intervention in American theater will figure in Chapter 4.

RACE AS MYTH WITH WHICH TO RECKON

Race is the overarching myth, or fantasy, in *Theater and Crisis*. Race's artificial—almost magical—power to hold the imagination has led Barbara J. Fields and Karen Elise Fields to apply the term "racecraft" for the "mental terrain" and "pervasive belief" that leads to policies, laws, and ideology around a purported—though imagined—ancestry (Fields and Fields 2012: 18). As Bottici argues, political philosophy is not merely rational, but it has also made use of the imagination, first through phantasy, and then grounding narratives that emerge from these fantasies. Bottici uses the example of race as just such a myth, although she focuses on its Nazi deployment rather than its original setting in the U.S.[28] Fields and Fields lend greater support to approaching race as myth. Even as myth, race is part of a national ideology, which "justif[ies] ends and means of organised social action" (Bottici 2007: 194).[29] Race toggles between national ideology and grounding myth for a subgroup within the nation. Bottici puts the case of such grounding as follow: "Thus, what makes a political myth out of a simple narrative is not its content or its claim to truth, but first, the fact that this narrative coagulates and produces significance, second, that it is shared by a group, and third, that it can come to address the specifically political conditions in which this group operates" (14).[30] "Black is beautiful" responded to the political conditions of the post-Civil Rights era, after the 1954 Supreme Court case, *Brown v Board of Education*, substantively demonstrated that the system of segregation codified in the 1896 ruling in *Plessy v Ferguson* had persistent adverse effects on people of African descent. "Black Lives Matter" produces significance, and "there cannot be a mobilisation of political action without a powerful set of images that assure those who are engaged in this action about the triumph of their cause" (Bottici 2007: 163). The "beautiful struggle" of Black life futures a cause, its triumph, and its aesthetics.

My treatment of myth in *Theater and Crisis*, as I have stated, is distinctly Judeo-Islamo-Christian and Greco-Roman, which allows me to handle specific stories on a broad yet specific scale. In Bottici's argument, however, there is an innate copiousness to myth. A reader might begin to wonder if anything falls *outside* of the category. Along with the image of the savage in political philosophy and the Nazi deployment of race, Bottici uses the general strike as an example of a political myth that functions for significance, grounding, and indeed as prophesy. In Marxist political theory, the general strike is inevitable (prophetic), and it also grounds workers in the inevitability of their cause. I will leave aside the wider possible applications of the theory. In *Theater and Crisis*, I am specifically interested in myth and race, which narrows the focus and prunes the examples. I take from Bottici the prophetic position of such stories as that of the Biblical Moses. Because of how seamlessly they all operate among Black artists, writers, and intellectuals, I set the Biblical stories alongside myths of Oedipus, Dionysus, and other Greco-Roman figures in ways not common in analyses of American drama. My approach leads to analyses of theatrical works like James Baldwin's *Blues for Mister Charlie*, a play that would not on its surface appear to be an instance of classical reception. As I demonstrate, however, the play draws from both Judeo-Islamo-Christian and Greco-Roman registers. Myth is a more meaningful framework for understanding *Blues* than any other within the repertoire of classical reception.

The payoffs of the approach that I offer to race and American drama in *Theater and Crisis* should already be clear, and they will be even clearer by the end. As I have begun to propose, myth and memory provide a more compelling framework for understanding the crisis of racial reckoning that surfaced in 2020 than previous ones, such as that of a terminal illness. Presenting the problem of race in the U.S. as a "cancer" is not a useful analogy, and the idea of America's "original sin" provides significance and grounding for some while alienating others. As myth, race is a story that we enliven, a drama that we perform. As such, drama as staged in theater plays is a useful site for the work of myth, especially as it pertains to race. Rather than the analogy to cancer or illness, psychoanalysis provides a better referent for working through race, given its narrative and performative dimensions. As with psychoanalysis, the collective work of racial reckoning can only happen as a process, one that is invitational and voluntary. The psychoanalytic process inevitably calls for a galvanizing therapist from time to time, and throughout more than half a decade, practitioners like James Baldwin, Amiri Baraka, and August Wilson have served in this role. More recently, the "BIPOC Demands" (2020) provide a multivocal, multiracial, and transgender call to action. I name the processes that takes place implicitly when we hear stories or take in images (or phantasies), or explicitly when these theatric therapists try to incite action, epiphanic encoding. In addition to matters of myth, history, haunting, and memory, I take up a fulsome definition of epiphanic encoding in the next chapter.

CHAPTER ONE

SETTING THE STAGE

The Two Pandemics, Epiphanic Encoding, and the Haunting of History (2020)

Two events from 2020, the year the novel coronavirus pandemic transformed reality, are corresponding priorities for *Theater and Crisis*. The first is the May 25, 2020 killing of George Floyd, cellphone video recordings of which soon went viral, viewed tens of millions of times by the time of this book's publication.[1] Floyd, a 46-year-old Black man, had been apprehended in Minneapolis, Minnesota for allegedly passing a counterfeit twenty-dollar bill at a local bodega, Cup Foods. My intention in citing the incident is not to retry Floyd's actions that day, his character, or the murder case. Derek Chauvin, the Minneapolis police officer who responded to the call, was found guilty on all three charges for which he was tried and began serving 22½ years in prison in 2021.[2] For the purposes of *Theater and Crisis*, I am interested in the symbolic, or spectacular George Floyd, how the small group of people immediately watching his death made meaning of it, and how the broader audience of the event's broadcast formed a kind of theatrical community.[3] Whether seen with sympathy, disgust, or some other emotion, viewers made Floyd's killing meaningful.[4] (See Figure 1.) There is a great deal to be said about the "cultural logic" of Floyd's murder (Goldsby 2006: 26),[5] or what the event signaled about the broader public's thoughts and feelings regarding race in the United States and elsewhere. For hundreds and thousands of people who watched, Floyd's suffering became encoded in ways that, upon viewing it or hearing the story retold, led to action.[6] The spectacle and its accompanying narrative, the communities that formed around it, and the subsequent actions of many became a contemporary theater with ritualized responses.[7]

The second event from 2020 that is of significance to *Theater and Crisis* is from the theater proper. In July of 2020, two months after Floyd's murder, a document began circulating online, called "We See You White American Theatre (WAT)," or "Principles for Building Anti-Racist Theatre Systems." The document, "signed by more than 300 artists and then endorsed by thousands online" (Paulson 2020b), lamented the message that Black, Indigenous and People of Color (BIPOC) receive in the theater across the United States that "this is not your artistic home." More than a set of complaints, the manifesto included a series of actionable demands in "a variety of tones and formatting styles employed to record our manifold voices and views," a technique "designed to hold the multiplicity and urgency we lay claim to given the persistent devaluation of our voices." These demands included symbolic actions, such as American Indian, Alaska Native, and Native Hawaiian tribal land acknowledgment for meetings and productions held at Broadway, Off-Broadway, and League of Resident Theatres (LORT). In addition, the demands extended to calls for fundamental institutional changes that impact hiring at every level of the industry of theater, from the costume shop to leadership and middle management. The document, the "BIPOC Demands" (2020) as I will refer to it, was attuned to the emotional needs of people who serve in the theater, such as the number of hours and workdays they commit to productions. The "BIPOC Demands," "if adopted, would amount to a sweeping restructuring of the theater ecosystem in America" (Paulson 2020b).

In addition to a chilling spectacle and an attempt to direct the gaze—"*we* see *you*" (my italics)—in Floyd's murder and the "BIPOC Demands" exists a dynamic between two entities: that between an analysand and analyst, to deploy an analogy that will be useful throughout this book, between a patient and a therapist.[8] The patient is the society, itself comprised of viewers and reactors to objects, things-in-the-world: in the case of George Floyd, a Black man suffering from an opioid addiction among other painful experiences, such as the death of his mother, now himself dying needlessly, insult added to injury.[9] As an agent or actor, he choreographs and performs the pain of so many, who see some version of their own humanity in what he projects. Seeing his distress during otherwise trying times, with COVID-19 shutting their doors for what would become 15 months, writers of the "BIPOC Demands," as analysts of the patient (who was not Floyd but society at large), effect a certain diagnostic distance from events. Rather than an object or thing-in-the world to be judged immediately, the drama being observed can simply unfold in terms of object relations; animate beings that emote will react to things-in-the world. The projection, the spectacle observed, could at first blush have been raceless, classless, and without any belonging to group, identity, or country, as an event seen and observed within a context—that is, as a social drama (see Turner 1979). George Floyd's murder evoked critical reactions across the culture. People analyzed, discussed the event, and drew conclusions, alone or with others, online, in protests, or in the comfort of their homes. In contrast to these somewhat spontaneous or effervescent reactions, what made the "BIPOC Demands" akin to the work of an analyst was its clinical diagnosis, its critical distance from the patient or the spectacle, and its attempt to redirect the audience's gaze and impact its behavior.

Framing the spectacle of Floyd's murder and the "BIPOC Demands" in symbiotic terms, as patient and analyst, distills several actions and reactions from 2020 that speak directly to the themes and arc of *Theater and Crisis*. There were countless other events from 2020 that constituted communities in noteworthy ways that deserve attention. The actions and reactions surrounding the performance of race, however, were so proliferate that news outlets such as *The Washington Post* devoted entire sections of their publication to "Race & Reckoning." Initially, racial identity was a compelling factor in how the pandemic was experienced, especially given the concomitance of employment, geography, and wealth. The two events that frame this book, however, were widely seen as catalytic of necessary recognition and transformation. As the analog of analysand and therapist suggests, they should also be read in episodic, ritual terms, like the ongoing, recurring interactions of psychoanalysis. Perhaps like many others, and especially given my training as a classicist, I looked to the past to find meaning, but myth and ritual provided more answers than history. That is, 2020 was not the first occasion when the killing of a Black person became a public spectacle in the United States, engendering analytical reactions from crowds, specialists, and in the theater.[10] After the 1955 lynching of Emmett Till in Money, Mississippi, his mother Mamie Carthan Till-Mobley allowed the publication of an image of his mutilated corpse in *Jet Magazine*, the media of the day akin to cellphone videos in 2020. James Baldwin's *Blues for Mister Charlie* (produced in 1964) was the way that he, by then a well-known author, processed the death. He hoped the play would address what he called the "stale, repetitious, and timid" spectacles he saw onstage in the American theater, and Broadway specifically. Although *Blues* itself was a noteworthy theatrical event, one I spend time on in this book, Baldwin's clinical analysis of American theater, in his 1964 preface to *Blues* and elsewhere, is less discussed but arguably as important, akin to the "BIPOC Demands." As historical and theatrical episodes in American life that expose an ongoing process of memory, myth, and racial reckoning, the "spectacular" events of Emmett Till and George Floyd,[11] and the analytical reactions to them, provide the critical and chronological frame of this book.

EPIPHANIC ENCODING: WHY CERTAIN EVENTS BECOME UNFORGETTABLE

The argument of *Theater and Crisis* is that the events with which I am concerned are noteworthy as instances of what I call "epiphanic encoding," which I will now elaborate. The murder of George Floyd and the "BIPOC Demands" became cultural flashpoints in a social drama because several surrounding circumstances led to their indelibility in the national consciousness. They became analytical moments in the life of the patient, which is American society. The degree to which the COVID-19 global pandemic impacted how people interacted with media will be studied for years to come. People were prevented from gathering in groups, rendering the theater itself a peculiar and curious institution worthy of focus and attention. Theater plays were either not performed or were broadcast from pre-recordings. In a few notable cases, such as Richard Nelson's Apple Family plays, the teleconference platform itself became part of the media. Whatever the case, the kind of encoding or memory-making with which I am concerned was happening before 2020, but the pandemic year intensified processes of media consumption, at-distance engagement, and memory-making. Theater, through the moving image in various media but especially live performance, is a premiere site of epiphanic encoding, but during lockdown, spectacular event concentrated in the streets.

Epiphanic encoding is a spectacular and theatrical phenomenon that, as I argue, emblazons—encodes through memory-making processes—events on the individual and collective conscience. An identification (and understanding) of the phenomenon of epiphanic encoding helps in the study of the spectacular and theatrical past, present, and future, in the United States and beyond. The phenomenon also reveals theater as one of humanity's foremost "memory machine[s]" (Carlson 2003). As has recently been argued, theater is one of humanities most "pro-social" venues (see Rathje et al. 2021).

Epiphanic encoding is an encapsulation of several narratological,[12] performative, or ritual processes that happen within groups or audiences as they live their lives, resulting from an accrual of information and emotions. The event, the epiphany, results from storytelling and mythmaking precisely because of the accretion of information, through repetition and across generations. As a simple example, a child knows that the heavyset man with the white beard is Santa Claus through repetition and image production, whether mental or in media.[13] Even as the young person grows into adulthood, the winter holiday can be evocative of this figure, and his manifestation can trigger long-repressed memories. This is the epiphany, with its accompanying emotions, sensations, and fantasies. The process of storytelling and mythmaking is the continuous encoding of Santa in memory. The epiphany helps this encoding of meaning through recurrence, and as a process, the mythic and ritual experience is simultaneously similar and somewhat different each time. Myth and ritual as processes of memory can offer more compelling explanations of cultural inertia or change than historical analysis. Studies of collective and individual memory have long spoken in terms of encoding, but my formulation of epiphanic encoding helps to encapsulate events in lived experience as theatrical, or spectacular, and theatrical events as potentially transformative.

As it pertains to the relationship between myth, memory, and race, George Floyd became an instantiation of epiphanic encoding. Consistent with how the event unfolded, three broad constants can be observed across the other historical hauntings with which I am concerned, and as we will see, the epiphany is a haunting, an uncanny recurrence (see Blanco and Peeren 2013). The haunting is the first constant, whereby through memory and recollection the event becomes, for many, an epiphany, "an illuminating discovery, revelation, or disclosure."[14] I use the term "epiphany" deliberately to include its religious connotation, as in the Catholic celebration of the revelation of Christ to the Gentiles.[15] Beyond Christian practice, epiphany, as the manifestation of a phenomenon akin to a religious experience, is the promised end of ritual or religious experience, although the embodiment is not always that of a single person or entity.[16] The epiphany is akin to a psychic fantasy, the "scene which is presented to the imagination and which stages an unconscious desire."[17] The fantasy can be "the channeling of unacceptable or unattainable desire into the imagination" (Rodriquez 2009: 206). Fantasy is necessary to object relations, which is a process whereby a subject reconciles mental projections and their relationship to other things-in-the world, to other subjects and objects.[18] The fantasy is an epiphany, a representation that relates to objects. George Floyd, like Emmett Till before him, is a martyr to many, which is the religious and ritual sense of an epiphany such as that of Christ. The epiphany distills several experiences because of the way his (in these instances, but the epiphany is not gender-bound) experiences manifest impressions already seen, felt, and to some degree understood. In sum, the epiphany triggers long-standing memories while encoding new ones. All epiphany relies, to some degree or other, on memory and recollection.

If the epiphany, the fantasy, or visual impression that haunts, is primary, of equal importance is the constant of the narrative that is crafted from it, which is a function of individual and collective practices. To return to the banal example of Santa Claus, stories of red-nosed reindeer and elves working away in a toymaker's workshop accompany the fantasy of a jolly, white-bearded figure. Memories of these stories are easily triggered and, like the fantasy itself, generate sensations, impressions, and recall. Similarly, George Floyd's murder was legible to many people as another manifestation of senseless violence accompanying Black life in the United States and elsewhere in the Western world.[19] The succinct and provocative formulation of "Black Lives Matter" (BLM), which Patrisse Cullors, Alicia Garza, and Opal Tometi spoke into existence after Trayvon Martin's 2012 murder, is a meaning-making, narrative formulation (see Cullors and bandele 2018). The point here is not to scrutinize BLM's methods or efficacy but rather to note how the idea distilled media and memory, as a narrative phrasing that encapsulates the fantasy or projection, which was the loss of a specific Black life that seems to corroborate experiences in the real world, namely that Black life has too often been a site of suffering and erasure. The narrative attempts to make sense of the fantasy. Like the analytical work that the "BIPOC Demands" does, BLM diagnosed the epiphany—Emmett Till haunts as Trayvon Martin, and then as George Floyd, as only three of wretchedly innumerable examples—through narrative. The diagnosis or affirmation that "black lives matter" does the analytic work, aiding the fantasy projection.[20]

What is striking about the events of 2020 is that communities confirmed, in real time and through their nightly protests, that in Floyd's murder they had witnessed again the needless suffering and erasure of Black humanity, that this had happened before, and that enough was enough. That is, with the assistance of the analyst—who, recall, asserted that "Black lives matter"—communities were able to encode the event, i.e., to generate meaning through the specter of murder. Floyd became an epiphany not only for African Americans, but for hundreds of thousands of people in the United States and elsewhere, many of whom were not necessarily Black. The epiphany was encoded, made meaningful, through narrative.

The fantasy and the narrative being the first two aspects of epiphanic encoding, the third is an epiphenomenon already evident in the #BLM slogan, namely the theorization of the event (which is a kind of metanarrative). To continue the analogy to psychotherapy, through an ongoing, ritual return, e.g., what happens in weekly therapy sessions, the therapist or analysand conspires with the patient to arrive at some new state of realization, having repeatedly assessed the fantasies and the stories being told. This is the function of analysis, such as a specific session in a series of visits to a therapist, that the "BIPOC Demands" played during the summer of 2020. Setting aside the tone of "demands," which might hasten an analysand out of the therapist's office, the "BIPOC Demands" was one of many instances in which the society, i.e., the patient, was directed to actions that would prevent the psychotic episode from happening again—psychotic, because what is more psychotic than an agent of law and order suffocating a citizen, albeit a subaltern, under the pressure of his knee? The "BIPOC Demands" is of interest because it engaged directly with theater, on some level aware that the theatrical observation of a societal process was squarely the matter at hand: "We *see* you" (my italics, now with different emphasis). Though it did so indirectly and within a context, the "BIPOC Demands" tied the specter of George Floyd to long-standing practices and perceptions that impact how Americans see one another. The document asks—demands—that the patient behave differently, henceforth. Whether the prognosis is positive is left to time to tell.

Epiphanic encoding happens during moments of cultural life when an event takes on the visage of a fantasy projection, a haunting, the uncanny impression that this has happened before. This encoding likely involves a person, such as George Floyd, because most hauntings are interpersonal. There is a diagnostic dimension to epiphanic encoding, wherein an analyst seeks to make sense of the epiphany, the fantasy projection. Epiphanic encoding has a ritual dimension because of recurrences, repeated hauntings, in response to which a metanarrative forms.

As I will demonstrate throughout this book, the events of 2020, and the critical response to them in theater, are only the most recent in what has been a cyclical, recurrent process of myth, memory, and racial reckoning in the United States. I begin this cyclical narrative in 1964 with Baldwin's *Blues* because of the significance of Emmett Till's lynching to American culture and the attempt to revisit it in theater. The play is paradigmatic of Baldwin's diagnostic work, before, after, and through *Blues*, to analyze—or to shrink, an appropriate term when we consider the stage as a miniature of life—American society.

EPIPHANIC ENCODING AND THE CLASSICS

As a scholar trained in the academic field of Classical Languages and Literatures, I might not come to mind intuitively for many readers as the specialist most able to make sense of the contemporary moment in American culture or its theater. What I will demonstrate, however, is that epiphanic encoding renders classical images and narratives relevant in unexpected ways. Even as the story of Santa Claus is not going to disappear from the culture suddenly, Saint Nicholas originating in the fourth century, the narratives and memories that crystallize in epiphanic encoding have deep and long-standing roots.[21] The way that fantasy projections work in terms of object relations encourages us, for deeper understanding, to look toward the past. The individual in psychoanalytic treatment—or the person talking to a friend about their feelings—turns to the biographical past to excavate material and understand its recurrence. Similarly, to understand ongoing patterns, the culture at large does best when it returns for insights to its collective past, excavating recent experiences, or doing deeper archeological digging, metaphorically speaking. In this context, images and narratives as long-standing as Greek and Roman or Judeo-Islamo-Christian ones are significant.[22] These are the embodied scripts that haunt the culture. Understood in this way, why Emmett Till's mother would use the language of Christ's martyrdom to explain her son's murder becomes more legible. As Smithsonian Museum Director Lonnie Bunch puts it, she "saw Emmett as being crucified on the cross of racial injustice."[23] Similarly, through the power of analogy, whether as a simile or metaphor, George Floyd can be imagined as a Christ figure. Bunch is not alone in this figuration;

the Smithsonian Institute features David C. Driskell's 1956 painting, "Behold Thy Son," which borrows from the crucifixion scene in its commemoration of Till (see Figure 2). A brown body outstretched on an imagined cross, the face in Driskell's painting is

Figure 2: *Behold Thy Son* (David C. Driskell, 1956)

reminiscent of West African masks from various cultural groups. The mask of veneration replaces the disfigured face of Till, melding Christian storytelling with an epiphany of Black empowerment.

Among professional classicists, a subfield broadly named Classical Reception Studies has emerged, which studies the affinity for, or legacy of, the Greco-Roman classics among contemporary authors and artists, and how these later authors influence what we know of ancient texts.[24] Theories of classical reception have aided in the understanding of performance fields, including dance, epic, tragic, and comic theater.[25] In theater, the classical and the modern,[26] which we might render in terms the vehicle and tenor, can be as easy to recognize as the title of a play. To use an example that I touch upon in Chapter 3, in the case of Wole Soyinka's *The Bacchae of Euripides: A Communion Rite* (2004), there is no question that the playwright, a Nigerian national who happens to be Yoruba, is offering a treatment of an ancient, classical text (or is somehow asking his audience to draw that play to mind), given the drama's title. Viewed as a push and pull between past and modern, Soyinka's play gains from some understanding of Euripides' *Bacchae*, but the modern adaptation also propels Euripides into a contemporary sphere, setting him in a space that illuminates his play in some new way while also reflecting contemporary realities for the audience.

An author like Soyinka might have any number of reasons for an affinity with ancient source material, but for the purposes of reception itself, these reasons are neither here nor there, insofar as they are difficult if not impossible to retrace. Reception is an ambivalent matter. Whatever Soyinka might say (or not) about his choice, the audience and reader must interpret, or intuit whether to take the artist's claim at face value. Indeed, the modern or contemporary author gains something by association between the classical and its afterlife. Soyinka's London audiences may flock to the play for its name recognition, as was the case with the New York-based theater critic Walter Kerr, who was disappointed with what he saw (see Kerr 1973). Soyinka gains recognition through his relationship to the source material, but there are risks as well. Kerr, who renders the postcolonial interests of the modern author secondary, if recognized at all, points to one risk in his review, namely that of making the vehicle (Euripides' *Bacchae*, in this case) the tenor.[27] Soyinka's interpretation of Euripides filters through Yoruba cosmology and Western philosophy.[28] Depending on the audience, however, aspects of his context can be clouded in reception, so overwhelming is the shadow that the past casts.

Strategies of disavowal among receiving artists and authors can encourage audiences to focus on the belated work rather than on its influences. On the one hand, affinity was beneficial to Soyinka. Contemporaries now talk about *his Bacchae* alongside the Euripidean original, and he gained an opportunity to alert his audiences to his cultural plight, writing in 1973 only shortly after Nigerian independence and in the wake of the country's bloody civil war, the Biafra War. As a counterexample, Toni Morrison, who during the same decade writes *Song of Solomon* (2004 [1977]), a novel with clear classical allusions, works in a mode of disavowal.[29] She publishes this novel in the milieu of the Black Arts Movement in the United States. *Song of Solomon* tested tenets of Black Power and African cultural and aesthetic independence from American and European hegemony. In it, Guitar, a friend to the novel's protagonist, Milkman Dead, belongs to an organization called the Seven Days, which assigns to its membership a retaliatory, sacrificial killing of a white person for every Black life taken on the same day of the week.[30] With such revolutionary roots, it is no wonder that Morrison would reject such Greek mythological motifs as that of Icarus as the source for the trope of flight in *Song of Solomon*. She would also disavow the Medea myth as relevant to her novel *Beloved* (2022 [1987]), which fictionalizes the potential sacrificial killing of children born into slavery by their enslaved mother, Margaret Garner.[31] Morrison was surely more interested in ensuring that her readers retain Garner's story from 1856 than that they reinforce the timeless value of Euripides' *Medea*. And yet, at the same time, there are unmistakable layers of classical and Judeo-Islamo-Christian images and narratives throughout Morrison's work. Morrison, however, wants to direct her readers' attention to the tenor, her primary concern, so she disavows the vehicle, which is in fact only one of many sources of inspiration.

The persistence of classical education in secondary- and post-secondary schools accounts for some of what Suzan-Lori Parks calls the "subterranean thing," (Shenk 2002), the inevitable association of modern and contemporary plights, such as that of Margaret Garner or postcolonial Nigerians, to classical figures like Pentheus or Medea.[32] Classicism (and its derivatives, such as Black classicism) refers to the primarily deliberate relationship between the European past and its incipient modernity. The periodization of the Renaissance, followed by an explicitly neoclassical age, augmented an already operational elevation of the classical past, with its foreseeable influence on future generations. As early as a text like Cicero's *De re publica*, there is a discernible, even powerful idea that liberal arts, the *artes liberales*, were emerging as cultural ideas and resources on topics as varied as beauty, sexuality, or the ideal form of government. Cicero looks to the past, specifically Plato, as essential reading, if his society is to understand how exemplary government might function. Within the American context, the notion of a "culture of classicism" has a long legacy among scholars and critics (Winterer 2004). In *Classica Americana: The Greek and Roman Heritage in the United States*, Meyer Reinhold writes that "mythology has, indeed, proved to be a major strand in twentieth-century classicism" (1984: 347). A slippage, however, is already evident in Carl Richard's *The Founders and the Classics: Greece, Rome, and the American Enlightenment* (1994).[33] This is the expectation of a benefit by association, where the modern author might not necessarily know much about the classical world but understands its value as signaling erudition.[34]

When we come to an author like James Baldwin, whose formal education ended at high school and who was not especially interested in the classical past for its cultural cache, a model beyond classical reception or classicism is evident. This is the kind of collective memory that is drawn upon at times consciously, but at times inadvertently, or unconsciously. That is, if the ubiquity of the classics is such that writers and artists felt the need to reference them even in passing, this ubiquity also occasions seepages into the unconscious, such that Greek and Roman myth, alongside Judeo-Islamo-Christian narrative, is present in the work of modern and contemporary artists, writers, and everyday people, even at times when neither they nor their audiences detect it consciously. Something as hard to grasp as the atmosphere of a poem, for example, can evoke a "fuzzy connection" to the classical past.[35] Put in another way, texts, ideas, and artifacts designated as classical are also part of a social or collective memory, which can recur in fragmentary or episodic ways.[36] As Baldwin famously wrote in "Stranger in the Village," "people are trapped in history, and history is trapped in them."[37]

For Baldwin, the Greco-Roman and Judeo-Islamo-Christian past as a feature of individual and collective memory is felt reality, even if jarring or traumatic. In "Stranger," he describes his experience in a remote Swiss village, where locals had none of the savvy he possessed as a world-traveler who lived for many years in Paris, France (and later, in Turkey and southern France). Nevertheless, these villagers still somehow had a sense of themselves as inheritors of "Western civilization," a phase Baldwin uses frequently and knowingly. In contrast to these Europeans, Baldwin is dispossessed of inheritance; he is a "bastard of the West" (Leeming 2015). Even in a remote Swiss village, Baldwin is the "nigger," an outsider not only to the local community, but also to the arc of European history. Baldwin understands that even here, the African, the Black person, is akin to Lucifer, the necessary nemesis of a particular mythology of death and life, a fallen angel of light, antithesis to a heroic (even salvific) storyline. The villager, on the other side, belongs. Baldwin argues that "the most illiterate among them is related, in a way that I am not, to Dante, Shakespeare, Michelangelo, Aeschylus, Da Vinci, Rembrandt, and Racine" (Baldwin 2012, 165).[38] Nevertheless, these authors make their way into Baldwin's life and work. They become in various ways his surrogates, for whom he substitutes personalized, psychological terms: father, mother, sister, and brother. It will be important (in the next chapter and later through the figure of Oedipus) to examine kinship as enviable but fraught in the way that Judith Butler articulates the trouble with such associations (2017).

Whether through kinship, which is vitally important to the binding lie that is race (Appiah 2018), or by some other trope, Baldwin implicitly argues that visitations from the past operate as components of individual and collective memory. This is the case whether writers or authors valorize the European classics or not. As such, individuals possess fragments of these memories, consciously and unconsciously, and viscerally give them value. Classicism as collective memory is operative in Baldwin's work, even if he does not chart it in the kind of expressed engagement with the classics evident among other authors.[39] Baldwin did not attend college, but memory was all around him in the people, places, and objects that he encountered. His grade-school teacher at Public School 24, Bill Miller, discovered his love of theater, and his early, adolescent writing garnered the attention of eminent figures, such as Fiorello LaGuardia, New York City's mayor from 1934–1945 (Leeming 2015). Prior to the year of Baldwin's entry to Frederick Douglass Middle School in 1938, the high school had a classics department and taught Greek and Latin. There Countee Cullen was his teacher. Cullen would have published *Medea and Some Other Poems* just a few years earlier in 1935, when Baldwin was eleven years old. From middle school, Baldwin went on to Dewitt Clinton High School in the Bronx, a place with notable alumni like

Romare Bearden, the collage artist whose *Odyssey* series remains one of the most poignant engagements with ancient Greece by any American artist. These biographical notes should not attenuate the focus on Baldwin only to those aspects of his work where the Greek and Roman classics might be present. Rather, they allow us a broader analysis of the memories and material he knew and with which he would inevitably work.

The classics in Baldwin are more a function of latent memory than of explicit analog, and this realization can impact how readers understand a play like *Blues for Mister Charlie*, as I argue in Chapter 2. Baldwin's experiences are "in the break" of narrative and psychological experience (Moten 2003). He recognizes his Americanness in at times traumatic terms. Broadly, Baldwin describes childhood trauma as his rite of passage. There was violence at every turn for young Jimmy. On the street corners in Harlem, "one would see a group of sharpies standing on the street corner, jiving the passing chick" (Baldwin 2012, 100).[40] A grown man solicited him for sex on those same streets when he was just a child, and he turns to the language of psychoanalysis to make meaning of these experiences.

Psychoanalysis is a salient feature of Baldwin's work, as it was—and remains—a powerful tool for untangling the knots of personal and collective memory and where they intertwine. As it pertains to the entanglements of psychoanalysis and classical myth, the Oedipus myth is a clear example of classicism's seepage into Baldwin's work. Broadly, the role of Freudian psychology in the writing of Americans of the mid-twentieth century is ubiquitous.[41] Baldwin racializes Oedipus, whom he writes that he knows about "not because of Freud but because of a poet who lived in Greece thousands of years ago."[42] Baldwin's incorporation of Freudian psychology, and the Oedipus complex in particular, is evident in such narratives as "Going to Meet the Man" (in Baldwin 1995b). The story opens with the impotent white character Jesse, a Southerner unable to make love to his wife until recalling the childhood memory that forms its substance. Jesse's father took him to see the lynching of a Black man when he was a child, and his triangular identifications—with his father, his mother (and the Black female substitutes for mother), and the hanged victim—arouse his sexual desire by the story's conclusion. Jessie's memories are "psycho-racial" (Kim 2017: 323), and his father "is transformed from his imaginary opponent into a racial ally whose mission is to cope with the possible threat" of Black sexuality (328).

Although "Going to Meet the Man" clearly explores Freudian psychology as it pertains to race, Baldwin's influences, and in particular his understanding of Oedipus, is not limited to this single story, and Baldwin cites multiple sources. Sophocles is in the background. In Baldwin's discussion of literary influence, he uncannily refers to Richard Wright as a writer whose "work was a roadblock in my road, the sphinx, really, whose riddles I had to answer before I could become myself" ("Alas Poor Richard," cited in Baldwin 2021, 285).[43] Baldwin is Sophocles' Oedipus, the figure whose fate is to kill his father, in this case Wright, at the crossroads. Elise Miller puts the case as follows:

> The allusion to Oedipus thus introduces a theme that preoccupies much of Notes of a Native Son—the black man's racial history is 'indivisible from himself forever' whether he remembers, represses, disavows, or distorts it ... Just as Oedipus's scarred ankles are evidence of his bondage, just as even his name (*Oedipus* literally means swollen foot) conveys a part of his history that he does not recall.[44]

Baldwin's deployment of the Oedipus myth in *Notes of a Native Son* demonstrates a deeper, perhaps even sublimated reading and a reluctance to dwell on the source of influence. The details of his reference suggest that he knows the story beyond Freud and has read Sophocles. Baldwin does not linger on these kinds of references but is satisfied to move on to his own concerns and contributions. In this case, he "assimilates" the story by "identif[ying] with

Oedipus's conflict" and "integrat[ing] Sophocles' play into his own biography" (Baldwin 2012: 632). At the same time, he is interested in "re-reading these texts through the lens of race," rather than paying homage to them.

At once the spectacle (as a racialized self in the United States) and the critic, Baldwin embodies and serves as an example of the processes encapsulated in the idea of epiphanic encoding. His experiences are projections, manifest as images and fantasies—the corner "sharpies," his father, Wright as father-figure, Oedipus, the Sphinx—that become part of his biographical narrative. Because he was an adept critic, Baldwin the analyst comes to make sense of these epiphanies; he transforms his own individual story into a metanarrative about being Black in the United States. He draws from disparate, fragmentary memories in his analysis, but no patient or analyst can make sense of the whole, all at once, at any time. The epiphanies, however, facilitate the encoding. And, the ancient past—as Greco-Roman myths and narratives, as Judeo-Islamo-Christian stories learned in childhood and repeated in his sermons as a young preacher (and those of other preachers he heard)—is a significant part of this encoding.

Encapsulating the classics in terms collective memory, epiphanic encoding accounts for classical presences—Greek and Roman myth, images, and narratives; Judeo-Islamo-Christian stories—not in term of reception or classicism, but rather as accruals of memory. The longer the accumulation historically, the more likely that the association will be visceral. Baldwin can refer to Wright as his sphinx, whether he is directly citing Sophocles' *Oedipus Tyrannus* or not. For memory, image, and the narrative work in tandem, which is why theater has been a particularly apt space for epiphanic encoding. The most effective plays and productions present a fantasy and tell a specific story whose narrative arc assists audiences toward broader truths. These plays consolidate identity, belonging, and a desire to act through the drama's mastery of images, myth, and metaphor. They draw on group dynamics at various registers in society, which in the U.S. has included concerns about race, gender, class, ability, and sexual identity. These plays accomplish epiphanic encoding, which is a communal, ritual process, notwithstanding the ostensible moves away from community that "post-" designates, whether post-Civil Rights, postcolonial, post-racial, or postclassical. These plays deploy metaphor in often stunning and disruptive ways, harnessing the knowledge of their audiences, whether conscious or unconscious, toward some new revelation.

Theater is the site for this study because epiphanic encoding occurs during moments of collective effervescence, which is as Susan Best puts it "the sense of a groundswell or bubbling up of shared feeling and the buoyancy and animation that groups make possible" (Best 2021: 108). Collective effervescence enables group cooperation, if even for a fleeting moment. Unlike the species of performance art that "invoke[s] social relations and social engagement without a clear idea of what that qualification means" (Best 2021: 123), performative events that accomplish epiphanic encoding are like a church altar call: the experience asks you to participate, to change your life, from the moment of performance onward.

EPIPHANIC ENCODING, HAUNTING, AND THE ETHICS OF THEATER

I have been talking about the process of epiphanic encoding not only in terms memory, but even as haunting. It is worth spending some time elaborating on how hauntology as theory relates to *Theater and Crisis*. Maria del Pilar Blanco and Esther Peeren (2013) have tracked the spectral turn, the shift in cultural discussions of ghosts, people coming back from the dead to discomfit the living, to haunting as a theoretical phenomenon that is speculative and yet still viscerally palpable.[45] Tracing studies of the supernatural from Freud's idea of the uncanny into the twenty-first century, Blanco and Peeren arrive at haunting as an ethical proposition, the haunting as a thing that returns repeatedly in order to be accounted for, corrected, and healed. By the late twentieth century, artists, writers, and theorists come to speak of ghosts in naturalistic yet tropic terms.

To say that Emmett Till haunts the culture, notable as late as the 2022 Hollywood film that bears his name, signifies something that is even more compelling than any literal ghost could be. His ongoing presence in the culture is, for many people, to borrow language from Blanco and Peeren applied more broadly, "a welcoming seen as ethical and enabling" (2013: 9). The ghost haunts the culture, especially those who ignore the significance of Till or fail to address the conditions that lead to the death of others like him, which by the twenty-first century no longer amount simply to segregation as a sanctioned system. Till's haunting may be "dispossessing,"[46] intended to highlight the potential failures of justice for Black people living in the United States, and the impact of this failure on all other persons in ethical proximity. George Floyd will be viewed by many people as similar to Till not because they deny that progress has been made in the United States since 1955. It would be unethical—disrespectful to the ancestral ghosts who fought and died for these changes—*not* to recognize advances in civil rights and equality of opportunity. The ghostly association, however, the haunting, asks where certain significant and necessary shifts have perhaps not yet occurred: are Black lives worth the same as their white counterparts? Is justice meted out in the same way for those who take a Black life as for those who take a white one? And what steps need to be taken to break the cycle of violence and misperception that led to Till's murder, and by 2020, that of Floyd? The haunting "demands justice, or at least a response" (2013: 9).

Returning to the psychological underpinnings of haunting that enabled Freud's notion of the uncanny (Blanco and Peeren 2013), epiphanic encoding homes in on specular and spectacular recurrences not as theoretical processes—like a seminar or conference where great minds discuss what should be done to change the culture—but rather as performative. Epiphanic encoding is a function more like riding a bicycle than memorizing the dates of historical events. Both are processes of memory, but the former is a result of performance and habit while the latter is dependent on logic and abstraction. Epiphanic encoding draws from every type of memory, and for this reason performative contexts (like riding that bicycle) are the situations in which the phenomenon is most indelible. Epiphanic encoding is fully embodied experience, whether bodies are in motion in protests across the country or moving onstage before an audience of rapt participants.

The concept of epiphanic encoding would render every public demonstration or every play admissible in such a study. As Marvin Carlson argues, "every play might be called *Ghosts*," since all theater bring a sense of déjà vu, and "one might argue that every play is a memory play" (2003: 2). The framework of myth, memory, and racial reckoning limits the scope of *Theater and Crisis* to a specific set of topics in the twentieth and twenty-first centuries involving theater and performance. Floyd's murder is at the epistemic center of the book because of the degree to which the event was a cultural flashpoint having to do with race, a haunting in the historical arc bending from the lynching of Till, though not beginning with that event. Floyd's murder was hard to miss, wherever one lived, or however one came to see it. In calling collectives to identity, a sense of belonging (or not belonging), and action, the specter of Floyd belied many assumptions about the current state of race relations in the United States, and perhaps in other parts of the Western world. By the early twenty-first century, through a series of historical "posts-"—post-Civil Rights, postcolonial, postmodern, post-racial, postclassical—some artists, writers, and scholars have signaled the end of certain communities (colonial, modern, or racial), so that even when groups convene, they can often signify what Best described, referring to particular instances of performance art as "empty version[s] of sociality" (Best 2021: 123). In the case of Floyd, however, at least momentarily, something in the culture seemed to have been mastered, made material, and projected into reality. Even before the making of meaning, before the narrative, the image of George Floyd being killed was epiphanic, a monstrous specter, a haunting, however one viewed the process of cause and effect leading to the event. In terms of myth, memory, and haunting, Floyd was the ghost of King Duncan appearing to Macbeth, whom Macbeth kills in Shakespeare's play, which is also to say a visitation of Clytemnestra, the mother of Orestes whom Orestes kills in Aeschylus' *Libation Bearers*. That is, as we will see in Chapter 2 in Baldwin's treatment of Till's lynching in *Blues*, the epiphany, the myth, makes meaning through encoding, which flattens past and present, fiction and reality, into memory, or haunting.

The idea of haunting is critical because, as Avery F. Gordon puts it, "haunting, unlike trauma, is distinctive for producing a something-to-be done."[47] Epiphanic encoding asks for ethical action. *Theater and Crisis*, as a book that raises questions of ethics and aesthetics, is also concerned with the question of what happened to the "beloved community" that Martin Luther King, Jr. envisioned.[48] As opposed to this ecumenical community, Floyd was the uncanny return of the repressed. The repetition of images, owing to the photographic and videorecording technology at hand for every owner of a smartphone, transforms the murder into a ubiquitous specter, an ever-present haunting. The haunting is a projection that actively seeks interpretation, a happening that asks for an ethical response on the part of the community that witnesses it. The interpretive or responsive tendency is the narrative, storytelling, or mythmaking process. The specter of Floyd was traumatic for those immediately at the scene, as it might have been for others watching the recording of him beg for life and expire. What is more, the trauma seeks meaning, the narrative, the "something-to-be-done." For many, the traumatic repetition of the scene, which was projected and replayed over the course of the year that passed between the murder and

Chauvin's conviction, provoked the memory of others whose deaths played out in the public sphere, including Till, Trayvon Martin, Sandra Bland, and Ahmaud Arbery, to name only a few. These memories encode meaning, which informs identity, the sense of belonging, and the actions people decide to take, on behalf of themselves and others. Shared meaning, through myth, memory, and haunting, makes collective action possible. In this way, all myth is political.

MEMORY, HISTORY, AND CHRONOLOGY

I have organized this book in terms of a chronological, historical arc from 1964–2020, from *Blues* to the epiphany of Floyd, not necessarily his expiring body, but certainly his resurrection in murals and aesthetic representations. By discussing the recurrences between (and including) the lynching of Emmett Till and murder of George Floyd in terms of memory, hauntings, and the communities evoked, my argument for epiphanic encoding challenges historical chronology. Rather than dividing between past and present, or before and after, epiphanies, hauntings, and memories recur. As we see with reactions to monuments and other centerpieces of collective commemoration, the epiphany serves, as Edward S. Casey puts it, "to ensure a future of further remembrance of that same event" (Casey 2004: 17). For historian David Blight, memory is social, whereas historical periodization "asserts the authority of academic training and canons of evidence."[49] History is derived, as Blight argues, "from schooling, religion, family, popular culture, or demagoguery" (Blight 2002); it can be indoctrinated or even officially revised. Memory, however, is tied to myth and ritual, allowing for a kind of spontaneity and effervescence. Ritual memory can oppose the official story. Memories refuse to die; they haunt.

In this analytic work of shrinking (and I also mean this as the psychological colloquialism) 56 years, the book encounters several periods that come to be celebrated in history as "post-." The Civil

Rights Act of 1964 and the Voting Rights Act of 1965 were to have marked the end of a period, closure to the American system of segregation. The 1896 Supreme Court decision of *Plessy v. Ferguson* sanctioned an apartheid system that the high court rolled back with *Brown v. Board of Education* in 1954. Yet there was Emmett Till in 1955, a haunting, or an epiphany encoded in the memories of millions of people, which signaled another set of realities. By the late 1960s, former European colonies across Africa, Asia, and the Caribbean were becoming independent, and historians look upon this period as a post-colonial one. Within the context of memory and identification, many American thinkers aligned with post-coloniality, notwithstanding the ways in which the United States masked its continuing colonial rule. Some Black intellectuals and political figures connected their plight in the United States with that of former African colonies and with the Vietnamese. While Muhammad Ali was asserting that he had no quarrel with the Viet Cong, Martin Luther King, Jr. was speaking of the Vietnam War in terms of the need for a "revolution of values" in America. I will explore this cultural turn more fully in Chapter 3.

This postcolonial period is also one in which the label of post-modern was ascendant, and yet in "Harlem is Nowhere," novelist Ralph Ellison examines the urban landscape (in Harlem, but as more broadly symbolic of any urban space with a concentration of Black inhabitants) as the "scene and symbol of the Negro's perpetual alienation in the land of his birth" (in Ellison 1995: 296).[50] The 1970–90s, a period of Civil Rights for Black Americans, saw several regressions in every area of social life, from housing, to health, and economic stability. Nevertheless, in the progressive march of history a post-racial period had purportedly arrived in 2008 (Baker and Simmons 2015), with the election of Barack Obama, the son of a Black Kenyan father and white mother from Wichita, Kansas, as the nation's first Black president. The murder of Trayvon Martin in 2012 was a haunting that triggered the trauma of the past. The lived experience and sacraments of millions of people across the

United States belied the march of history, the official story of post-racialism.

Myth, memory, and racial reckoning halt the march through time, demonstrating the extent to which the experiences of millions of Black Americans are out of time.[51] Ritual time, as opposed to linear progression, helps to account for differences between histories, national stories, and lived experience. Rather than a chronological advance through time, and progress, these experiences evidence traumatic breaks, where recurrence dominates over attempts at closure or admonitions simply to move on. Those who wish to understand would heed what the protagonist characterized as the "boomerang of history," in Ellison's National Book Award-winning novel, *Invisible Man* (Ellison 1980 [1952]), the Faulknerian idea that the past is never dead and is not even the past. What is more, memory as a collective, ritual experience seeks participation, beyond simple intellectual understanding. It is ecumenical—the altar call at a church service that expands the flock. Epiphanic encoding is effervescent, ritually urging a broader awakening to the visitations of the past that require accounting, atonement, and expiation.

OUTLINE OF CHAPTERS

Notwithstanding an awareness of time and memory that resists historical periodization, *Theater and Crisis* is organized primarily in chronological terms. In societies we structure our lives in terms of decades and events (e.g., 13th birthday, 16th, 18th, or 21st birthday, one's thirties, forties, fifties, etc.). We do this even if collective memory resists narratives of progress, newness, or posts-. The tension between historical or narrative progress and the regress of memory and haunting is persistent across these chapters, a representation of how time functions in reality. In the next chapter, the turn back to the historical past allows an excavation of the places and artifacts that still feature in the culture, or at least still matter to the people and emotions that haunt the present. After 1955, Emmett Till was a spectral recurrence that haunted James Baldwin until the first production of *Blues for Mister Charlie* in 1964 (Baldwin 1995). Till is for Baldwin a visitation, a memory encoded epiphanically. Through *Blues*, Baldwin seeks to commit society at large to a project of racial reconciliation, hoping for the culture's religious conversion to the observance of the terror of Till. Till becomes mythic in his fictionalization, and to grapple with the lynching, Baldwin turns to ancient mythological themes like kinship and betrayal, vengeance, and sanctioned punishment. In Baldwin's panoramic scope of Western civilization, similar ghosts to that of Till include figures from Shakespeare's *Macbeth*, a play Baldwin saw as a child and explicitly references, and from Aeschylus' *Oresteia*, the mythology of which is alive in Shakespeare's play. Like the ghost of Emmett Till, who appears in Baldwin's play in the equally ghostly form of the character Richard, already dead in the first scene but present through flashbacks, the visitations of figures from these plays include Shakespeare's Three Weird Sisters and Duncan, and Aeschylus' Clytemnestra. These ghosts seek retribution and justice, which are complementary though not identical phenomena, potentially antagonistic processes that *Blues* foregrounds.

Through *Blues* and throughout his writing, Baldwin acts as both patient and analyst. Haunted and in need of succor, he processes the events of Till's murder through his essays and this play in particular, but he also wants to provoke recognition in his audiences. His call for an American theater outside of the stale, repetitive, and commercial dramas he laments broadens his analysis beyond *Blues*. Like Agamemnon from Aeschylus' play and Macduff (and others) from Shakespeare, Till is epiphanically encoded as myth in society. In *Blues*, Baldwin attempts to direct this encoding through the character Richard. The figure of Till and his haunting presence arrive at a metanarrative, a potential ethical recognition that makes conscious sense of the memories that often recur unconsciously. As haunting, this sense-making process disrupts the neat historical narrative of the advent of Civil Rights through the legislation of *Brown v. Board of Education* in 1954, which historically might be seen as ushering in a post-segregation period. Till's murder a year later alerts observers to a cyclical return that denies historical progress.

As it turns out, *Brown v. Board* was only the beginning of a decades-long struggle. The next three chapters span the late 1960s into the 2000s and seek to understand what disrupted the linear historical gains of the Civil Rights Movement. If history had a kind of reckoning in the Civil Rights legislation of 1964 and 1965, the Civil Rights Act and Voting Rights Act, respectively, the culture seems to have been at times regressive, such that the epiphany of Emmett Till could return in George Floyd. These two figures are not the same, but they are projections of unreconciled experiences. In Chapter 3, I am interested in the regressive aspects of the cultural revolution of the 1960s and 1970s, an Age of Dionysus (as much as an "Age of Aquarius"), the quintessential Western epiphany of sexual and cultural revolution. The latent presence of classical paradigms in *Blues* prepares us for the Greek god Dionysus as the epiphany in Chapter 3. In classical mythology, among many other attributes of Dionysus, or Bacchus, is the paradigm of the return of the repressed. The god is "twice-born," having been ripped from his mother's womb and sewn into the thigh of Zeus. He is dismembered, that is, lynched, but made whole again. He is home-grown yet exiled and returns to claim his rightful place. There is likely no other figure better to symbolize the Black American in the cultural currents of the 1960s and 1970s. Dionysus is ever-present in American culture during this period but not appreciated as a potentially Black encoding. This is also a time in which performance as theory comes into its own, especially through Richard Schechner (e.g., Schechner 2000), who was among the first to develop a theory and practice of performance, as we see in his play *Dionysus in '69* (Schechner 1970). Through *The Euripides of Bacchae: A Communion Rite* and other writing like "The Fourth Stage" (reprinted in Soyinka 1990), Wole Soyinka directly engages with Schechner to center the subaltern, anti- or postcolonial personality. Performance is gestural, punching through the artifices of society to uncover raw—Dionysian—realities. During a period that saw the Vietnam War and other social upheavals, Dionysus (or Bacchus) is an epiphany of revolution. He is a subaltern presence that in the U.S. is Black. Even beyond the U.S., Dionysus could be encoded as a figure for this postcolonial period, as Soyinka's *Bacchae* demonstrates.

In this chapter, the reader encounters the raw energy of the late 1960s and 1970s through narrative attempts at epiphenomenon, or analysis. Dionysus figures in the analysis as well. As it pertains to theater, Schechner was one analyst, and through his intervention of Environmental Theater, he sought to channel the energy of the culture toward productive ends (Schechner 2000). Soyinka was another. In addition to *Bacchae* and elsewhere (1990), Soyinka criticizes the fixation of the West on a sexual—rather than revolutionary—interpretation of Dionysus. In the United States more directly, Amiri Baraka wanted to jolt theater out of complacency. His *The Revolutionary Theatre* (1965) is a precursor to the "BIPOC Demands." Himself a force to be reckoned with, Baraka's approach was an awakening for practitioners like Ntozake Shange, whose *for colored girls who considered suicide / when the rainbow was enuf* was an important dramatic event at the end of the 1970s (Shange 1997). Shange centers the subaltern spirit, in this case as the Bacchic chorus figured as multihued, women of color. As Susan Best (2021) argues, however, the performative turn by the late 1970s had become a place of individual expression rather than communal or ethical movement. *for colored girls* presents the Bacchic chorus of women and asks for the audience's emotional energy, but it does not require the community's ethical response. Critics like the Public Theater's founder Joseph Papp sympathized with the subaltern women presented in *for colored girls* (Turan and Papp 2009), but the performance asked nothing more of him as a white male viewer. The play does not ask him to join in the ritual theorization of Dionysus, as Euripides' *Bacchae* does of Pentheus.

Papp's basic instinct was correct that a society where Dionysus rules is not a peaceable or sustainable place. A constant state of revolution is not a formula for civil society. If the 1960s and 1970s brought many events difficult to contain from the standpoint of historical periodization, in the U.S. (and certainly in the United Kingdom), the 1980s and 1990s could be viewed as a turning point, with conservative governments reining in previous excesses. The Reagan Administration rolled out its War on Drugs. By the 1990s, leaders were waging a full-fledged War on Crime, which Richard Nixon had initiated. Notwithstanding the official moves in government, people across the country were experiencing other realities, and their irrepressible memories counter official narratives. If Dionysus was a figure for the revolutionary energy of the 1960s and 1970s, wherein the Black subaltern was quintessentially Bacchic, Oedipus becomes a recurring epiphany during the 1980s and 1990s. The War on Drugs and War on Crime exposed cursed youth, the unwanted, Black children across American cities. Baldwin had cast the nation through ties of kinship, to varying degrees imagined. As kin, however, the racial offspring had always been a problem, a "bastard" in Baldwin's language. It is no coincidence that in contrast to the War on Drugs and the War on Crime, the rhetoric of family values also becomes prevalent during this period. The family as conceived during the 1980s and 1990s was white, and in the Black child, the American family was exposing and abandoning its most vulnerable youth. Oedipus, the Theban baby that Laius and Jocasta expose in Sophocles' famous plays, is a fitting epiphany for the period. During this period, an Oedipus adaptation on the American stage becomes the most influential play for future encounters in dramas in the U.S.: Lee Breuer and Bob Telson's *The Gospel at Colonus* (Breuer and Telson 1986).

In Chapter 4, I argue that *Gospel* and other adaptations of the Oedipus story on the American stage, including Rita Dove's *The*

Darker Face of the Earth (Dove 1994) are epiphanies that represent various official evasions of the racial problem in the U.S. In the case of *Gospel*, the fantasy of a fully actualized Oedipus, the old man at Colonus, reconciled to his past and ready for transfiguration in the next life, skips over the troubling presence of Black youth in a city like New York. Offstage, in real life, the violence of childhood exposure manifested again in the City in the murder of Michael Stewart earlier the same year (1983). Stewart, age 25 at the time (a boy), was apprehended by police officers and accused of spray-painting graffiti on property, although none of the artist's friends knew him as a "tagger." He somehow experienced extreme violence during the arrest and suffered a heart attack in custody. Stewart died violently on September 28, 1983, and his family settled a civil suit in 1990 for $1.7 million. At the time of the criminal trial against the police officers, however, an all-white jury acquitted them of charges related to Stewart's death. The officers, as representatives of the state, stand *in loco parentis*, and yet their duty to protect the family often did not extend to Black youth (Schanbert 1984). Stewart—a real-life Oedipus—became an important visitation during this period, and Jean-Michel Basquiat's artistic representation during the same year, *Defacement*, immortalized Stewart's killing (LaBouvier et al. 2019).

Within this context of the defacement of Black youth in 1983 (outside of time in its constant recurrence if we consider Till before Stewart and others after him), the phantasy of a mature Oedipus in *Gospel* is curious, amounting to a kind of evasion. A similar evasion is evident in Dove's *Darker Face*, despite its representation of a militant, revolutionary Oedipus resonant with Toussaint L'Ouverture of the 1791 Haitian Revolution. In Dove's play, Oedipus, named Augustus, belongs to another time, a fantasy projection that makes the revolutionary past present. The presence of the past is ghostly, but in this sense, Augustus also ghosts the realities of Black youth living in the 1980s and 1990s. With *Gospel* and *Darker Face*, each dramatic experience escapes the present, but not to represent haunting, ethical ghosts. The idea of an anti-Oedipus, from Gilles

Deleuze and Félix Guattari (2009), helps to reckon with the phantasy projections of the period, figures like the Welfare Queen, who disrupts the idea of family values. Although it might be argued that Oedipus onstage and other projections owe nothing to the cultural moment, the therapeutic intervention of August Wilson (1997) gives the lie to ideas of color-blindness, and color-blind staging of theatrical characters, which also came to prominence during the period.

From an analytic perspective, August Wilson directly called into question the use of Western symbols (like Oedipus) to represent for Black Americans. In his 1996 speech for the Theatre Communications Group (published in 1997), he lays out practical steps for the patient, American society, and for theater, performative spaces purportedly, blind to the personal and cultural narratives of millions of Black Americans. Given the Oedipal projections of the period, and specifically an American public discourse celebratory of colorblind society, it is noteworthy that Wilson would reject the idea of colorblind casting. The language of the BIPOC Demands echoes and deliberately calls upon several tropes first presented in Wilson's "The Ground on Which I Stand" (1997). At the end of Chapter 4, I briefly discuss one work that does not evade the Oedipal plight of subaltern youth, Luís Alfaro's Oedipus, who is an incarcerated Hispanic man. He is an ethical haunting, but he belongs to twenty-first century. It is noteworthy that Alfaro develops *Oedipus el Rey* during the period in which Barack Obama would be elected to the presidency (Alfaro 2020).

Many people saw Obama's presidential election in 2008 as the beginning of a new era. It was to be a period of several posts-— postmodern, post-Civil Rights, post-racial, and perhaps even post-gender. Despite the promising dawn of the twenty-first century, however, it would soon become clear that, as Faulkner put it, the past is not dead. Spectral presences from the past hover over the period. Of the many violent specters that could haunt the 2000s, in Chapter 5 I focus on Brandon Teena, the trans man killed in

Humboldt, Nebraska in 1993; and Matthew Shepard, the gay man killed in Laramie, Wyoming in 1998. In the latter, we have a clear case in which a real-life murder haunts the theatrical stage, like what we saw with Baldwin's *Blues* and the lynching of Emmett Till. These killings in fact had much in common. In the wake of Shepard's killing, President Obama signed Civil Rights legislation in 2009, named the Matthew Shepard and James Byrd, Jr. Hate Crimes Prevention Act. In addition to protecting against "crimes committed because of the actual or perceived" race or color, the law extended to "gender, sexual orientation, gender identity, or disability." Through this Act, Obama tied together race, sexual orientation, and disability as sources of violence-producing difference. This development would ostensibly appear on the dramatic stage, as Shepard—Matt—was being encoded epiphanically as a Christ figure. Playwright Moisés Kaufman and his partner Jeffrey LaHoste staged the play, *The Laramie Project*, for their Tectonic Theater Project in 2000. It was a staggering success, and by 2010 the company was developing *The Laramie Project: Ten Years Later* (Kaufman et al. 2014). The two plays offer a therapeutic intervention that had an undeniable role in the transformation of Matt into a cultural icon. At the same time, the plays repressed the ties that Obama signaled in his 2009 legislation, those between race, color, gender, and sexual orientation.

In this chapter, through the model of memory, haunting, and recurrence, the 2000s can be seen as a period of various regressions in broader narratives across culture in the U.S. One such regression occurs onstage in the disentanglement of race and gender in the *Laramie Project*. Matt was HIV+. Coming out of the 1990s, it would be strange to talk about the HIV/AIDS crisis without notice of the entanglements of that disease with race. By 2000, to represent HIV/AIDS as a gay, white man's disease would require a series of repressions. I will trace those repressions in both plays, *The Laramie Cycle* (the 2000 play and the 2010 one). Whether inadvertent or strategic, the representation of HIV/AIDS through

Matt in *The Laramie Project* (Kaufman et al. 2014) signaled a new, heteronormativity in American culture. Whiteness is normative. Theater practitioners talked about diversity in color-blind casting. Theater companies like the Public Theater hired George C. Wolfe, a Black artistic director who also happened to be gay. At the same time, they staged plays that reinforced a white normativity, like Ellen McLaughlin's adaptation of Euripides' *Helen* (published in 2004), which I also discuss in this chapter. If McLaughlin's *Helen* was working through the normativity of its titular character as a white woman, *The Laramie Project* represents the normalization of ties between white men and their sexuality. For this reason, Brandon Teena troubles the paradigm, as a transgender man killed like Matt, but a symbol that evades heteronormativity, a term I will discuss.

By setting *The Laramie Cycle* against the backdrop of the murder of this trans* man, I enable what international relations and gender scholar Rahul Rao calls a theoretical "trans-ing" (2020), which reveals the knottiness of events that seem otherwise independent of each other, in this case race and gender (or queerness). These spectral figures of Brando, Helen, or Matt, trans-—they "cross over," in the sense of gender, but also in theoretical terms. The trans* relationship between and among spectral subalterns exposes connections between and among cultural events. The ghosts of Teena and Shepard reveal the problems that inevitably return when an individual or culture prioritizes a single set of memories over others. These epiphanies are tied together with the ghost of Emmett Till and other specters of Black Americans maimed, mutilated, or killed, even into the 2000s. As a documentary theater, *The Laramie Cycle* dramas are tied together with the project of Anna Deavere Smith, whose 1992 play, *Fires in the Mirror* (published in 1993), was a theatrical intervention in killing of Gavin Cato. Cato was a 7-year-old Black boy who was struck by a car in the Crown Heights neighborhood of Brooklyn, New York. A member of an Orthodox Jewish community of Crown Heights was driving the car, and controversy ensued between Black protestors and the community they held responsible. In this chapter, I offer that in the sphere of social dramas, a trans* awareness allows us to see the latent possibilities that linger in the culture, as classical presences in contemporary spaces, even for subaltern people in a majority population in the U.S. In this case, as with Till, the epiphany is figured as a martyred Christ.

Throughout *Theater and Crisis*, I show that like individual memory, cultural memory draws from Greco-Roman myth, as well as from the Judeo-Islamo-Christian storytelling dominant in the West. This latter register is sometimes a neglected cultural reality in the scholarship of classical reception. Nevertheless, Biblical stories function in the culture as prevalently (if not even more transparently). As we come to the contemporary scene in Chapter 6, I foreground one of the first plays staged during Broadway's 2021 reopening, which features Christian symbols. First performed at Chicago's Goodman Theatre in 2017, Antoinette Nwandu's *Pass Over* is a drama that shows epiphanic encoding through imagining a young Black male character as the Biblical figure Moses (Nwandu 2019). The play features two Black men in continuous dialog on a city street corner somewhere in the United States. *Pass Over* has been compared to Samuel Beckett's *Waiting for Godot* (Akbar 2020b). The play reworks mythic figures to embody existential American concerns with race and violence. Because the play has a pre-pandemic iteration and a subsequent one that responds to the events of 2020, and given its presentation of racial interactions in phantastic rather than real terms, it was a fitting vehicle for the reopening of commercial theater in 2021.

In this chapter, I argue that the 2021 adaptation of Nwandu's *Pass Over* epitomizes the role of mythological fantasy in the process of epiphanic encoding. From the standpoint of the processes of presenting dramas onstage, moreover, *Pass Over* was one of the productions sensitive to the issues that the "BIPOC Demands" raised. The production process foregrounded care of the artists working to stage this play. This vision of care is not far removed from the Edenic ending of the 2021 play, which moves from the ghostly violence in its 2017 counterpart to an epiphanic vision of Moses and a Promised Land. Nwandu's comments on *Pass Over* move from the metaphor of cancer, with race relations in the U.S. needing "chemotherapy," a trope consistent with race as one of the pandemics in the country, to a healing imaginary. Unlike *Gospel at Colonus*, however, this phantasy does not elide the true cost of racial violence. Rather, it encodes the toll of race on Black and white bodies while offering a therapeutic intervention into this dysfunction, one closer to psychotherapy than chemotherapy.

As *Theater and Crisis* ends, the Conclusion returns to the pandemic year, 2020. Considering the preceding recurrences of myth and memory across the last half-century, Richard Nelson's pandemic-year plays, *What Do We Need to Talk About?* and *And So We Come Forth*, provide theatrical instantiations of a family finding meaning through storytelling. The Apple family, a group that projects pandemic experiences onto a makeshift stage, in this case the recognizable Zoom teleconferencing platform, evolves as they deal with quarantine and then the nationwide protests of the summer of 2000. They approach the issue of race indirectly, but their conversations about the past and the protests surrounding monuments betray an anxiety about threats to these characters' own meaning and significance. Although their conversations mark the Apple family as white and politically liberal, their concerns are consistent with those of others who began to shut down in the face of protests and the racial justice discourse that arose. By 2021, a backlash to the centering of race was discernible in the U.S. This contentious relationship to race found its grounding in Kyle Rittenhouse, whose individual actions became meaningful to a group of people who saw in him an epiphany with which they could identify. The Apple family is not the type to condone Rittenhouse's violence, and yet their concerns echo those of the groups that did. Rittenhouse became a Christ figure, similar to how George Floyd had been encoded as a martyr. Mythological narratives have no ultimate claims to truth, any more than do memories, and yet they project a set of realities that can be negotiated in common—or, as I am arguing, in performance.

The epiphany or fantasy is a psychological theory, but students of classical myth, literature, and narratology might be drawn to the central place of myth and storytelling, as it pertains to the idea of ethical action embedded in epiphanic encoding. Readers across the cultural divide might note (in the idea of encoding) that classical narratives continue to matter, but they matter in a particular way. In theater, works that master encoding, which is to say master metaphor, succeed in drawing audiences into an ethical or beloved community. At best, such theater is not didactic; it does not direct its audiences how to think about the questions that these hauntings bring to the surface.[52] Rather, the most successful theatrical works encode fantasies in a way that draws from myth and collective memory to generate meaning for their audiences, beyond the particulars of the subjects or characters represented. These audiences are transformed into communities. What to do with the ethical questions raised, or the love generated, is left to us, the community, to determine.

CHAPTER TWO

JAMES BALDWIN'S *BLUES FOR MISTER CHARLIE* (1964)

Kinship, Punishment, and Vengeance on the American Stage

The ghost of Emmett Till, the innocent Black teenage boy whose life and death fold onto that of too many similar stories, some before 1955, and others well into the twenty-first century, haunted Baldwin from 1955 to 1964. Unearthing this ghost in *Blues* was work he—and the nation—needed to do. Emmett's legendary status and the representation of his life onstage are instances in an ostensibly linear story that folds untidily upon itself as we consider its haunts in such visitations as the 2020 murder of George Floyd.

On July 2, 1964, Congress passed the Civil Rights Act, which outlawed discrimination by color, religion, sex, or national origin in schools, employment, and public settings.[1] The single law could only begin to gesture toward a reconciliation between various groups in the United States, so long-standing and persistent in the law and society were the specters of the past. The 1964 judgment had an emancipatory precedent, *Brown v. Board of Education*, the 1954 Supreme Court case that banned racial segregation in schools,[2] effectively overturning the "separate but equal" practices that had been legally sanctioned in the 1896 Supreme *Plessy v. Ferguson* case.[3] As with all other times in American history, the courts were the site of the enactment of real-life contestations over rights and justice during the Civil Rights movement of 1954–1968. In contrast to the courts, theater could be ground for make-believe and fantastic projections about what could be, a place where audiences might imagine the impact of race in America on the individual psyche and its associations. Theater, which could manage projections of the self, was a place to unearth the psychological fruit growing from real-life relationships. If the courts signaled where the culture was going, James Baldwin envisions theater as the place where people might become themselves, realizing the entanglements between the past, the present, and one another.

Baldwin's play is a daring exploration of theater as just such a social hothouse. *Blues*' provocation, the events leading to its development and the aftermath of those catastrophes, would be a decisive test of America's appetite for racial reconciliation. *Blues* is an important experiment in Baldwin's broader study of race and reconciliation in America from 1964 to 1972, years spanning from the play's publication to that of *No Name in the Street*, Baldwin's 1972 post-mortem on the Civil Rights era.

In this chapter, I situate *Blues* within several adjacent and equally important contexts for understanding the play. First, *Blues* is best read within the broader framework of Baldwin's writing and reflections because this perspective helps us to make sense of his sensibilities and symbols, and his condemnation of the continuing avoidance of true reckoning and reconciliation across American history. Through *Blues*, Baldwin also encodes Emmett within a bloody, unjust American saga. Baldwin's character Richard is a fictionalization of Emmett, making of a person an epiphany, part of a larger American saga, bloody and unjust. Moreover, family kinship—the American South, with segregated white and Black families and their forbidden encounters—becomes entangled with a broader collective past within the U.S. and beyond. Emmett became myth, a "legend" in Baldwin's language.[4] Emmett is a scapegoat whose bloodshed had done little to expiate previous wrongs or prevent future ones. The culpability of Emmett's assailants was plain for anyone to see (Tyson 2017), but time and again, justice would prove blind to the humanity, dispossession, and pain of Black claimants.

Theater is another critical frame through which we might view *Blues*. Many artistic media transfigure myth and memory, but for Baldwin theater was to be the site of an important therapeutic intervention into the cultural status quo. Within the broader context of this book, Baldwin emerges as an astute and ancestral critic of American theater. Where laws fail, Baldwin makes a plea for compassion in the court of public opinion, through theater. He turns to the blues as a performative, choral call for audiences to experience the lives and feel the anguish of others, as if they were our own. Baldwin's status as a theater practitioner, his "flesh-centered imaginative work" (Mitchell 2012), is important to the contextualization of the play within his literary corpus and beyond. Although Baldwin only staged two complete plays of his own in his lifetime,[5] the other being *The Amen Corner* in 1954, he was an incisive theater and film critic. After 1964, he "directed a play on prison life in Turkey—though he spoke the language haltingly—and supported friends putting on a production of 'Hair'" (Fahim 2017). In 1976, we find strong signals of Baldwin as a performance theorist in *The Devil Finds Work*, ostensibly a book of film criticism (Baldwin 2011). His relationship to theater criticism in America, as it pertains to race and even more broadly, is significant. Baldwin's critique of the state of play in American theater in the 1950s and 1960s provides a precursor to August Wilson's speech "The Ground on Which I Stand" (Wilson 1997) and has an important place alongside the 2020 "BIPOC Demands."

Beyond American theater per se, Baldwin signals that *Blues* attends to larger "ghostly matters," an attention to which can "radically change how we know and what we know" (Gordon 2008: 27).

If there is an American lineage from Emmett Till to George Floyd, there is also a broader heritage into which the American is born, historical and theatrical ghosts we ignore at our detriment. The blues of Baldwin's heritage is also the Greek tragic chorus transported to the United States, another ghostly matter.[6] In my analysis of *Blues* in this chapter, I am particularly interested in Baldwin's relationship to the European and American theatrical heritage, evident first in his formulation of "Western culture" or "Western civilization" throughout his writing.[7] More immediately, Baldwin's theatrical imagination includes William Shakespeare's *Macbeth*, although he came to appreciate the playwright with great struggle (Baldwin 2010: 65–69), and Aeschylus, whose *Oresteia* has important but heretofore unexcavated relevance for *Blues*. Baldwin was not content to see himself as an inheritor of Western heritage. Rather, he believed that the world was coming to recognize not only the European past but also other, new classics, such as those evident in the writings of Léopold Sédar Senghor, the writer of negritude and first Senegalese President from 1960–1980 (see Senghor 1998). At the same time, Baldwin reckoned with the European past as an inescapable part of a collective memory, ghosts he would have to exercise on the nation's behalf.

STAGING BALDWIN'S RAGE

First performed on April 23, 1964 (Leeming 2015), *Blues for Mister Charlie* grapples with Emmett Till's 1955 lynching in Money, Mississippi through the figuration of family, the tangled kinship bonds between Black and white people in the American South. Scenes of civic and familial reckoning, the home, the Church, and the courtroom are prominent in the play, and they are sites of action in Baldwin's theatrical and social memory. More broadly, the theater serves a metaphysical function in Baldwin's imagination. These institutions haunt his writing, but his 1976 essay *The Devil Finds Work* most poignantly imagines the Church and the theater in juxtaposition (Baldwin 2011 [1976]). As it pertains to theater, young James crafted his first play in his preteen years (Leeming 2015). For Baldwin, there was in theater a "wonder", a sleight-of-hand to dramatic representation. At the same time, theater is "powerful on a more dreadful level" (Baldwin 2011 [1976]: 41). In Baldwin's descriptions of theater (and film) in *Devil* and throughout his writing, he betrays his fascination with make-believe, the realm of mimesis that consumes everything and orders the world anew, in each person. As he puts it, people "are each other's flesh and blood" (29).[8] This formulation, which recurs throughout *Devil*,[9] pertains to theater but emerges from Baldwin's experience of the Christian sacrament of—metaphorically in the Protestant Church, and by transubstantiation in Catholicism—eating Christ's flesh, drinking his blood, and becoming one with his body and the body of other Christians. Baldwin recasts Christian iconography as mythic symbolism (Bottici 2007), where he imagines Macbeth as equally important as Christ. Baldwin's grade-school teacher Bill Miller took him to see *Macbeth* as a child, and even as an adult he hearkens to a kind of transubstantiation on the American stage: "Flesh and blood had proved to be too much for flesh and blood. For, they were themselves, these actors—these people were themselves. They could be Macbeth only because they were themselves" (Baldwin 2011: 33).

Through mythic epiphanies, Baldwin examines his own relationship to institutions within the "Western civilization" to which he often refers, an idea that broadens the scope of American experience—and Baldwin's critique of it—beyond 1964, temporally and spatially. The formulation of Western civilization mirrors Baldwin's own sense of what constitutes home. His departures and returns home to the United States throughout his life figure in his imagination and literary output.

Race is a haunting issue in this landscape. Baldwin's fixation on race led critics like Robert Brustein, a staple in American theater of the twentieth century who figures later for August Wilson, to call him angry, enraged, or deranged (Menand 2021). Race renders Baldwin a "stranger," the Negro in the remote Swiss village whose inhabitants he imagines belonging to the West, being at home, in ways that he never can.[10] By projecting his experience as an American onto what he imagines as Western civilization, Baldwin proposes that rather than anomalous, America is merely one manifestation of broader designs beyond the United States. In this way Baldwin anticipates a Black Atlantic well before Paul Gilroy's 1993 formulation. These include associations between Europe and whiteness, Africa and blackness, and concomitant perceptions of superiority and inferiority—ultimately, power, colonialism, and the potential of a post-coloniality.[11] Baldwin's Black Atlantic perspective will have more bearing in the next chapter, when we see how he reflects global Blackness back onto American society in his search for a composite subaltern culture, one that would reconstitute the mixed-heritage American—indeed, the broader Western—family.

Despite his international roaming, his hearth, his home, was in the United States, even in its brokenness and injustice. He returns home to the U.S. to visit the segregated South in 1957, two years after Till's murder, from the émigré status he held in France beginning in 1948. As late as his 1964 preface to the play, he writes that the 1955 lynching of Emmett lingered in his mind. The lynching "would not let me go" (Baldwin 1995a). In addition, his friend the Civil Rights icon Medgar Evers was killed in Mississippi in 1963. Baldwin was indeed enraged. The killing happens in the same year Baldwin published his judgment of the Negro's chastisement in the United States, in their national home. Baldwin calls down a cosmic vengeance, "a vengeance inevitable—a vengeance that does not really depend on, and cannot really be executed by, any person or organization, and that cannot be prevented by any police force or army" (Baldwin 1992a [1963]: 105).[12] As we will see, this vengeance is that of the Erinyes, the ghosts who guard familial bloodletting in Aeschylus' *Oresteia*.

The language Baldwin applies to the institutions of the Church and the theater conveys his sense of urgency, his fiery passion for their sacred and ritual roles in society. He imagines public institutions, even the American courts, as collective extensions of familial, domestic space, where the individual can be reconciled to community. Christianity held this promise and gave mythic language to hope. The Church is the house of God, home an underlying trope of James Baldwin's theoretical corpus, including *Blues*. It is worth recalling that home is also a spatial and speculative framework at the foundation of the "BIPOC Demands." Whereas the writers of the demands seek to counter the implicit message that people of color receive across American theater that "this is not your artistic home" ("BIPOC Demands" 2020: 3), being each other's flesh and blood transforms a nation into a house of kinfolk. For Baldwin, where the Church had failed, theater could be the central, unifying hearth, a place of domestic safety and sustenance made public for national gathering. In terms of epiphanic encoding, Baldwin was imagining a site for the work of myth, for the past figured in the present and futured in terms of reconciliation. Such a process would have to happen in story, phantasy projections, before it could be imagined or made real in the surrounding world.

Throughout *Devil* and across his writing, Baldwin commits these institutions—the Church, the house, the theater—to his imagined national identity. The tropes are rooted in his own understanding of self and longing for family. He never knew his biological father, but he held a deep love for his siblings, and curiosity about his mother formed some of the material through which he imagines the world outside himself, his idea of the space "between the world and me," as he put it.[13]

At this intersection between the world and the self, Baldwin imagines a journey into a collective memory. I have named the work of myth in the past, figured in the present for an imagined future, epiphanic encoding. Being one another's flesh and blood is also to be haunted by and bound up with a certain past and present beyond oneself. Baldwin's childhood and family life were points of origin for his Christianity and idea of the West. He transmutes his attempt to reconcile his "bastard" status, as a man taken in by David Baldwin, his mother's husband but not his father, into a broader cultural bereavement. David forced young James to abandon the theater, his first love, for the Church, and Baldwin became a young preacher. Baldwin would later leave the Church, but the institution never left him. Outside of his own home, he is a "bastard of the West," and this status outside of the familial hearth is the driving force in his unrelenting quest to be at home in America and, more broadly, the world. The secular sources that inspired Baldwin as a child also never left him. He ultimately expresses his frustration with the West's projections of race, which disrupts familial ties and shatters home.

In the world of Baldwin's West, the biblical imagery of vengeance, destruction, retribution and, ultimately, terror permeate the visual and intellectual landscape. In his reflections on American society in the wake of the murder of Dr. Martin Luther King, Jr., for example, Baldwin returns to the image of blood, this time not as connective tissue across the U.S., but rather now as retribution: "The suffering of the scapegoat has resulted in seas of blood, and yet not one sinner has been saved, or changed, by the despairing ritual. Sin has merely been added to sin, and guilt piled upon guilt" (Baldwin 2007 [1972]: 54–55). Baldwin's "scapegoat" describes Black death, not as victimization but as the object of ritual sacrifice, of a "despairing ritual." The Church figures here, as we see in "sinners to be saved," but something beyond Christianity is being signaled, as we hear in the "sin ... merely ... added to sin," and the "guilt piled upon guilt." The "seas of blood" that Baldwin sees pouring out on American streets owe to Aeschylus and Shakespeare as much as to Christianity. Baldwin evokes Lady Macbeth's unclean hands: "Out, damned spot! Out, I say!—One, two ... The thane of Fife had a wife. Where is she now?—What, will these hands ne'er be clean?" (Shakespeare, *Macbeth*, Act 5, Scene 1, 25–27 and 30–32).

As I argue in this chapter, the mythic past helps Baldwin to encode contemporary figures, by which he in turn projects new epiphanies for American audiences. Such epiphanic encoding is not an appeal to history, but rather it is a ghostly matter. Shakespeare is undeniably part of this epiphanic, mythological past.

Moving deeper into the past, although Baldwin does not cite Aeschylus (beyond naming him in "Stranger in the Village"), I argue that the Greek playwright is also part of the material that blends indiscriminately in his work, such that his relationship to source material is not easy to trace.[14] Nevertheless, Aeschylus is part of Baldwin's "frightful" imaginary (Baldwin 2011 [1976]), and he uses his understanding of the West to convey the full psychic force of horrifying violence for which there must be an accounting. We see Aeschylus at play through images of home (the *oikos*), sacred spaces of worship (Agamemnon's tomb, Apollo's temple), and the courtroom (the Areopagus).

Through *Blues*, Baldwin brings the urgent conversation about race to American theater, one that goes beyond what he sees as the anemic representations on stage up to 1964. As he writes in his introduction to *Blues*, race has "the power to destroy every human relationship" (Baldwin 1995a). It is a collective crisis, a plague, and yet American theater proves to him ill-prepared to represent adequately the sickness or its potential cure. Baldwin does not "have much respect for what goes on in the American Theatre" (Baldwin 1995a). He is, however, an adept playwright, theater critic, and theorist of performance. Baldwin's critique of the theater is coterminous with how he views the Church, whose myths had lost their power, so "the true believer goes elsewhere" (Baldwin 2011 [1976]: 29). Rather than the Church, the ritual of theater-going and acting are now the sites of the host, the flesh and blood that all share as part of one body. That is, for Baldwin the American theater could pick up where the Church had failed. Actors in a Shakespeare play perform a fundamental ritual of life and death: "They could be Macbeth only because they were themselves" (33). Throughout

Baldwin's writing, dread, terror, and destruction recur as necessary and, ultimately, restorative. He echoes Aeschylus in these figurations. For Americans to be themselves or anything else, they would have to encounter the dread of the past, the reality that "revenge is a human dream" (40). Since "the story is revelation, not resolution" (42), it would be important first to tell American stories that spoke to many truths. American theater, however, like the Church, was failing to rise to its ritual potential.[15] Baldwin takes the violent, real-life event that made Emmett legendary and delivers its enactment, Emmett's flesh and blood, to onstage revelers in a communion ritual.

A GHOSTLY READING OF *BLUES FOR MISTER CHARLIE*

It is fitting that Baldwin should set his autopsy of Emmett Till's lynching in Plaguestown, U.S.A., given the urgent calls in the U.S. even some 65 years later to address racial relations as a public health emergency (see Chapter 1). By this account, the plague is still ravishing the population. In 1955, at 14 years old, Emmett was visiting relatives in Money, Mississippi, from Chicago, Illinois, and was accused of whistling at (or making lewd comments toward) a white storekeeper, Carolyn Bryant Donham (see Tyson 2017). Her husband Roy, along with an accomplice, J. W. Milam, dragged young Emmett out of his uncle's house by night, slaughtered him, and tied his body to a heavy gin mill, so as to sink it to the bottom of the Tallahatchie River (see Ginzburg 1996). Carolyn later confessed to lying about Emmett's behavior: "Nothing that boy did could ever justify what happened to him" (Pérez-Peña 2017). Beyond the gruesomeness of the crime, Emmett's cousin, who was present, would characterize the lynching in terms of a disorder in the American justice system, given the acquittal of the perpetrators: "It's important to people to understand how the word of a white person against a black person was law, and a lot of black people lost their lives because of it. It really speaks to history, it shows what black people went through in those days" (Pérez-Peña 2017).

Notwithstanding the acquittal of Roy and Milam at the time, the case has continued to bend slowly toward the long arc of justice. Attempts to reopen and retry the assailants have persisted well into the twenty-first century.[16] In the 1950s and 1960s, however, the acquittal of Till's murderers was a sign to many of the failure of the American justice system when it comes to non-white subjects.

As early as the days and weeks after his death, justice for Emmett would have to be extra-judicial. The enactment of truth and reconciliation in the court of public opinion was an immediate matter historically, which Emmett's open-casket funeral highlighted, his mangled face and decaying body the ever-present habeas corpus for the world to judge.[17] Over sixty years later, the ritual repetition of Emmett's death reaches a religious pitch in the performative space of the Smithsonian National Museum of African American History and Culture, which opened its doors in 2016. The "those days" to which Till's cousin refers in 2017 are relived daily, as the crowds that gather mount onto a podium containing Emmett's reconstructed casket, a memorial that marks the culminating experience of the visit.[18] Visitors to the museum are able to relive his mother Mamie's humanization of her son and perhaps understand why she allowed the image of Emmett's disfigured face to be printed on the cover of *Jet Magazine.* The prominence of these images transformed Emmett into a touchstone for the Civil Rights Movement. The disfigured image, however, is distilled through the figure of the pietà, the suffering of Christ. (See Figure 2.) As we saw in the last chapter, Lonnie Bunch, who was director of the museum in 2015, reported that Mamie "saw Emmett as being crucified on the cross of racial injustice."[19] The murder of Emmett Till became a symbol of the brutality that accompanied—and still attends—being Black in America. The communities that bear witness to his ritual significance transformed his body into a sacrament of veneration, or a haunting for those who would prefer to move on.[20] Till becomes a mythic figuration, a phantasy, an epiphany encoded in personal and national memory.

Emmett's open-casket image conveyed what a performative experience, that of reliving the premature funeral of a teenage boy, could do for the living, who might undergo "something much deeper" than either guilt or revenge, to return to Baldwin's description of the theatrical experience (Baldwin 2011 [1976]: 40).

Moving back to this space of theater from the museum, or from the courtroom that failed to condemn Till's murderers, if the American stage was to be more than entertainment, it would have to encounter protagonists like Emmett and his murderers. The theatrical work would have to depict these men beyond a flattened humanity, on either side of the terrible act. To seize its "power on a more dreadful level" (Baldwin 2011 [1976]: 41), theater would have to be deeply invasive, operating beyond a treatment of cancer to reconstitute the memories and intentions of the body politic. Baldwin wanted *Blues for Mister Charlie* to operate on this mythic, psychological level.

Regarding the play's title, the blues provide a compelling metaphor for Baldwin to use because the musical genre itself does the work of myth by transforming painful emotions into melody, harmony, rhythm, meaning. By naming theater as a laboratory where this emotional, mythmaking process can take place, Baldwin asks whether the institution could do more than the Church, more than the courts, to unite American communities. The site of theater would accomplish this unity because it is a "memory machine" (Carlson 2003). The courts had failed, and in 1964, Baldwin did not have the museum in Washington, D.C. as a comparable institution.

The theatrical blues of Baldwin's play, however, are not for Emmett. They are, rather, for Mister Charlie, the white Americans who perpetrate these crimes or those who absolve the perpetrators. Mister Charlie might well be in the audience watching *Blues*, participating in the ritual. He is certainly onstage, embodied in

Baldwin's characters. Mister Charlie shares with others, who might be black, female, young, or old, public space, whether the streets, the home, the shop where Emmett went to buy a Coke, or the court of law.

Reading *Blues* for setting, characters, kinship, and justice is a case study in how Baldwin saw theater to operate as a pivotal institution for racial reconciliation in the United States. Baldwin's was a reckoning, not out of any hatred of others or impulse to retaliate. Rather, theater as a collective, ritual space, the public hearth, was an ancient reality, one resonant with the Greeks, reverberant in Shakespeare's England, and present in other traditional cultures.[21] Baldwin draws from these ancient myths in manifest and sometimes unspoken ways, practicing something akin to signifying on his predecessors and influences.[22] In what follows, I trace the mythic entanglements of *Blues* to a foundational work of theater, Aeschylus' *Oresteia*, which is itself an important if hidden subtext to Shakespeare's *Macbeth*. As we know, *Macbeth* is in Baldwin's blood. Through a reading of setting, character, action, and retribution, I reveal the play's potential role in epiphanic encoding, the evocation of individual and collective phantasies that seek their teleological resolution.

SETTING

The streets (and shops where business is transacted), the Church and the courtroom are important spaces where the national community congregates. Baldwin echoes those settings in the fictional world of *Blues*. Stage directions separate the Black and white characters of the imagined Southern town, Plaguestown, in keeping with the laws and practices of segregation. Through "the dome of the courthouse and the American flag" and "the Church, and the cross," Baldwin presents American theater with two other storied institutions, or spoiled inheritances: a system of justice, one that by the end of the play has failed Black people; and Christianity, a sacred social practice that Black people embrace in vernacular practice but that Americans have used to justify enslavement. These are the settings that the characters inhabit. Their ghostly embodiments include fathers and sons, daughters and lovers, mothers and enemies, the kinship ties and surrogates that run throughout all of Baldwin's writing.

Music (as figured in spirituals or the blues) is a mythic form that distills these familial experiences into something meaningfully recognizable to others. As we have seen, *Devil* shines an illuminating light into Baldwin's worldview as a point of comparison to *Blues*, an important source for understanding how Baldwin casts the blues, generally, as a domestic—American, but also familial—artistic form, in the essay. As elsewhere in his writing, *Devil* resounds with metaphors of home and kinship. One section in *Devil* melds Church and home, opening with an epigraph of the words of a black spiritual song:

> I found a leak in my building and:
> my soul has got to move.
> I say:
> My soul has got to move.
>
> (Baldwin 2011 [1976]: 93)

In the refrain presumably sung in Black Churches, the singer trades the old building that "keeps sinking" and "mov[es] home," to a "mansion in the sky," an eternal place, built by "another builder." Home is also a unifying symbol of the Church – e.g., the house of God, heaven as a "mansion in the sky" (John 14:2), the congregation as the family of God—and Baldwin will take it to be an important trope for the nation as well.

It is telling that Baldwin deploys the domestic symbolism of Black Christian life to reconcile a broader public to its imagery. As he puts it in *Devil*, it is "through the creation of the black Church that an unwritten, dispersed, and violated inheritance has been handed down" (Baldwin 2011 [1976]: 113). Black inheritance is figured through blood ties of the "violated," a subaltern collective within the U.S. and across the African diaspora that often expresses itself in Christian symbols (Gilroy 1993). At the same time, Christianity is part of a broader heritage of Western culture, an institution that Black people have transformed to speak to their circumstances. Baldwin puts the case as follows: "The custodians of an inheritance, which is what blacks have had to be, in Western culture, must hand the inheritance down the line. So you, the custodian, recognize, finally, that your life does not belong to you: nothing belongs to you" (Baldwin 2011 [1976]: 114).

Baldwin characterizes the Church as a home that Black people built. Western Christianity wrought slavery and Black denigration (as the children of Ham) (Genesis 9:25–27; 10:6–20), but Baldwin inverts this reality. Rather than condemning the Church, he argues that its true "custodians" are Black. He looks to the Church as a possible place to reconcile the outcast status of Black people in "Western culture." Just as "nothing belongs" to Black people, the Church does not belong to Europeans either.

It is noteworthy that Baldwin does not look only to the West for the Black form of Christianity. The West is the site of Black estrangement or bastardization. Rather, Baldwin uses language of return, to something *before* the West: "The blacks did not so much use Christian symbols as recognize them—recognize them for what they were before the Christians came along—and, thus, reinvested these symbols with their original energy" (Baldwin 2011 [1976]: 113). In his notion that blacks "recognize[d]" Christian symbols and "reinvested" them, Baldwin points to antiquity, a time *before*, even if this antiquity is undefined and without distinct location.[23] Baldwin's antiquity may be that of the early Christian Church, but it is also mythic, an a-historical time and place that is prior to but also ever-present in the contemporary. Ritual return, rather than historical study, helps us to locate this antiquity. Baldwin's language of antiquity, including African retentions, or even the European past, is not fulsome; it is not a fully actualized idea. The mythic setting of this antiquity folds onto the present through characters and their actions, as we will see. American Emmett, figured fictionally as Richard in *Blues*, is an epiphanic return of Agamemnon or King Duncan, blood that has been shed and that cries out for a justice that the Christian Church, with its emphasis on forgiveness, cannot offer. Thus, Baldwin discerns a time "before the Christians." He seeks a return to this "original energy," and in *Blues,* the Church that the West built will not prove to be sufficient.

In contrast to the Church, the courtroom offers the potential for justice, but it too fails. Just as Baldwin looks to something prior to the West for his idea of Christianity, he will reach to an unnamed antiquity for justice considering the bankruptcy of the courts. As it pertains to justice, Baldwin gropes for a time "before," and it is here that I point not only to Shakespeare, but more distantly to Aeschylus. In Aeschylus' *Oresteia*, Baldwin's search for a cosmic justice prior to Christianity finds a compelling destination.[24]

A quick sketch of Aeschylus' trilogy is worthwhile. The *Oresteia* also begins in the home, the vernacular *oikos* that establishes right relationships between and among kin, such as the stable marital relationships that do not result in violence to a spouse. This violence, however, is exactly what unfolds in the home. After Clytemnestra kills her husband Agamemnon on his return from war in his namesake play, an act she presents as retribution for his previous murder of their daughter Iphigeneia to secure the war's success, the setting moves to Agamemnon's graveside in the second play, *The Libation Bearers*. This is a setting of spiritual observance, like the Church, as Agamemnon's daughter Electra, along with a chorus of women, brings libations to his gravesite and prays for atonement. The setting of home is never too far in the background. Agamemnon's son, Orestes, whom his mother sent away as a child to prevent his retribution, reenters the *oikos* disguised as a stranger. He continuously alludes to sacred space, the temple of Apollo at Delphi, which is echoed in the Cross and

Church of *Blues*. Orestes receives word from Apollo, who stands in as a surrogate father, that he must avenge Agamemnon's death. Within the *Oresteia*, the temple of Apollo is the penultimate setting, where the last play in the trilogy, *The Furies*, opens. Like *Blues*, this third play ends at the court of law, in this case the Areopagus. The Eryines, maidens who cry out when kindred blood is spilled, pursue Orestes there, after Apollo advises him to seek out justice in Athens.

By the *Oresteia*'s conclusion, Orestes moves from suppliant seeking protection from the Eryines to defendant. Although he kills his mother, the Eryines spare his life, which would have been the appropriate price for his act of spilling kindred blood. The final judgment in his favor, however, preserves the possibility of future retribution. The Eryines become Eumenides, a euphemism for the bloody pursuers of justice, "the kindly ones." If legal, sanctioned punishment fails to maintain right relationships between and among persons, the inner nature of the Eumenides, as seekers of blood, remains. They are ready to hunt.

It is no accident that the *Oresteia*'s domestic, religious, and legal setting correspond with *Blues*' home, Church, and courtroom. Baldwin cites Aeschylus as a Western forebear and need not lead us beyond the "fuzzy connection" or rhizomic roots he suggests (Hardwick 2011). The *Oresteia* is as clear an antecedent to *Blues* as *Macbeth*, the more explicitly referenced play in Baldwin's repertoire. Shakespeare's play begins with the haunting of the Weird Sisters, and in *Blues* the audience encounters Richard primarily as a ghost because he has already been killed when the play begins. Ancestry and displacements from home are themes of *Macbeth*, the "blood for blood" of Aeschylus' play, notable in translations contemporary to Baldwin, corresponding with Lady Macbeth's "damned spot:" Phillip Vellacott's 1962 translation of the *Oresteia*, which I will cite more fully later, is worth a quick juxtaposition: "This was the god's command: 'Shed blood for blood, your face set like a flint. The price they owe no wealth can weigh.' My very life, he said, would pay, in endless torment, for disobedience" (Aeschylus, *Libation Bearers*, 278–80).[25]

In the context of justice at the familial hearth of the United States, Baldwin called for fire in 1963. By 1972, he had seen enough of Black bodies becoming sacrifices, the "seas of blood" pouring out in the streets. Like the Eryines and Lady Macbeth, he declares, as we saw, that "sin has merely been added to sin, and guilt piled upon guilt" (Baldwin 2011 [1976]: 54). *Oresteia* offers an alternative resolution to justice delayed, albeit not a comforting one.

CHARACTER

Shakespeare might not point Baldwin to a time "before the Christians" for characterization, but Aeschylus certainly would. Aeschylus represents familial ties prior to Christianity, before dichotomies of public and private, nation and home, or even Black and white overlaid the ritual realities beneath the surface. Baldwin animates the stage with characters who are more deeply connected than these polarities permit them to realize. He sets his play in a Southern town in America in the 1950s and early 1960s, which he populates with the kinds of people Emmett might have seen, encountered, or himself been (see Leeming 2015). These characters are also approximations of those Baldwin encountered when he accompanied Medgar Evers on his interviews pertaining to a killing similar to that of Till a year earlier, in 1963. Southernness, however, belies deeper entanglements with other kinfolk in Northern states. Baldwin conceives of America as one house, one family, and one nation.

Baldwin goes to great lengths to establish all characters as kin, full human beings, and potentially good people, although given to prejudice and anger, revenge, and hatred. These are Shakespearean emotions, from which no human being is exempt. As Baldwin puts it in his analysis of Shakespearean language, "once one has begun to suspect this much about the world—once one has begun to suspect, that is, that one is not, and never will be, innocent, for the reason that no one is—some of the self-protective veils between oneself and reality begin to fall away" (Baldwin 2010: 55). The language of the world and the self ("between the world and me") is resonant in the "self-protective" veil that obscures reality, perhaps the same veil that W. E. B. Du Bois uses to describe a "double-consciousness" between Black people and others during segregated times.[26] On either side of the veil are people who are not innocent, which is the designated role of victims, but who are fully human, in all the complexity that Shakespeare was adept at conveying.

A few central examples of the complexity of characterization in *Blues* convey the Shakespearean depth Baldwin hoped to reach, as well as the ancient, familial entanglements between and among characters.[27] In the play, Richard is another Emmett, if a bit older, a young man in his twenties struggling to find his way. He is a person whom his family loves—one might call him a generally good or likeable person—but many grievances plague him, including what he believes is the wrongful death of his mother at the hands of white people.[28] Because he has lived in the North (in New York City, as opposed to Emmett's Chicago), he is somewhat eccentric, different from other Southerners, daring, for example, to carry around pictures of white women in his wallet. These stories characterize him in like fashion to Emmett (Tyson 2017). Since he is already dead at the play's opening, the audience encounters Richard as a ghost, like how people interact with Emmett and later apparitions, whether Trayvon Martin, Sandra Bland, or George Floyd.

Richard's white counterpart and murderer is Lyle Britten. Lyle is a fictional parallel to Emmett's killers. The complexity that Baldwin adds is that he resists (or at least intends to resist) turning Lyle into a caricature, a point relevant to acting as much as to the script.[29] The stage directions are as follows:

> He's an honorable tribesman and he's defended, with blood, the honor and purity of his tribe!
>
> (WHITETOWN: *Lyle holds his infant son up above his head.*)

Baldwin's stage directions quickly signal his intention, the "honorable tribesman" in parentheses, a father lovingly playing with his son, even as he is about to slay another's child. It would be easy to make Lyle into a caricature, the ignorant Southerner who murders Negroes because he does not know better. Baldwin's stage directions indicate otherwise.

In these characterizations, Baldwin reaches for his theatrical predecessors. In Aeschylus as in Shakespeare, knotted and complex ties of blood haunt households, just as they do in America's racial family. The language of the "tribesman" and defending the "honor and purity" of kinfolk orient *Blues* toward ancient practices. In the *Oresteia*, Orestes is exiled from home because he would otherwise be the "avenger," the *dikephoros*, literally the "bringer of justice," for his father. As we have seen, in the first play, Clytemnestra and Aegisthus send the son away to prevent retribution for the slaying of the father. After Orestes' return and murder of his mother in the second play,[30] the son wanders from house to house for purification. Even outside of the language of an exile who might emigrate to another home or country, he is wild, more like a beast than human (*Eumenides*, 451–2).

My aim in juxtaposing Lyle to Orestes is not to suggest these characters as exact counterparts. What Orestes adds to an understanding of Lyle is complexity. Orestes is not an innocent—he, after all, kills his mother—any more than is Lyle, but a caricatured villain cannot truly have a blues. Like the ancient character, Lyle sees himself as protecting his blood lineage through retributive murder. As much of a challenge as this might be, Baldwin puts his audience in the mode of an ancient, ritual drama of blood for blood. Through Orestes, we have a kind of ghostly presences haunting the stage, a kinsman facing a similar dilemma of drawing his own blood. That is, Lyle as Orestes is killing his own flesh, if America as Baldwin saw it is one body, one family. Orestes serves to illuminate Richard as well. In *Blues*, Richard is the outcast, wandering from place to place, akin to the wild man-child. Richard suffers a societal abandonment, presumed guilty from the moment of his birth, and his handling of such an identification, his internalization of the phantasy (as bastard), leads to his often-erratic behavior.

Lyle projects phantasies of what he is supposed to be, the "honorable tribesman," which he draws from society. The kinship, or brotherhood between Richard and Lyle—in a word, their *sameness*—is a proposition seemingly absurd on its face but one consistent throughout Baldwin's writing. Lyle embodies the "utterly inevitable species of schizophrenia" that Baldwin attributes to American identity, another of "the many manifestations of the spiritual and historical traps, called racial, in which all Americans find themselves and against which some of us, some of the time, manage to arrive at a viable and honorable identity."[31] Just as no one is innocent for Shakespearean characterization, everyone is entangled in Baldwin's *Blues*. Race is the most evident entanglement of identity, though there are others, such as gender: both the sense of what constitutes masculine honor, and how alterity is engendered through women.

Freudian psychology is another mode of characterization for Baldwin, one unavailable to Aeschylus or Shakespeare. Lyle's primary relationships are with mother, father, and child, the nuclear family of Freudian triangles. When he looks at Richard, Lyle sees his son, through a projection of difference, i.e., that which is not his own son. That is, Lyle's dyadic relationship with his son becomes triangulated through Richard. Lyle's inability to see Richard's humanity, even as he fetishizes his own son, is tied up in his own sickness, what Freudian psychology might call his neurosis leading to psychosis. This mental state is what Baldwin calls schizophrenia.

Triangular desire in the United States involves racial and gender identity, and in *Blues*, Richard's girlfriend Juanita is a Black, female embodiment, although the central characters are gendered masculine. Juanita has her own wants and desires but is also a site for the projection of the desires of the other characters, Black and white alike. Christian symbolism is at play in Baldwin's representation of gender as it is elsewhere. Within the Church, the female might be seen in various figurations of Mary, the mother, a contrast to embodied sexual desire, represented in *Blues* not only in Juanita, but also in white women. Kinship is pivotal here as well, as the honorable tribesman defends his wife and child. Freud recognizes kinship as an important human entanglement, manifest most clearly in the Oedipal complex. The masculine psyche in Freud and in Baldwin's writing bifurcates the gendered woman as goddess or whore. Roy Bryant's fantasy in 1955 about the purity of his wife Carolyn and Emmett's supposed violation of it—again, a triangulation of desire—leads to the lynching. Roy's home has supposedly been violated, and murder sets it right.

Although Freudian psychology amplifies certain tendencies of gender representation, the polarities in nineteenth- and twentieth-century theoretical writing have their own expression in Aeschylus. There is, for example, a somewhat binary representation of women throughout Aeschylus' *Oresteia*. In the *Agamemnon*, the doubles are Clytemnestra and Cassandra, the former the betrayed wife turned avenger, the latter the retreating concubine turned illuminated prophetess. For Orestes to accomplish matricide in *The Libation Bearers*, the maternal impulse moves from Clytemnestra to the wetnurse, the child's true nurturer. The new justification of Clytemnestra's murder is that she was not Orestes' effective mother; the nursemaid was. Such is the importance of kinship relationships and blood ties.

If Baldwin truly believes that "one is not, and never will be, innocent," then he must also realize, perhaps to a greater extent than Freud, that gender is a projection of the individual psyche.

The white man's fantasy of the violation of a sexual taboo, a rape of innocence that shatters the home, is at the heart of lynching narratives across American history, even if these stories have little bearing on reality (see Patterson 1999). In *Blues*, Lyle protects hearth and home through his murder of Richard, a triangulation like that which led to Emmett's lynching.[32]

It is worth noting the extent to which the taboo of miscegenation, different from Freud's incest taboo in its implicating of race, conceived as something other than kinship, further complicates psychological triangulation in *Blues*. Lyle's passion for his family corresponds with—and his love for his wife is bound to—his hatred of Black men. The triangulation of desire could also be projected otherwise. Parnell, for example, the white journalist who is a friend to both the white and Black townspeople, has taboo desire for Black women (rather than a hatred of Black men), like the protagonist in Baldwin's story, "Going to Meet the Man" in his short-story collection of the same name (Baldwin 1995b [1965]) Tellingly, taboo masks itself as that which is forbidden, but taboo is profoundly familial. It must be: the *familial* relationship with his mother is what makes Jocasta taboo to Oedipus. As I have stated, however, miscegenation is not incest, prima facie, because relationships between Black and white people are not customarily conceived of in kinship terms. Kinship is a phantasy. In *Blues*, Parnell captures the irony in his expression of desire to sleep with Juanita, who is Black, describing the feeling as "like you woke up and found yourself in bed with your mother!" (Baldwin 1995a [1964]: 126). The language of taboo is fundamentally Freudian, and it renders miscegenation an incest fantasy. Along with taboo prohibitions, distortions are necessary to create enough distance from the forbidden, as if she were kin.[33] Ultimately, the racial fantasy exposes the artificiality of kinship in the first place, a position that Judith Butler (2017) has most articulately advanced.

Baldwin's proposition is that characters in *Blues* are entangled in ties of blood, like the characters in a Shakespearean drama or in

Aeschylus. Just as in Aeschylus' three plays, choruses of old men, female suppliants, and goddesses of retribution, respectively, reveal collective desires through song, Baldwin creates a blues for "Mister Charlie," the titular figure who does not appear in the play but is the aggregate of all white characters. Emmett does not need a new blues in this play. Black people, themselves made kin through race, already know the pain of the racial experience in America. But what of those in the United States who have not processed their lack of innocence, in fact denying any consciousness of race at all? As Meridian, the Black reverend and father of Richard in the play says to Parnell, "You're Mister Charlie. *All* white men are Mister Charlie!" (53).[34] Through these blues, Baldwin seeks to understand Lyle's cruelty, how within his honorable identity he might have become so murderous. The twisted nature of racial entanglements must be understood not only for its impact on Richard, but also for how it nooses Lyle himself.

NARRATIVE AND ACTION: KINSHIP, HISTORY, AND RACE

Kinship is an operative reality—though an artificially constructed one—in *Blues*, as it is across American life. Its bond is blood. Baldwin conceives dysfunction in the family as sickness, which it might be said is also in the blood.[35] The play's setting in Plaguestown is a sign of the miasma. In Plaguestown, Black and white people live separately, although they comprise one country, manifestly each other's flesh and blood. American ties of blood, across race, class, and creed, go beyond the symbolic. From as early as the days of slavery, masters transgressed the artificial boundary of skin color and conceived so-called Black offspring. Throughout his writing, Baldwin uncovers the shame of white people who would conceal their Black children, Black people who pass as white, or white people whose cultural heritage is tied to slavery, despite their denial. This denial reifies the myth of race through an evasion of kinship, which is also constructed. The morass constitutes a collective cultural tragedy (see, e.g., Rankine 2005). In Plaguestown, surrogate relationships expose the artificially of kinship, as we see in Parnell's cooption of Benita into an Oedipal fantasy. Surrogacy, a substitute to familial relationships, is further acknowledgment of how broadly kinship across the U.S. could be conceived. The epiphanies that encode race, such as those of Lyle and Parnell, could be re-encoded otherwise. Baldwin knew about how moveable kinship could be from his own life, given the surrogacy of his father David and his more broadly conceived status as a "bastard" of the West. Where kinship ties break down, surrogacy can also be healing. Baldwin recognizes that his condition is not entirely unique. All people are at once part of a family and alone, bereft of actual ties and transgressive of others—between the world, and themselves. Although in segregated America and well after this historical period, people repress ties of kinship and deny heritage, unconscious desire erupts indiscriminately. Heritage finds the individual, not the other way around. Having been found, we become custodians of traditions and values. In the context of American society, however, the lies people tell to deny human ties of kinship, real or surrogate, threaten to destroy any possibility of group cohesion (Appiah 2018). Myth, however, reinscribes the community.

As it pertains to the mythic kinship ties of *Blues*, it is worth reiterating that surrogacy is also at play in Baldwin's predecessors, such as the *Oresteia*. Orestes is orphan of a once-great household (246–7), which can only be raised again by divine aid (262–3). Apollo is his surrogate, steadfast father-figure, a substitute after the murder of Orestes' father, Agamemnon (269).[36] Apollo's surrogacy supplants supposedly natural blood ties and the binding force of reciprocal violence. He takes the place of the father but, in this role, can no longer advocate for Orestes, once the young man has killed his mother, although throughout the narrative, seemingly natural ties of blood, such as maternity, come into question. As we have seen, the play disrupts Clytemnestra's role as Orestes' mother. The nurse nurtured him, another surrogate in place of his traitorous mother. It becomes clear throughout the classical trilogy that surrogates can play as central a role as kin.

There is, ultimately, a human and ethical responsibility for individuals tied by bonds of kinship or surrogacy within the environment. In the case of plague, which is a miasma or communal contagion, Orestes takes responsibility after some degree of evasion.[37] In *Blues*, Meridian puts the case of responsibility, and its potential evasion, as follows:

> What hope is there for a people who deny their deeds and disown their own kinsmen and who do so in the name of purity and love, in the name of Jesus Christ.

This line corresponds with Baldwin's idea of white cultural schizophrenia. Despite being inextricably bound to Black people, white Americans "deny" their responsibility and "disown" their kin, however imagined. Whatever the repression and lies, however, kinship and surrogacy render Americans as being of the same hearth, moving the ties of blood from the home to public spaces, whether they be temples, churches, or courtroom. Baldwin would add to these national institutions the theater.

DÉNOUEMENT: FORGIVENESS, PUNISHMENT, OR REVENGE?

Lyle's real issue is a false projection, his invention of the "nigger" as a threat to stable kinship ties. In a psychotic delusion (not dissimilar to Orestes'), he believes he is protecting the honor of his family. Baldwin wants his audience to see Lyle as an honorable tribesman, who succumbs to a phantasy because the violation of the home, real or perceived, would require retribution (as is the case with Orestes). While a full study of revenge, retribution, and punishment is beyond the scope of this chapter, it is worthwhile to draw from distinctions between justice, punishment, and revenge. Danielle Allen's seminal study of these topics, which takes Aeschylus as its point of departure (Allen 2002), is an excellent point of reference. We might apply Allen's analysis to lynching of Emmett Till, which is retributive from the killer's perspective. In Allen's formulation of revenge, Roy Bryant perceives an "injury or harm or slight" in Emmett's behavior toward Carolyn, and the asymmetrical distribution of power between Emmett and Roy places the Black boy on the losing side of the equation. In *Blues*, Baldwin's fictive tribesman Lyle takes justice into his own hands in response to a similar slight. Richard entered the shop of Lyle and Jo Britten, the white man's wife, to buy a Coca-Cola. His tone with Jo, a perceived slight, provoke Lyle's anger. This reaction is extreme but "passion is commonly thought to generate responses to wrongdoing that are neither impartial nor commensurate to the wrong." Lyle's behavior aligns with Allen's notion that "revenge is personal." It involves "a particular emotional toll" (Allen 2002: 18). Although initially meant as an interpretation of the *Oresteia*, Allen advances a definition of vengeance and retribution that is not bound by time or cultural context. Her analysis could easily describe the murder of Trayvon Martin at the hands of the more powerful George Zimmerman in 2012, as the Black boy clung to a bag of Skittles candy. For Allen, revenge and retribution pertain to a mode of justice that has to do with who has the right to punish, or as Allen puts it, who gets to touch the body, or habeas corpus.[38]

Courts of law in early European and later Western societies promise a finality to punishment, an end to the reciprocal violence that is a feature of the *Oresteia*. Baldwin would have realized that the Christian concept of forgiveness holds the same promise as the court of law, that of a resolution, a completion of justice. In *Blues*, although justice in the courts has failed, as it has for Emmett Till, the black preacher Meridian (apparently a vehicle of forgiveness) initially rejects endless retribution:

> I do not wish to see Negroes become equal of their murderers.
> I wish us to become equal to ourselves.

Considering the court's failure to punish, Meridian seems to turn toward release, but his use of the term "murderers" makes it clear that justice, defined as the legitimate, passionless judgment of "an impartial judicial actor" (Allen 2002: 18), has failed.[39] The judge in the courtroom has the authority to punish, but in the case of Lyle, as with Roy Bryant, he does not. It has been clear, however, that justice has rested on a dilemma, namely that Lyle might be compelled to violence, but he must also be punished.

Blues is again resonant with Aeschylus' *Oresteia* as it pertains to its conclusion, the failure of the legal, sanctioned punishment. Revenge and retribution are, to paraphrase Baldwin's usage, tribally sanctioned, and the second play of the *Oresteia* conveys the impact of this potentially endless cycle through Orestes. In addition to compelling Orestes' murder of his mother,[40] Apollo warns him that the Eryines will pursue him. The longer quote from Phillip Vellacott's 1956 translation of the play, which Baldwin could well have known, echoes with the Shakespearean language that also snakes its way into Baldwin's "seas of blood:"[41]

> This was the god's command: 'Shed blood for blood, your face set like a flint. The price they owe no wealth can weigh.' My very life, he said, would pay, in endless torment, for disobedience. First he revealed what things men must perform, to soothe anger of spirits of earth; then if such anger rise, what plagues break forth: the spreading scab whose rabid teeth eat at the flesh till human shape is gone; the white fungus that flowers the scab. But when, he said, a father's blood lies unavenged, and time grows ripe, the neglectful

> son sees yet more fearful visitations, as, towards eyes that strain and peer in darkness, come the attacking Furies, roused by inherited blood-guilt, armed with arrows of the dark, with madness, false night-terrors, to harass, plague, torment—to scourge him forth from his city with brazen lash, in loathed and abject filthiness.
>
> (Vellacott 1962, *Libation Bearers*, lines 278–90)

The passage is descriptive and vivid, no single translation conveying the force of Aeschylus' language. Vellacott's rendering insists on "blood for blood," drawing out the "killing by turns" (*antapokteinai tropon*) in the text. Despite the necessity of Orestes' vengeance, revenge is itself not healing. The language of wrath and plague in the passage points to a possible source for Baldwin's own setting of Plaguestown, even as Vellacott seems to draw from Shakespearean language to amplify his translation. The Erinyes will haunt Orestes, the mother's blood a stain difficult to undo. Orestes returns to the status of exile, the lash (*plastiggi*) touching his body as it might that of an enslaved person, until the judgement, the sanctioned punishment, of the authorized party in the third play, which is Athena.

In *Blues* as in the *Oresteia*, punishment is the legitimate, passionless judgment of "an impartial judicial actor" (Allen 2002: 18). Unlike revenge, which is impassioned, punishment is legal and sanctioned. The breach of justice in the *Blues* comes with a reminder that judicial processes are not, in fact, final, even if they purport to be. Rather, punishment is an "unfolding drama" of "strategic actors" in contest about what is deserved (Allen 2002).[42] As such, the power of vengeance is not banished at the end of *Blues*, any more than it is at the conclusion of the *Oresteia*.

The ending of *Blues* suggests a similar right to vengeance as that of the Erinyes:

> Meridian: You know, for us, it all began with the Bible and the gun. Maybe it will end with the Bible and the gun.
>
> Juanita: What did you do with the gun, Meridian?

Parnell:	You have the gun—Richard's gun?
Meridian:	Yes. In the pulpit. Under the Bible. Like the pilgrims of old.

As *Blues for Mister Charlie* closes, we learn that Meridian keeps a gun, which fittingly belonged to Richard because it is his blood that cries out for justice, "in the pulpit, under the Bible. Like the pilgrims of old." Meridian returns us to the potentiality of the Eumenides to revert to their role of Erinyes once again, breaches of justice spilling from the courtroom back to the wild. This violence is contained at the pulpit, the site of religious utterance. The pulpit, a sacred site, would return us from the courtroom, which has failed, to the primal world where spirits act, much like the Erinyes would depart the Areopagus, should bloodshed not find rest.

Through *Blues for Mister Charlie* Baldwin represents ancient principles of violence, retribution, and punishment, prior to the Church or justice system in the United States. He certainly found these realities of human emotions and their ritual significance in Shakespeare, but a hidden transcript to his theatrical production is Aeschylus' *Oresteia*. Aeschylus, whom Baldwin names among the Western authors from whom he, as Black, was estranged, nevertheless haunts Baldwin's American stage. Shakespeare is a surrogate descendant of Aeschylus through whom Baldwin in turn receives his literary inheritance. The *Oresteia* helps in understanding the deep, ritual realities that precede America's—or the West's—construction of justice and belonging. In 1964, Baldwin brings these realities to the dramatic stage through *Blues*.

A RECKONING: 1968–1972

In the aftermath of George Floyd's murder on May 25, 2020, newspapers and social media across the United States were either calling for a racial reckoning or stating that the day of reckoning had finally come. If readers of American history were to eschew linear time, even momentarily, it might seem as though perhaps the country had been here before. The months and years after James Baldwin staged *Blues for Mister Charlie* were a time of reckoning, at least for him. In the aftermath of Emmett Till's murder, Medgar Evers had been slain in the South in 1963. By 1965, Malcolm X's own Black kin slew him, a sign of the familial entanglements (themselves artificial) attending vengeance and violence in the United States. In the house that is the American nation, Martin Luther King, Jr.'s death would follow in 1968, an assassination that shook Baldwin to the core.[43]

Blues brings the darkness of American conscience to the theatrical stage, where perhaps deeper psychological work could be done than history might allow. In this way, Baldwin hoped *Blues* would be epiphanic, helping to encode new ways of being in the world among Americans. *Blues* was the work of myth, but during its months onstage, its mixed critical reception echoes the contradictions that Baldwin knew he would have to face in attempting to stage such a harrowing American event as Till's lynching. The play's reception was indicative of the human tendency toward denial, which leads not to revelation but to haunting. Like Richard's ghost hovering at the beginning of the play, reencoding the Erinyes of the *Oresteia* or the Weird Sisters of Shakespeare's *Macbeth*, Emmett's ghost will continue to haunt the culture until justice is served.

Aesthetics confront history in *Blues*, but the question remains as to whether the play was an effective intervention. Writing for *The New York Times* on April 24, 1964, Howard Taubman felt the play "makes valid points as if they were cliches," even if it has "fires of fury in its belly, tears of anguish in its eyes and a roar of protest in its throat." The play "throbs with fierce energy and passion." This is Aeschylean grandeur. That said, Taubman laments that Baldwin "does not worry about the niceties of legal procedure." Judging from the foregoing reading of *Blues*, Taubman might have missed the larger points the play raises about the disruption of punishment, the American legal system's failure to prosecute justice for blacks. Indeed, Baldwin's *Blues* "is a summons to arms in this generation's burning cause—the establishment in this country of the Negro's full manhood" (Taubman 1964) The summons might be timeless, as Baldwin's call to arms in 1964 did not resolve the hostilities of later generations.

This is not to say that Baldwin's theatrical incitement is without flaws or that Taubman and others should not have mounted critiques. For Taubman, Baldwin fails to represent white Southerners with the same humanity as Black people covet for themselves: "Southerners may talk and behave as he suggests, but in the theater they are caricatures." Much of what Baldwin writes as shorthand in the text would have to be fleshed out onstage. Any caricature, however, is in some ways of America itself, as a mythic construct built on the artificiality of kinship. In 1972, Baldwin wrote of his visit to the South in the 1950s that "the South was a riddle which could be read only in the light, or in the darkness, of the unbelievable disasters which had overtaken the private life ... I was not struck by their wickedness, for that wickedness was but the spirit and the history of America" (Baldwin 2007 [1972]: 55).[44] The "spirit," as Baldwin put it elsewhere, is ancient. Whatever this analysis is, it is not caricature, although it would take excellent direction and dramaturgy for the personalities in *Blues* fully to live. There is a telling evasion in Taubman's review, a refusal—or resistance—to countenance the naked reality of American violence, which does not only operate in the South. On this level, Taubman's observations are also consonant with Robert Brustein's, who could only hear Baldwin's anger.[45]

Taubman is a single reviewer whose own likes and dislikes would certainly influence his take on the play, but more broadly his language evidences tendencies that Baldwin already noted. From Baldwin's perspective, Taubman's review might exhibit a kind of "schizophrenia," a word that Baldwin reserves for discussions of race. The grandeur of Taubman's comparisons betrays the nature of his quibbles. He likens *Blues*, for example, to Clifford Odets' 1935 play, *Waiting for Lefty*, which grapples with another of America's ongoing tensions besides race, that between capitalism and socialism. *Blues*' call to atonement could challenge the audience into discomfort, and Taubman's reaction on the racial register of the play is but one example. Nevertheless, he ends his review with praise, suggesting that Baldwin's play had been a proverbial light onstage in 1964: "The Actors Studio Theater, which has been stumbling in darkness all season, finally has arrived at something worth doing." Although Baldwin "has not yet mastered all of the problems and challenges of theater," the play takes on a topic that is "one of the momentous themes of our era" with "eloquence and conviction" (Taubman 1964).

Although Taubman's review was primarily positive, the original run of *Blues* would close on Broadway on August 29, 1964. The cause of the relatively short run seems to have been as much a failure at the level of production as any artistic failure (Leeming 2015). Baldwin's idea of ritual, namely that the theater might function like the Church in processes of collective expression and catharsis, meant that audiences had to be democratized; real flesh and blood had to be in the room, at the performances. The uptown, Harlem patrons would be as welcome as the Broadway crowd, in Baldwin's dream of an integrated audience. He had insisted on ticket prices that would allow Black people (some of whom might not otherwise have been able to afford the play) to sit alongside white audience members. The lower ticket prices could well have contributed to the interruption of the run, as much as the difficulty of the subject matter. Baldwin was upset with the Actors Studio and his longtime associate there, Elia Kazan, for the premature closing (Leeming 2015).

Despite his disappointment, Baldwin would not abandon the theater. Theater remained one of the primary spheres of interest for Baldwin with which this chapter opened, which include the American cultural realities that produced an Emmett Till, Baldwin's relationship to a broader Western (classical) cultural heritage, and his own process of working out the distance between the world and himself through his writing. Although he only produced one other play of his own, theater and performance remained of critical interest to him. By 1969, he was in Istanbul, Turkey, directing John Herbert's 1967 play, *Fortune and Men's Eyes*, at the invitation of Gülriz Suruni (Zaborowska 2009). His observations about theater, performance, and ritual would continue to influence how he wrote about the American scene, especially in the aftermath of the Civil Rights Movement and the endless bloodshed and violence that continued well into the 1970s.

Throughout this chapter, I have shown how essays like *The Devil Finds Work* (2011 [1976]) themselves untangle Baldwin's relationship to his times, particularly as it pertains to race and American identity. Published in 1972, *No Name in the Street* conveys something of the state of play after the assassination of Martin Luther King, Jr. As I have noted, Baldwin would have by then lost Medgar Evers, Malcolm X, King, and many others to violence. Those Black people closest to him who survived the fury would be trailed by the Federal Bureau of Investigation (FBI) or Central Intelligence Agency (CIA), themselves falsely accused of violence, or they would succumb to some other form of ferocity. Baldwin would continue to talk about the situation "in the streets" in ritual terms. Theater remained an important interest because of the way it exposed naked realities, like the bloody processes of true retribution. After 1968, a time of reckoning had come, as far as Baldwin was concerned.

Baldwin encourages an understanding of the "dark gods" beyond Christianity and Western civilization, those gods of vengeance who would be sure to remind Americans of the seeds we had sown, forces like those of Aeschylus' *Oresteia*. He borrows this idea of darker gods from Bobby Seale, co-founder of the Black Panther Party:

> Bobby Seale insists that one of the things that most afflict white people is their disastrous concept of God; they have never accepted the dark gods, and their fear of the dark gods, who live in them at least as surely as the white God does, causes them to distrust life.
>
> (Baldwin 2007 [1972]: 136)

By one interpretation, the "disastrous concept" of God is the Christianity that justified slavery, rather than what Black people make of this religion through syncretism. In this case, theater again served to unmask mythic reality. Dark gods are those who activate the gun under the Bible at the pulpit, preserving vengeance in light of miscarriages of justice. Consistent with the language of these infernal gods, a "miasma of lust and longing and rage" (69) and "miasma of fury and frustration" (127) hang over America, which has produced killers within its own household, slaughterers of prophets of peace like Martin Luther King, Jr.

As Baldwin sees it, racial reckoning would be inevitable. In his singular focus on Baldwin's anger, Brustein and others miss the poignancy and rich language that Baldwin was transferring from self to the collective. While he might indeed have been angry, he is also quite refined in his thoughts and references, knowing that the problem existed in the world and not in himself. As in *Blues*, the work of myth in Baldwin's writing operates within a metaphorical household:

> When the heir of a great house repudiates the house, the house cannot continue, unless it looks to alien blood to save it; and here were the heirs and heiresses of all the ages, in the streets, along with that blood always considered to be most alien [that of Black people], never lawfully to be mixed with that of the sons and daughters of the great house.
>
> (Baldwin 2007 [1972]: 187)

In this passage, again we find processes of surrogacy and kinship, along with the taboo of miscegenation. We have seen, however, that this alienation is based on a lie. Black people are as much heirs of the American house as white people. More broadly, the continuation of the "Western house" depends on "how one treats one's flesh and blood" (185).

Beyond the violence done to well-known figures like Evers, Malcolm X, and King, Baldwin would throughout *No Name* linger over how the institutions and individuals across the United States treated lesser-known brethren. Vengeance is warranted when citizens like Baldwin's longtime associates, William Maynard, Jr. or Tony, who later took the name Djata Samod, are put in prison for no just cause. This example is worth our notice both because of the attention Baldwin gives it and for what it further reveals about how Baldwin thought about the theater.

Tony was arrested in October 1967 on the false accusation of an April 3 killing of a white official, Marine Sergeant Michael Kroll. Tony walked free in 1974 but not before spending over six years in some of the most bone-chilling prisons in America. Prior to the callous ruination of his life, Tony had been a chauffeur, secretary, and attendant, roles in which he had served Baldwin. Tony also wanted to be an actor, so it is no coincidence that Baldwin would linger over his example. Baldwin's preoccupation with Tony's plight is in keeping with an esteem he expresses, in *Devil* and *No Name*, for the work of thespians, who bring "revelation" through storytelling (2011b [1976]: 42).[46] Tony's story might also have served as the inspiration for Baldwin's 1974 novel, *If Beale Street Could Talk* (Baldwin 2006 [1974]).[47]

Ritual and storytelling are bases for how actors might come to play their broader roles, if there is as much a place in society for the poet as there is for the revolutionary. Throughout American society, Black people had become a kind of scapegoat, as Tony's example and that of countless others show, including Emmett Till and King. The idea "that the scapegoat pays for the sin of others," however, is "only legend" (Baldwin 2007 [1972]: 54). Baldwin places into this category of legend the story of Malcolm X, about whom he was writing the script for a movie in the early 1970s. Baldwin distrusts legends, including what others might say about Malcolm X, because "we, in Harlem, have been betrayed so often" (93). In contrast to the myth, Baldwin finds Malcolm to be "gentle," just as he will later add complexity to the treatment of figures like Huey Newton. As Baldwin puts it, "people surrounded by legend rarely look the parts they've been assigned" (173). Through theater and his short stories, novels, and essays, Baldwin would come to conclude that language "might be made to bear the burden of my experience if I could find the stamina to challenge it, and me, to such a test" (Baldwin 2010). A poet, not a revolutionary with arms, Baldwin calls language to account for the ills of his society. He sees that the poet has a role to play alongside the revolutionaries like Bobby Seale and Huey Newton in harnessing wrath. As Baldwin put it, "something awful is happening to a civilization, when it ceases to produce poets" (*The Cross of Redemption*, 51).

The publication of *No Name* in 1972 allowed Baldwin to communicate his clear-eyed judgment of the United States. The "commercial speculations" of theater were only a manifestation of the broader American society, and by 1972 the country was sick even beyond what Baldwin could diagnose in his 1964 *Blues*. As an émigré traveling the globe, he could see that this sickness was extensive beyond American borders, a pathology of Western civilization, but its manifestations were endemic to the United States.

As for the idea of civilization, this was a category by nature—and damnably—European, or white, since it was Europeans who imposed the categories of savage and civilized on their colonial subjects. Having traveled the world, Baldwin sees the impact of this colonial apparatus in Algeria, which the French had possessed, as well as across the African world. These countries, however, were rising. For Baldwin, Senghor's negritude movement represented the possibilities of new memories, new classics, of which Senegal was only one of many examples. With this clarity of distance, Baldwin in the late 1960s and early 1970s was beginning to write about the United States as a colonial power.[48] As with the rest of Western civilization, an American reckoning was coming, even if the hour had been postponed. America's day of judgment was not just a fantasy for African Americans. White youth of the era of the Vietnam War were "heirs" to this great Western house who were "repudiating" their country. The promise of what would come after the apocalypse, the destruction by fire, would be not another cycle of vengeance, but a post-colonial and racial reckoning.

CHAPTER THREE

TELEVISING THE REVOLUTION IN POSTCOLONIAL AMERICA, 1969–1977

Richard Schechner's Dionysus in '69, *Wole Soyinka's* Bacchae, *and Ntozake Shange's* for colored girls who have considered suicide / when the rainbow is enuf

I have been calling the murder of Emmett Till a lynching, even though "the word 'lynching' potentially misidentifies the range and aims of punishments targeting African Americans precisely because the state routinely allowed extreme, and often lethal, measures of discipline to be executed on them" (Goldsby 2006: 17). Indeed, there was punishment for Emmett because of a perceived slight, but there would be none for his assailants (Tyson 2017). The state absolved the murderers, Roy Bryant and J. W. Milam, of any wrongdoing, confusing kin relationships with roles of plaintiff and defendant, as we saw in the last chapter. As a spectacular, even spectral practice, the lynching of African Americans affirmed their marginal status in the United States. In the last chapter, I advanced the idea that Black people in the U.S. have not been treated as kin, although nations are imagined communities, fabricated ties of blood (Anderson 2016). In civic terms, Black people are not citizens, and when citizens, not Black. This is an ambivalent, bipolar experience, and what has not heretofore been adequately captured in cultural criticism is the bivalent nature of Blackness in the U.S., a "Plaguestown" that sees Black people as the miasma, the untreatable, irresolvable stain that simply must be expunged. The African American is an insider/outsider, and as I will demonstrate in this chapter, no epiphany in the Western imagination conveys the paradox of the insider/outsider better than Dionysus.

Blackness impacts the broader American culture, but first it makes non-persons. American poet Robert Pinskey put the case succinctly in his 9/11 remembrance of 2005, where he cites of Gwendolyn Brooks' poem, "Boy Breaking Glass." He asks: "What if victims and thugs, large numbers of the bereft and the violent, are who they are because in some deep way they are not part of our society" (Pinskey 2005). No accidental object of Pinskey's observation, Brooks' "Boy Breaking Glass" helps to transform the reciprocal violence of the titular subject, the protestor turned rioter, presumably Black, into "a cry of art." Brooks published the poem in 1968, amid the urban unrest that would accelerate after the assassination of Martin Luther King, Jr. (Brooks 1994). Like Dionysus, the boy revels in what seems to be destruction, the "broken window" that he has shattered: "'I shall create! If not a note, a hole. | If not an overture, a desecration'." The boy reflects this desecration back onto the "you" who "'threw away my name!'" Previous analyses have seen Brooks' poem as an "attempt to repair" violence, albeit an attempt that always fails (Best 2018: 57). The poem's epiphanic potentiality (of the return of the repressed) lies in how it "stubbornly ... resist[s] reparative suture" (57). The "victims and thugs," as Pinskey puts it, are in Brooks' able hands distilled into artform, perhaps even encoded as Dionysus, especially if we consider the 1960s and 1970s in the U.S. as an age that reveled in the god's bivalent nature as simultaneously generative and destructive.

Resonant with "Boy Breaking Glass," Bob Thompson's 1964 painting "Triumph of Bacchus" (Figure 3) renders the multi-hued collective revelry that inevitably would represent the possibilities for a post-Civil Rights—post-Bacchus—America.[1] As the summary by the Whitney Museum of American Art in New York describes it, the figures, ranging from humans to satyrs and nymphs, are in "flat, bold, unmodulated colors."[2] This is the Biblical prophecy, the epiphany that "the wolf also shall dwell with the lamb, and the leopard shall lie down with the kid; and the calf and the young lion and the fatling together; and a little child shall lead them" (Isaiah 11: 6). Thompson's is a cultural revolution without arms, after Dionysiac miscegenation. I take his painting as a sign of the

Figure 3: *Triumph of Bacchus* (Bob Thompson, 1964)

times, and I use it to encapsulate through image the Bacchic symbolism pervasive in the 1960s and 1970s. As a Black artist, he provides an embodiment of the Dionysian age not broadly discussed in terms of race. Thompson might also help us in understanding the other Black Dionysian embodiments from the period, such as that of Amiri Baraka.

In this chapter, I am interested in the figure of Dionysus as epiphany, a ritual recurrence that crystalizes the revolutionary potentiality that reached a kind of acme in the 1960s and 1970s. Although the ubiquity of the Greek figure in the 1960s and 1970s has been widely discussed, no study considers race or the subaltern figure as Dionysus, although the shift, evident in Brooks' and Thompson's art, points to the epiphany's revolutionary potential for the entire culture.[3] Richard Schechner's *Dionysus in '69* was aware of the myth's symbolic significance, but it repressed the real site of revolution in the U.S.: not the sexual revolution, but the revolutionary presence of a Black subaltern spirit. Wole Soyinka's *The Bacchae: A Communion Rite* (2004) sought to address Schechner's racial forgetfulness. It did so, however, from the perspective of Yoruba culture in the postcolonial, African setting of Nigeria, although Soyinka was well-aware of happenings in the U.S. Postcolonial perspectives such as those Soyinka expressed were available as therapeutic tools within the U.S. through such authors as James Baldwin, Amiri Baraka, and Ntozake Shange. As it pertained to the representation of cultural processes onstage, Soyinka's example of Dionysus as Ogun in Nigeria's cultural transformation was already present in Baraka's insistence upon a revolutionary theater in the U.S. If Americans failed properly to diagnose the violence in the streets, Baraka—like Brooks—translated this violence into poetry, and yet his therapeutic intervention was deemed an unwelcome provocation, taken more as the raging of an angry Black man than as a Dionysiac visitation, an artistic epiphany that called his theatrical audience into ethical reckoning. There is, of course, every reason to believe that Baraka eschewed European symbols, but Dionysus is nevertheless at the core of his "Revolutionary Theatre."

Dionysus embodies the immanence of America's cultural revolution, the possibility that disparate and conflicting strands of memory either disappear completely or bind in stronger ways than ever before. The idea of immanence is itself ghostly—imagine Emmett Till as ever-present in American culture—pointing in temporal terms to the time between past and future, a present not static but full of the potential for transformation, whether destructive or creative. Such immanence conveys well the racial situation in the U.S. during the period.

Schechner's performative turn and Environmental Theater impacted the culture in significant ways, and theater post-1969 continued to engage with performance art. As Susan Best (2021) argues, however, performance art tended to move away from urging collective action; racial reconciliation was consequently not the objective. The boy breaking glass remained at the margins of the society, brought to centerstage only when ritually remembered. Although Best does not discuss Black subjects (nor does she discuss Schechner), her study is consonant with what I argue here. I include race in the turn away from ethics in performance art. I will end the chapter considering Ntozake Shange's play (see Shange 1997), which shifts the audience's perspective from the god Dionysus to the Bacchic chorus of women deemed revolutionary. Centering Black female embodiment onstage was a necessary and important shift, but by the 1970s the performative impact had become interior and personal, not collective, and public. The performative turn brought a complete othering onto the strangest of (non-)Americans, the Black female subject, an estrangement that absolved audiences of their ethical responsibility to be one with the epiphany.[4]

Immanence not only signals the possibility of the ever-presence of Till in the culture, but the idea of immanence can also be applied to classical symbols and myths. The mythic symbolism around disgraced U.S. President Richard Nixon is relevant. In the climax of Peter Morgan's 2007 play, *Frost/Nixon*, a dramatization of the momentous 1977 interviews between television personality David Frost and Nixon, Frost homes in on the Watergate burglary that led to Nixon's resignation.[5] He asks Nixon about his knowledge of the event and his complicity in the cover-up. Stage directions convey what 45 million viewers saw during the five-part series, this being the third: "*Nixon is struggling for air. His face is ravished*" (Morgan 2007: 74). Responding to Nixon's declaration that "when you're in office, you have to do a lot of things that are not, in the strictest sense of the law, legal," Frost doubles back: "Wait a minute ... did I hear you right? Are you really saying that there are certain situations where the President can decide whether it's in the best interest of the nation and do something illegal?" (74). Nixon's answer has become infamous, the undoing that the country had waited three years from the time of his resignation to witness: "I'm saying that when the President does it, that means it's not illegal."

Nixon's confession—or his denial of the capacity for guilt—was certainly historic, and Morgan reads it as a coda to an already eventful era. Concurring with Frost, Morgan sees that the transformation of Nixon the interviews engendered was important for its potential impact on its viewership. Morgan is insistent upon the *Frost/Nixon* interviews as cathartic, reconciling the country to its recent past and providing a sense of closure. (The word "cathartic" is used of these interviews too often to realistically cite.) The play invokes mythic ghosts through Greek tragedy to describe the event (the interviews) from 1977. Early in the drama, Jim Reston, the historical figure and author of another 2007 book on Nixon and a character in Morgan's play, puts the case as follows:

> Aeschylus and his Greek contemporaries believed that the gods begrudged human success, and would send a curse of 'hubris' on a person at the height of their powers; a loss of sanity that would eventually bring about their downfall. Nowadays, we give the gods less credit. We prefer to call it self-destruction.
>
> (Morgan 2007: 4)

Nixon himself becomes epiphanic, taking on the visage of the legendary downfall of a tragic character. Nixon's ravished face conveys his "self-destruction" of 1972, relived at the apogee of the interviews with Frost.

At the beginning of the play portraying these interviews, the character Nixon reveals that he "tend[s] to perspire" (3), and this flaw plagued his performance at the 1960 Presidential Debate against John F. Kennedy, who went on to win the presidency.[6] On camera, which can reveal a tragic or comic mask, the face becomes an appendage. The face as mask is captured after the act of hubris, the "loss of sanity" that brought the downfall now broadcast and repeated for the television audience, frozen in time. Reston recalls that the President was at the height of his powers in 1972. He "brought the war in Vietnam to an end, achieved a diplomatic breakthrough with the Russians, had been the first Western leader to visit the People's Republic of China and presided over a period of economic stability at home" (Morgan 2007: 4). He had high approval ratings and was poised to be re-elected in a landslide victory. Rather than experiencing a glorious second term, however, he becomes a tragic persona. On camera, his face appears fragmented, the searching eyes, the worn texture of skin, the hand to mouth in contemplation. His disembodied (dismembered) face is further fragmented into its emotive parts: deep-set eyes, fixed brows, and mouth agape.

Reston cites Aeschylus, and we might think back to the *Oresteia* in the previous chapter as a structure for encoding American kinship and tragic reckoning. As we saw with James Baldwin's *Blues for Mister Charlie*, retribution is revealed to rely on ancient rites of blood, which Aeschylus and Shakespeare help us to understand. Similarly, a Dionysiac turn makes Nixon's amorality, his refusal of guilt and rejection of legality, legible; Nixon's power is Penthean, as both men embody an equation between the state and its guardian. The prompt of Aeschylus' "Greek contemporaries" provides a segue to Euripides' *Bacchae*, with its specific resonance for the 1960s and 1970s. In Euripides' play, Dionysus arrives at Thebes as a foreign god, although he is in some ways native to the land, as a child of Semele.[7] Dionysus, or Bacchus, is an outcast who causes a frenzy among the women when they worship him by the countryside. The character Pentheus, the ruler of Thebes who is Dionysus' cousin, fears Dionysus' engendering of sexual waywardness and his potential to upset the governing of the people. His character is tyrannical and uncompromising, but he is also willing to appropriate Dionysian power—of persuasion, of culture—for himself. Nixon is like Pentheus in these self-destructive impulses and in his unraveling.[8]

Frost/Nixon might well have in its broader symbolic background Richard Schechner's gesture toward mythic memory in *Dionysus in '69* (Schechner 1970), the adaptation of *Bacchae* staged on the cusp of Nixon's first election to the presidency in 1968. The 1970 Brian De Palma film of those performances ends with the ancient god Dionysus' signal toward Nixon specifically: for the character in the role, fingers formed in a peace sign in each hand, arms raised over head creating a third V for victory (De Palma and Schechner 1970). Dionysus' gesture in Schechner's play moves the phrase "Dionysus in '69" from sexual and chronological position to political slogan. Classical scholar Froma I. Zeitlin, who saw *Dionysus in '69* at the Performance Garage, recalls that the play was "nothing if not a child of its time" (Zeitlin 2004: 49). She posits that "in fact, until the 1960s, Bacchae had never been performed in any version on a commercial stage in the United States during the earlier twentieth century" (49). Dionysus' migration to the U.S. is itself a significant event, begging the question of what environment precipitated the need or desire for his presence. This Dionysus of '69 trolls Nixon, but the disgraced former President is not the only target of Bacchic destruction. Dionysus is the revolutionary epiphany of the period in the U.S., a reckoning that included race, even if a racial dimension of Dionysus was not immediately visible in the performance.[9]

More than *Dionysus in '69* itself even conveyed, the revolutionary tenor of Euripides' play had much to offer the collective spirit of the 1960s and 1970s, as is also evident internationally in the adaptation of the *Bacchae* that Wole Soyinka staged in 1973 (see Soyinka 2004). During this period, Dionysus is involved in what Gayatri Chakravorty Spivak might call a ghost dance, "an attempt to establish the ethical relation with history as such, ancestors real or imagined" (Spivak 2013: 323). Although Schechner's performances highlighted a sexual dimension to Dionysiac revelry, Soyinka interprets the Dionysiac spirit in terms of a deeper revolution that might be expressed sexually but that is more fundamentally the potential transformation of the culture at large.[10]

Whereas previous treatments of Schechner and Soyinka convey the latter's re-racing of Dionysus in a broadly African context (Lecznar 2020), I would like to press upon Dionysus as an embodiment of an American racial revolution, which was as much a cultural process as a potentially military one. In the U.S., such a revolution would involve race, but it is not enough to say that American Dionysus would be a racial embodiment. For the 1960s and 1970s, Dionysus is the epiphany to be encoded as the mythic memory, present by virtue of his characteristic, revolutionary potentiality even when not named. From the perspective of racial reconciliation, what has been missed in previous studies is the immanence of cultural transformation in the U.S. that Dionysus manifests. By 1968, the U.S. was federally and legally primed for social integration, but Pentheus' resistance, as it were, imposes a practical order opposed to the organic processes operating in the culture. Far from an indictment of one leader, whether Nixon or anyone else, there were countless Pentheuses among the citizenry, including Bryant and Milam (Till's lynchers), and Byron De La Beckwith, who slayed Civil Rights' leader Medgar Evers. Each of these Pentheuses was resisting the changes that would come with the Dionysiac epiphanies of the Emmett Tills and Medgar Everses, respectively.

Dionysus' visitation in the U.S. in 1969 is the acme of an historical period, but my use of the mythological and dramatic figure is revelatory of an immanence, which is more than a question of temporality or chronology. That is, the fundamental cultural revolution that is always possible is not for a leader, a Pentheus, to declare or legislate, although declarations and legislations can set tones or upset constituencies. Rather than resting in the hands of a single person, Dionysiac revolution is more like a psychological process, the guiding of unconscious phenomena toward their narrative potentiality. Historical periodization directs streams of information to contain events—e.g., a post-Civil Rights era, a postcolonial era, post-racialism, etc. However, cultural memory resists periodization. Ritual or cultural memory recurs. Memory functions like a ghostly visitation. History is akin to the already dead, or a past. Memory is not dead; it recurs.

The ghost dance to which Spivak refers calls up spirits from the past in a way that hearkens to the possibility of a different future. Within a colonial culture with a Black subaltern, the assassination of a leader like Dr. Martin Luther King, Jr. would always ever be not only possible, but likely.[11] There would be no post-Civil Rights return to an original glory (e.g., an Eden) because the ghost dance is an ongoing process, wherein the broader culture recognizes the presence and potentially destructive power of its past, ghosted into its present through epiphany. As we will see by the end of *Theater and Crisis*, civil war is as present and parallel to the culture as are Civil Rights.

As it pertains to the flattened (dead) past of history (which still helps us to contain events), I find useful a mode of "post-" not often discussed in the context of the U.S., namely the postcolonial. In this regard, Soyinka, a Yoruba from the newly declared postcolonial country of Nigeria (from the perspective of 1973), is continuously relevant to the discussion. Baldwin and others demonstrate an awareness of the U.S. as a colonial power, as they express what Paul Gilroy (2006) might call a postcolonial melancholy, an affective ambivalence, an attraction and repulsion, depending on the topic, to (or from) what has been lost. Although by looking to the possibility of an American postcolonial reality Baldwin might seem to impose a periodization in the U.S., the histories of colonialism offer an alternative American history, one that recognizes the country's imperialist activities.[12] Historical periodization might seek to declare American colonial activities as dead or past, but the internal subaltern performs a ghost dance on American power. The ritual realities of the culture are much more complex than historical periodization will allow. Understanding the stories that the culture tells and images it projects—its myths and epiphanies—is revelatory beyond historical periodization. The boy breaking glass is Emmett Till. In 1957, he was Johnson Hinton, and in 1962, he was Ronald Stokes, each of whom had been brutalized by police, in New York City and Los Angeles, California, respectively.[13] He might also be encoded as Dionysus.

SETTING THE REVOLUTIONARY STAGE: "PRINCES AND POWERS," VIETNAM, AND BLACK LIBERATION

Throughout *Theater and Crisis*, the analogy between individual personality and group dynamics has helped to break from historical periods and to reveal the processes of memory and recollection behind these dates. Although memory resists simple periodization, it is easy to see why the American political and social geographies would be felt as seismic shifts by 1968, the year that King was killed. Views that might seem to have been extreme in the 1950s, such as James Baldwin's anger about the state of interracial relations in the U.S., were becoming more mainstream by the 1960s. If television could highlight aspects of Nixon's face during those interviews as anguish, images of Emmett Till's mangled and disfigured face had also been impactful (Nodjimbaden 2015; Thompson 2016), alongside those of Black children like Ruby Bridges, the girl who desegregated an elementary school in New Orleans, Louisiana, in 1960, frozen in time in Norman Rockwell's iconic 1964 painting, *The Problem We All Live With*. The domestic cultural revolution was being televised alongside international crises, such as the Vietnam War, which Baldwin sarcastically called America's struggle against communism for the "domination of the world." Whereas prior to the triumphs in 1964 and 1965 (the passage of the Civil Rights Act and Voting Rights Act, respectively) King's focus had been domestic, his commentary on Vietnam during Lyndon B. Johnson's presidency was different. His position was now in some ways indistinct from that of Malcolm X, at least as it pertained to King's critique of America as a colonial power. For King, the 1964 Nobel Peace Prize came with a responsibility to speak out wherever he saw injustice, and Vietnam was "not just." More than a haphazard foray into international politics, King's remarks were measured and methodical. In addition to the question of justice, in practical terms struggles on the international front threatened domestic advances toward social uplift for Black people and the white poor in the U.S. King lamented the massive spending on the Vietnam War, which led to an unprecedented national deficit and inflation.[14] These trends had a pernicious impact on social programs like Johnson's Great Society (Johnson 1964). Johnson began escalating the United States' involvement in Vietnam when he became president in 1963 after the assassination of John F. Kennedy, even as he signed the Civil Rights Act of 1964.[15] King believed that America was putting imperial interests over and above the pastoral care of its domestic flock.

Internationally, the 1960s and 1970s marked the height of regime changes across Africa and Asia, what historians periodize as a postcolonial era, or the era of decolonialization (Getachew 2020). Already in the 1950s, Baldwin was speculating about the lessons from these events for the U.S. One of his clearest inscriptions of the United States as a Western colonial powers came in "Princes and Powers," his report from the September 1956 conference of Negro-African Writers and Artists at the Sorbonne in Paris (Baldwin 1992b [1961]). In the essay, Baldwin aligns the plight of Black Americans with these international struggles. First, one idea unified the conference participants, notwithstanding the array of cultural differences and national situations represented, which included delegates as diverse as Aimé Césaire, Leopold Senghor, a Haitian national, African Christian, and Richard Wright, the American atheist living abroad; this one idea was race. They were Black and as such shared the "fact of their subjugation to Europe" (15). Black people in the United States, however, were in a paradoxical situation, given their "uncomfortable awareness" of their national status (48), the inconceivability of their liberation from the nation to which they belonged. Black people in the U.S. had no native language of their own, for the most part, whatever vernacular inflections existed.[16] What constitutes a people, where there are no distinct ethnicities and no land? Baldwin's answer is cultural, not military. He recognizes that whatever their potential relationship to nation, Black people globally were debating questions of "religion, tradition, and imperialism" (45), as Richard Wright put it during his address to the conference. Through colonialism, European powers, which now included the U.S. and Russia in their struggle for world domination, had remade all African peoples, indeed the entire (global) South.[17] All were "related to Europe." The traditions of African peoples now melded with those of Europe. Because of the "double-edgedness" of this reality, politics, as George Lamming saw it (42), had become the only common ground for Black people across the diaspora, an arena of pragmatic civic and economic gains alongside the expansion of private life and indulgences. Politics, however, obscured the Dionysiac possibility of a deeper unconscious resistance, the unwillingness to settle on political and economic compromises. Dionysus might stand in for the unconscious desires repressed for the sake of politics and economics. And this repressed desire in the form of Dionysus was certainly present.

A clear undercurrent at the conference was the idea that culture, quite apart from politics or economics, could be revolutionary. Black people in the United States were born in an "open" and "free" society with "possibilities" (20),[18] but these possibilities would seem to come at the price of assimilation. Broadly, European colonialism meant the African would, to greater and lesser degrees, "replace his habits of feeling ... and thinking" with those of the oppressor (16). From Baldwin's report, much of the conference was spent trying to determine what remnants of African cultures were left after assimilation, in each of the circumstances, whether in practices such as voodoo in Haiti, or Yoruba culture and stories across the continent, as two examples brought up at the conference. Whatever the case, Black people in the U.S. were living under a colonial power, not colonized by occupation but by extraction, existing as a subaltern within a national context.[19] Black Americans would always be citizens in quite a different way from majority culture. Despite these realities, Baldwin weaves together an American Black experience out of disparate parts; being a "bastard of the West,"[20] albeit undesirable, is still an affective relationship, a bloodline. Black people in the U.S. were seeking to make their presence felt across the broader culture, and the Civil Rights movement had been working toward deeper American integration, toward "remak[ing] the world"—in fact, remaking the nation—in the image of the subaltern, grafting the African onto the "all men" that had been created equal (29). Like Dionysus, the Black presence in the U.S. was simultaneously always home-grown and foreign, always domestic and at the same time otherworldly. Cultural remnants of African remained, remade in Black bodies and re-enlivened generationally (Thompson 1984).

The Dionysiac idea conveys the dilemma of how such a presence as that of Black culture in the U.S. could ever be successfully integrated into the society. Although memory resists simple periodization, the alternating currents of resistance and assimilation would come to a momentary, tragic resolution with King's assassination. If Baldwin was on the periphery of the United States in the 1950s, both in terms of his exile status and his thought (himself a type of Dionysus), his perspectives on American coloniality were becoming more mainstream by 1968. Baldwin saw the U.S. as a burning house into which he did not want to integrate (Baldwin 1992a).

Moving closer to Baldwin's position before the assassination, in his speech at Riverside Baptist Church in Harlem (King 1967b), delivered a year before his assassination, King expressed that America's "adventures like Vietnam" were incongruous with campaigns to end poverty, likening a country that spends more on war than on social programs to one undergoing "spiritual death."[21] Like Baldwin, King came to see the U.S. as an imperial power encompassing the West—the white man's burden—across the globe. The U.S. had become "the greatest purveyor of violence in the world today." King extends his nonviolent philosophy and practice "toward little brown Vietnamese children." He rejects the idea that the nation should be the watchdog of the world. He seeks instead a "brotherhood of man." King's language of revolution is at times jarring, but unlike Malcolm X, he stops short of military options. Black people have no military power or land and are part of American society, even if an internal minority. Culture, however, was potentially more revolutionary than might be imagined.

Whereas postcolonial revolutions were taking place across the global South, what was needed in the United States was a "radical revolution of values."[22] Rejecting America's "militarism," King calls for a return to domestic policies that would uplift the country's poor people, who were most apparently but not exclusively non-white. His call to "recapture the revolutionary spirit" is a plea to turn back the hands of time to 1954, when the U.S. was transfixed on its own transformation, namely the country's renewal of its foundational Constitution, which was in a way supplanted in 1965. King resisted the easy simplification that aligned the war in Vietnam to American efforts to resist communism. He fended off the accusation that anti-war sentiment was un-American.[23] As he put it, "I oppose the war in Vietnam because I love America" (King 1967a). On April 4, 1968, King succumbed to an assassin's bullet. The historical record names James Earl Ray as the man who shot and killed him, a day after the Civil Rights icon's famous "Mountaintop" speech, which he delivered in Memphis, Tennessee, at a union strike of black sanitation workers. Resistance to cultural change aligns Ray's white supremacy with Bryant, Milam, and even Nixon, as the American Pentheus. As incongruous—or conspiratorial—as it might seem to align such figures as the assassin Ray with the executive-in-chief of the U.S., it is now a well-known truth that through the FBI the state had been tracking King, and even wished for his death (Pollard 2020). Whatever the reason for the assassination, the loudest voice for cultural revolution in the U.S. had been silenced.

STAGING REVOLUTIONARY CULTURE: ANTICOLONIAL DIONYSUS AND THE PERFORMATIVE TURN

The idea of hauntings from the past, as mnemonic recurrences, has been a theoretical tool to which I have returned as a trope of collective memory. The ghost dance "attempt[s] to establish the ethical relation with history" (Blanco and Peeren 2013: 311). but it also suggests an immanence, the potential that the future will be different. What would this different future, this relationship between and among groups from disparate backgrounds, be in the U.S. in 1968? Ghosts visit the present with a something-to-be-done, such that the future is different. As Spivak puts it, "the ghost dance can never 'work' as the guarantee of a future present. Yet it is the only way to go at moments of crisis; to surrender to undecidability (since the 'agent' is the ancestral ghost, without guarantee) as the condition of possibility of responsible decision, to transform religion into militancy" (Spivak 2013: 324). As a visitation, Dionysus challenges at a precise moment of "undecidability."[24] The "possibility of responsible decision" is applicable to the direction of postcolonial cultures during the 1960s, including the U.S., which was postcolonial by virtue of its legislative shift, its incorporation of subaltern people through civil and voting rights. The transformation of "religion into militancy" is evident at various cultural flashpoints (324), including the unrest in cities across the U.S. in 1968 in the wake of King's assassination. Racial miscegenation would be one of the phantasms of the period, as such promiscuity, to borrow the Penthean projection, can unravel a social order.[25] The protests of the 1960s toggle between sexual liberation and social unrest, as the proponents of the former see themselves as aligned with the actors on the latter scene.[26] Intriguingly, in the Frost/Nixon interviews the former President "go[es] on and on about the 'war' he faced at home, with protesters 'bombing and assaulting police officers'" (Morgan 2007: 61). Nixon is in the position of Pentheus, imposing order to avoid a Bacchic revolution in his own home, as it were. The political leader, Nixon's Pentheus, seeks to quell the conflict through military intervention, whereas social insurgents militarize sexuality.

Dionysus in '69 captured much of the spirit of the period, but in two ways it failed to speak fully for the moment. Soyinka conveys the first: the play was an extraordinarily white affair, drawing from non-European cultures but neglecting local, domestic hybridity in its obsession with aligning European ghosts (Bacchus) with the newly discovered primitivism of Asmat social practice.[27]

Zeitlin sees that the foundations for the performative turn were already laid from the 1940s through the 1960s, but Schechner built on this grounding with "concepts from anthropological theory and studies of primitive ritual to develop the idea of an Environmental Theater, which was to be realized through his Performance Group" (Zeitlin 2004: 52).[28] Books on the Asmat ethnic group of Indonesia were being published, and Schechner was gaining inspiration about ritual and performance outside of the West. As Adam Lecznar puts it, "Dionysus is no longer an ancient Greek god from whom one could draw a clear link back to ancient Athens: it is through the medium of the Asmat ritual that the Performance Group can create their own, modern, vision of the figure" (Lecznar 2020: 157). Zeitlin sees the play "whose impact reached far beyond the spare and vast space of the Performance Garage" as the most important performance on "a commercial stage in the United States" during the period (Zeitlin 2004: 49). The play was part of a "convulsive moment in American social history toward the end of the 1960s" (49).[29] *Dionysus in '69* set the stage for many more performative endeavors in the United States, including Ntozake Shange's choreopoem, *for colored girls who have considered suicide / when the rainbow is enuf*. However, *Dionysus in '69* appropriated non-European cultural forms while suppressing the social conflicts raging at home, which, as Soyinka understood, were not ultimately sexual.

If its extraordinary whiteness (notwithstanding its anthropological rooting in non-European culture) was one of its failings, its focus on sexuality—with little regard for sexuality's cultural power through miscegenation—was the second missed opportunity in the Dionysiac epiphany. By focusing on Dionysus as a figure for sexual revolution, the myth in Schechner's hands bears similar limitations to Pentheus' misconception of Bacchic revelry in Euripides' play. Sexuality might be a site for cultural activity, but it only manifests more deeply held norms. Sex, as the women of Aristophanes' *Lysistrata* know, can be a figure for war, or vice versa: love transformed into militancy. As important as the symbolic sexual revolution was, there were armed revolutions taking place around the world.

Soyinka was a first-hand witness to the process of state-building and violence in Nigeria. Having become a nation in 1960, Nigeria fell into civil war by 1967, when Emeka Ojukwu declared the independence of the Republic of Biafra. The Biafra region was an Igbo stronghold, and after a series of coups and countercoups, Nigeria plunged into a war that claimed anywhere between "one and three million people" (Nossiter 2012). (The population of Biafra was approximately 13.5 million at the time, about 26 percent of the population of all of Nigeria, which was 52.3 million.) Ojukwu belonged to the Igbo ethnic group, a powerful minority owing to their status under British rule. Writers like Chinua Achebe, who was also Igbo, would come to discuss the conflict in ethnic terms,[30] although the relationship of Ojukwu and his opponent, Head of State Yakubu Gowon, to the English, French, and American colonial powers was a factor. War ensued for the better part of three years, during which time Soyinka (a Yoruba) was held in prison. Soyinka knew the true devastation of revolution. During the Biafra War, "as many as 6,000 a day starved to death once the federal government blockaded the ever-diminishing Republic of Biafra" (Nossiter 2012).

Although the focus in the U.S. during these years was on the Vietnam War, America was certainly a focal point for people in Nigeria fighting for various forms of liberty. The U.S. could not be ignored on the world scene. Just as Black Americans looked to postcolonial African countries for their inspiration, so their cultural struggles in the U.S. inspired postcolonial Africans, including Nigerians.[31]

Soyinka responds to Schechner through his *Bacchae*, which addresses Dionysus' cultural whiteness, as a European phenomenon, and Schechner's inordinate focus on sexual revolution over a cultural one that sometimes manifests militarily. The play premiered in London, England, at the Old Vic of the National Theater Company, and primarily draws from Soyinka's social rooting in Nigeria of the 1960s. Although the situation in the U.S. might have seemed remote to the play in 1973, Soyinka revealingly points to the broader U.S. context and the role of Nixon in his later discussion of his play:

> As I explained to some of my company, "You say you have difficulty looking for some parallels [to Pentheus' downfall] in America. But what do you call what happened to Richard Nixon? If ever there was a tragic character, that is it. Begin from there."
>
> (Appiah 1988: 783)

Soyinka is keenly aware of Schechner, directly taking on criticisms of *Dionysus in '69* that were already circulating. In his review of the play for *The New York Times,* Roger Greenspun described how the Performance Group "by turns chant, or dance, make love, plot murder, whisper to the audience, or among themselves hold group therapy sessions" (Greenspun 1970). Plunging into the perceived essence of the Bacchic revelry, the actors stage their nudity and sexual exploration in "audience-participation orgies." Soyinka echoes the critique of Schechner's physical, sexual language that was in circulation: "How, except as a groping toward the ritual experience (alas, only too often comically misguided) could we describe the theatrical manifestations of the so-called 'Liquid Theatre' or the more consciously anthropological 'Environmental Theatre' in America?" (Soyinka 1990: 6). Soyinka's phrase "comically misguided" would make clear that his use of "groping" was pejorative. "Groping," a curious term among critics, was (as we will see) Amiri Baraka's 1965 description of the search for enlightened behavior among white Americans, a desire for cultural mooring (even for ethnicity) deeper than the notion of whiteness would allow. For Soyinka, Schechner's play gropes. It is not the ghost dance it could have been, were it to have communed with the ancestors in ways that Schechner seems to have known was possible, given his use of Asmat ritual and his description of the actor as shaman in *Environmental Theater* (Schechner 2000). *Dionysus in '69* is reduced to the sexual position without its deeper political and economic potential domestically. That is, culture can be revolutionary, but the coming American revolution was to an important extent in the hands of the Black subaltern.

Soyinka conceives of his play as a corrective to Schechner's. While eschewing some of the more reductive and essentialist tendencies of the negritude approach of many of his African contemporaries,[32] Soyinka roots his Dionysus in a Yoruba ancestor, Ogun, born out of the revolt of an enslaved figure.[33] Soyinka amplifies subaltern voices. He invents a chorus of enslaved people alongside a Slave Leader.[34] His play opens with the image of the "bodies of crucified slaves" (2004: 1),[35] which would be visually arresting for the viewer. Fears of a slave rebellion fester, from the very opening. As the Slave Leader urges, "let them reckon ... not with the scapegoat bogey of a slave uprising" (3). In addition to the layering of the narratives of enslaved people onto Euripides' *Bacchae*, Ogun is a revolutionary spirit that, among other powers, presides over rum. For Soyinka, Ogun is the "first actor" (Soyinka 1990). This role is consistent with the actor-as-shaman; Ogun is Dionysus, and he represents any performer who taps into the primal essence of human existence.[36] Soyinka links his Dionysus to slavery because the creation of Ogun himself is the act of a slave.[37]

Since the ghost dance disrupts temporality, making the past present and anticipating the future's imminence, it is worth lingering on the "fourth stage" of Soyinka's essay, a framework outside of linear time. On the fourth stage, Ogun acts to expose hidden truths. The fourth stage is Soyinka's way of conveying a difference between European temporality and Yoruba cosmology:

> It is necessary to recall again that the past is not a mystery and that although the future (the unborn) is yet unknown, it is not a

> mystery to the Yoruba but co-existent in the present consciousness. Tragic terror exists therefore neither in the evocation of the past nor in the future. The stage of transition is, however, the metaphysical abyss both of god and man.
>
> (Soyinka 1990: 149)

In language and lived experience, we might consider the past, present, and future each as a temporal stage. In Soyinka's Yoruba, however, past, present, and future are "co-existent in the present consciousness."[38] Soyinka offers that Yoruba temporality upsets Western conventions of time, as ancestors (or orishás) coexist in the present. Ogun is a shaman because he occupies an out-of-time, ahistorical field. The fourth stage, the "stage of transition," where the living meet the dead, is the site of the tragic enactment. The transition between past and present, or the dead and the living, and present and future, or the living and the unborn, is the "metaphysical abyss both of gods and man." "The Fourth Stage" advances a theory akin to the psychological principles of the unconscious, where past, present, and future (such as past behavior as predictive) are simultaneous, indiscriminately projected fantasies. Like the unconscious, the fourth stage is revolutionary in its power to upset normative perceptions of reality and time.

Ogun is for Soyinka the realization of the Bacchic visitation, the fantasy projection that performs its ghost dance. It is noteworthy that Soyinka presents his iteration of Dionysus in terms of the processes of culture, rather than as sexual or military revolution. The revolution that Ogun brings is not even primarily the regime change of military activity that Soyinka witnessed in the Biafra War, the upheaval that is a constant during postcolonial times. Rather, the revolution is realized in much the same way as individuals recollect the disparate experiences of their past, as shapeshifting fantasies that perform ritual dances in the person, in the mind and body. These fantasy projections are the encoding of memory later recalled, often indiscriminately.

Further nuance to Soyinka's perspective on the role of culture, which performs a psychological revolution in the individual as it encodes memories through epiphany, can be found in *Aké: The Years of Childhood* (1989).[39] It is significant that the narrative perspective in the memoir is that of a child because the recollection of childhood memory allows unconscious experiences to flow freely (like ghosts dancing indiscriminately) as they do in dreams. Through the encoding of these memories, culture can be revolutionary, infiltrating the colonizer's attempts to subdue, control, or neutralize. Soyinka characterizes his childhood as an imaginative reality where Christianity, Yoruba, and colonial educational structures blend to produce his personal culture (his identity) and that of his family and, ultimately, his nation. Aspects of this cultural identity that find their way into the *Bacchae* are not only Ogun as Dionysus, as "The Fourth Stage" portends, but also the ritual celebration of the New Year, which in the play becomes melded with Christian communion. In *Aké*, Soyinka describes the new year as a time when his family would travel to the ancient town of Isara: "Smoked pork, the flavour of wood smoke, red dust of a dry season, dry thatch. New Year was palm wine, ebiripo, ikokore ... a firmer, earth-aged kind of love and protection" (67). To Soyinka's childhood memory, "our women were darker in Isara, much darker." These ancient places and realities rub up against the European world, such as when a "box" suddenly appeared in the house playing "God save the King" (108). This gramophone was like an "Oracle," which people gathered to listen to, dropping whatever activity in which they were engaged to hear its pronouncements. From the perspective of a child, what Soyinka remembers are not only the voices of Paul Robeson and Marian Anderson, but also Christmas carols and "a massed choir of European voices—the Hallelujah Chorus," all "permanently interned in the same cupboard" (1989: 108). By telling of these experiences from the perspective of a child, Soyinka avoids the easy distinction between traditional values and modern society, that of the primitive and the civilized, the African and European. To a child, all experiences are primary, memories blending indiscriminately and magically.

This world of childhood memory is where Soyinka places Yoruba traditions and his introduction to Ogun. His grandfather initiates him, and he first resists by repeating things he no doubt heard from his Christian mother, such as the idea that "Ogun is the pagans' devil who kills people and fights everyone" (1989: 140). In contrast, Soyinka's grandfather told him that "Ogun protects his own" (140). Young Soyinka encodes the epiphany of Ogun as protector alongside his mother's sense of awe at the divinity, her Christian repression of this revolutionary force as destructive. It is telling that young Soyinka merges the memory of his grandfather with that of the Anglican Canon he encountered as a child, each a pillar of society left to be reconciled only in his imagination: "Father's eyes twinkled with inward merriment. Except that his eyes were much larger and brighter, he had the same trick with his eyes as the Canon, they wrinkled at the corners almost half-way to his ears when he was amused" (140). To Soyinka the child, his grandfather and the Canon are guides, and he continues to hold them together mentally as reconcilers of seemingly contradictory truths. In the same way, the melding of Ogun with Christian symbolism is what we see in Soyinka's *Bacchae*, where the festival of the New Year and the "communion rite" of the play's title becomes a sacrificial ritual to Ogun. Pentheus' head is delivered to the insurgents, the enslaved, the subaltern, for all to see.

Alongside his Yoruba cultural figures, Soyinka understands classical Western symbolism in terms of collective memory. Just as Ogun is his ancestor, conceived in such a deeply personal way that the god "protect[s] his own," so the Christian Canon holds the child's imagination with "twink[ling] eyes." In Soyinka's postcoloniality, to speak of European culture in opposition to Yoruba ancestors is senseless; both are mnemonic and evocative in a free play of ideas and associations before they hold power within society. Given this framework, Dionysus is as much Soyinka's own as

Ogun, and therefore it is Soyinka's prerogative to highlight areas where his perspective illuminates hidden or neglected insights about how the culture has received Dionysus. This blending of mnemonics is epiphanic encoding. Soyinka takes the childhood phantasies, the voices and images "permanently interned in the same cupboard" (1989: 108), and they become part of his conscious and unconscious reckoning. This reckoning, this ghost dance, forges an unprecedented future because the phantasies are juxtaposed in ways heretofore nonexistent. Soyinka presents a postcoloniality that opens possibilities for what epiphanic encoding could mean in an American postcolonial context.

STAGING THE REVOLUTION IN THE U.S.: THEATER FOR WHOM, AND TO WHAT END?

Ghost dancing is therapeutic work, a reckoning with the past that engenders a different future. This ghost dance is what the epiphany of Dionysus occasioned in the U.S., although the phantasy fails at its best identification, which is the subaltern cultural presence because Dionysus is always simultaneously inside and outside of the culture, as sameness, and difference. The modern American dilemma of race is epitomized in *Dionysus in '69*, especially in the way that it represses the transformational potentiality of the racial subaltern into its sexual fixation. With its focus on sexual revolution, the play ultimately fails to serve in the encoding of new experiences that would address race relations in the U.S. Such an encoding would have to call upon white audiences to experience the epiphany of the Black person—beyond victim or thug—in the same way that Soyinka experienced the various cultural epiphanies of his childhood. The deeper revolutionary change that miscegenation can represent—and is therefore often also feared and repressed—failed to materialize. Rather than the promiscuous cultural mixing Soyinka celebrates, *Dionysus in '69* represents a one-sided, white sexual liberation. As Baldwin saw, by virtue of their subaltern position Black people in America watch white behavior their entire lives, whereas white people had often not learned the language or symbols of the oppressed. This claim is manifest in *Dionysus in '69*. What is missing from the play is the revolutionary potential to integrate the culture. For revolution to happen, the community of Black and white (and other) people in the U.S. and other Americans must "watch each other watching," and such cross-viewing is never achieved in *Dionysus in '69*.[40] Baldwin had attributed to theater the potential to be the space where this cross-viewing could happen. The theater could, in his analysis, offset the segregated spaces where communities gathered, serving as a sanctuary where revelers become each other's flesh and blood, witnesses to a shared set of social realities. The theater could be a place for "true believers,"[41] the church having failed to spark the transformation—the revolution in values—that King hoped would occur. Baldwin's perspective of American theater required that "Mister Charlie" (from the previous chapter) not just listen to his own blues, but even find deeper catharsis and healing across a racial divide. Mister Charlie enters the "private lives" of Americans, believing in a single solace for the society: "The only hope this country has is to turn overnight into a revolutionary country and I say 'revolutionary' in the most serious sense of that word: to undermine the standards by which the middle-class American live" (Baldwin 2010: 14). Here again, Baldwin points to something akin to King's "revolution in values." Discussing the segregated stalemate in the United States in the 1950s, he argues that in whatever way this revolution comes, "it will be bloody" (15).

Blood and fire are Baldwinian images evocative of Euripides' *Bacchae*.[42] In a broader sense, Baldwin translates the postcoloniality apparent in Soyinka's work, directing his vision to the plight of Black people in the U.S. as a subaltern. If Soyinka's critique of Schechner played out more in the context of a Nigerian, postcolonial culture, others in the U.S. had to take up the revolutionary posture. LeRoi Jones/Amiri Baraka offers just such a provocation.[43]

Baraka had been counted among the Beat poets until his split with that group and initiation of the Black Arts movement, when he "rose from the ashes of Malcolm X and Martin Luther King Jr." (Reilly 1994: x). In 1965, even before King's assassination (and a year after Baldwin's *Blues* opened in NYC), Baraka published "The Revolutionary Theatre" (Baraka 1965). This is a Dionysiac, therapeutic intervention in the U.S. that anticipates both Schechner and Soyinka. The editors of *The New York Times*, where Baraka had originally sent the essay, claimed that they "could not understand it" and therefore did not publish it. Even *The Village Voice*, a countercultural, alternative weekly newspaper that was a decade old at the time, refused to run "The Revolutionary Theatre." Like Baldwin's observations, the manifesto was meant for white audiences, and Baraka held nothing back. Although Baraka preceded Schechner and Soyinka with this publication, there is compelling reason to believe that Dionysus was also at the heart of Baraka's message, as an epiphanic projection that captured the spirit of the decade. His work of the same period as "The Revolutionary Theatre," *The System of Dante's Hell* figures a protagonist akin to Nietzsche's Dionysus (Baraka 2016 [1966]).[44]

In "The Revolutionary Theatre," Baraka never directly names the European specter of Dionysus, but as we have seen, his Bacchic "groping" anticipates the language of Schechner and Soyinka. On the surface, Baraka seems to uproot himself from the European cultural soil in which he grew. He changes his name from LeRoi Jones to Amiri Baraka, divorces his white wife, and quite literally dons African garb. Although his Black Arts framework would be threatening to established American norms and would seem set apart from the mainstream, it drew from selfsame symbols of the Europe from which he sought to distance himself. The characteristics of Beat Generation poetry were Bacchic. These include sexuality, psychedelic drugs, and the merging of Eastern and Western forms, all of which would come to realization in Schechner. In *System of Dante's Hell* (2016 [1966]), Baraka is obsessed with sexuality as well, and yet the miscegenation and homosexual anxiety that permeates that novella stays home, as it were, unlike Schechner's *Dionysus in '69*. That is, Baraka's foci are domestic, beginning in his hometown of Newark, New Jersey, and never straying far from American soil, although Dante, Odysseus, and other European ghosts also haunt that work.

Throughout "The Revolutionary Theatre," Baraka dances between the idea of revolution as a cultural, metaphorical mode, and the revolution of theater as violent and real. The treatise arrests time. Throughout the piece, the repetition of "The Revolutionary Theatre" at the beginning of most sentences—replaced at times by "it" or "this"—reverberates in Gil Scott Heron's 1970 recording, "The Revolution Will Not Be Televised" ("The revolution ... The revolution ... The revolution").[45] Baraka seeks an onstage hero who demonstrates "not sad sentimental groping for a warmth in our despair." Just as Heron's poem will later echo Baraka's words, Baraka anticipates Soyinka's notion of "groping," the "warmth in our despair" evincing the corporal "groping for the ritual experience." Declaring what the Revolutionary Theatre "is" and "should" or "must" do, Baraka rhythmically seeks to "force change." The Revolutionary Theatre "should be change." Baraka calls for the Revolutionary Theatre to "cleanse them [white American theatergoers] at having seen the ugliness." He seeks to replace the "sad sentimental groping" of white American theatergoers with a kind of Aristotelian catharsis, which echoes Baldwin's call for white self-realization: "You cannot lynch me and keep me in ghettos without becoming something monstrous yourselves. And furthermore, you give me a terrifying advantage" (Baldwin 2010: 17). The terror for which Baldwin calls is that of the beheaded Pentheus. As Baraka puts it, "White men will cower before this theatre because it hates them."[46] In Bacchic fashion, Baraka wants to set the stage for Pentheus' reckoning and the culture's—Agave's—recognition. This requires the contemplation of harsh realities: the beholding of a dismembered Pentheus. These harsh realities are, however, the truth behind the veneer of civil society, and Dionysus identifies as this truth, in that he too was dismembered.[47]

Although not often read together, Soyinka, Baldwin, and Baraka each sought a therapeutic intervention at a point of cultural crisis. Each sees theater as an important site for this therapeutic work. Each becomes a guide, attempting to shift unconscious processes into conscious, epiphanic awareness. Like Baldwin, who wanted to press beyond the spiritless commercialism that he saw as endemic to theater in NYC, Baraka asserts that "the Broadway theatre is a theatre of reaction whose ethics like its aesthetics reflects the spiritual values of this unholy society." He calls out a society that "sends young crackers all over the world blowing off colored people's heads." Although his language seems quite apart from that of Baldwin and King—imagine King using the word "crackers" to describe white people—each ultimately conveys a similar prophetic message, a Jeremiad: America must change or suffer grave harm. Baraka's "Revolutionary Theatre" is steeped in the language of kinship (which is consonant with Baldwin) and ritual. He blurs the lines between society and stage, shadow and act, insisting that "all theatre is social theatre." He calls for the "American Artist" to be more than a "super-Bourgeois," not simply reflecting everyday taste but challenging the middle-class audiences that attend the theater. Theater was to reflect reality back onto its audience and thus precipitate change.

Baraka gives a sense of the Dionysiac character that he wanted to see onstage, the character who, like Dionysus, would visit a symbolic destruction of the old ways. In addition to black revolutionaries like "Crazy Horse, Denmark Vessey, Patrice Lumumba," Baraka cites his own hero Clay, in the play, *Dutchman* (2002 [1964]). Baraka's *Dutchman* demonstrates the extent to which the Black Arts Movement had set the terms of the debate for Black theater, moving into the late 1960s. Clay was Baraka's fiery Othello, who had tried on the attire of his oppressor, literally and symbolically, only to find that he would never be accepted within the mainstream of the culture. Like Dionysus, Clay is simultaneously of the culture and foreign. Clay is the "Dutchman," in his European suit and tie at the beginning of the play, a captive in Western wrapping. By the end of the drama, Clay is killed by the white woman on the New York subway train. Joseph Papp, who led the Public Theater and founded Shakespeare in the Park, put his objection as follows: "I never did any of LeRoi Jones's plays, although they were very good plays, because I felt they were too much just attacking whites for being white" (Turan and Papp 2009: 213).[48] By tapping into the idea of a revolutionary theater, Baraka was raising the possibility of a Dionysiac potential in American life, one where the culture as a whole sees itself and can move from recognition to a realignment of sentiments and behavior. This was unpalatable for many whites, however, too jarring in its presentation even if the message was noteworthy.

Before turning to Shange by way of conclusion, it is worth noting the inside-outside response to cultural integration evident in Baraka's proposition. Papp found Baraka to be extremely jarring. As was also evident in Brustein's critique of Baldwin's anger, these men (primarily) found the mirror that Black writers held to them too distorting. The catharsis Papp and others wished to see was that of *another*. It was one thing to watch Black people struggle through their own issues. It was quite another to have Black people bring psychological miscegenation, wherein they were intimately bound up with the phantasies of their white counterparts. This psychological resistance would explain, in part, why in contrast to Baraka, Papp found Charles Gordone, whose play he would produce in 1969, "more evenhanded, more universal" (Turan and Papp 2009: 213).[49] Gordone's *No Place to Be Somebody* succeeded at least in part because what the play presented was a process of Black catharsis, Black assimilation to norms and expectations, rather than a process whereby the white or hybrid audience moves toward an unprecedented position (Gordone 2019 [1969]).

Individual identity—as Black, white, brown, male, female—would be important to any encounter within community, any dyadic or communal relationship. Baraka's Clay is coming into a recognition of his condition, his social death, but that individual evolution finds its mirror in Lula, the white woman who kills him. Likewise, Gordone's Black characters come into their own, but that process does not lead to, in Baraka's words, "white men ... cower[ing] before this theatre." As Papp puts it, *No Place* was "a play about black people that didn't put the blame for all of their problems on white people" (Turan and Papp 2009: 213). Papp's sensibilities were affirmed in the consensus of theatrical taste; Gordone won a Pulitzer Prize for Drama in 1970, becoming the first Black person in the United States to win the award.[50]

Like the "Boy Breaking Glass," Dionysiac theater, as expressed in Euripides' *Bacchae* long ago, is a revolutionary theater. Revolutionary theater as Baraka defines it would "show victims so that their brothers in the audience will be better able to understand that they are the brothers of the victims, and that they themselves are victims, if they are blood brothers." Rather than making whites the "blame," as Papp felt, Baraka wanted whites to see themselves as also the victims, or as Baldwin put it, "we are each other's flesh and blood" (see Chapter 2). Baraka's solution, however, his pill as it were, was too bitter, his therapeutic intervention too harsh for his white audiences. On the other hand, Schechner's *Dionysus in '69* was too removed from American culture, at least as it pertained to the subaltern voices of Black people in the U.S.

FOR COLORED GIRLS ...

I will end this chapter with Ntozake Shange's groundbreaking work. Through her eminently successful *for colored girls who have considered suicide / when the rainbow is enuf* (Shange 1997), the ensemble piece where seven women, each wearing her own color and fully embodying the pain and joy of Black life, Shange wanted to project "black women in the world as a historical and metaphorical reality" (Shange and Ross 2014: 488). *for colored girls* is attuned to the ritual and performative dimensions that Schechner brought to the American stage, and it was also a drama that foregrounded racial embodiment in the U.S. Like Schechner's Environmental Theater, Shange's poem was performance art, "unique" as well as "unrepeatable, and to some extent improvised" (Anderlini 1991: 86). Bringing the performative turn to the bodies of Black and other subalterns, the chorus of women become *for colored girls'* protagonists. The foregrounding of their experiences had a lasting impact. *for colored girls* is often revived, notably in the post-pandemic, 2022 Broadway production. The play also underwent a 2010 film adaptation, albeit a treatment with which Shange was not delighted.[51] Though groundbreaking, the play was not the revolutionary theater for which Baraka had called. *for colored girls* countenanced a double-edged innovation on the American stage. By the time of its staging in 1976, the performative turn had ushered in a future for theater, placing representation and identity center stage. The plurality of identities in the U.S., however, resulted in the further atomization of the culture. There would be no unifying epiphany for an integrated American culture, no mythic figure or dramatic frame that could contain the whole.

Like Baraka, Shange was steeped in the language of postcoloniality. She calls upon the potentiality of the voices of "colored" persons within the culture. In her 1991 interview with Serena Anderlini, Shange conveys her worldview and her focus on postcolonial identities:

> Shange: The neighborhood where we grew up during segregation—as if there wasn't any now!—had Haitians, Nigerians, people from Togo, Jamaica, Panama, Costa Rica, East India, the Philippines and Japan. We all had to live with each other because we couldn't live with the white people: my friends'

> parents were from countries that were still colonies. When we were almost teen-agers these countries attained so-called independence: we experienced colonial history; my parents told us about it, but it was also all around us.
>
> (Anderlini 1991)

Shange sees the experience of being in the U.S. in terms of "colonial history." Whiteness is the neutral position against which colored people act. The plurality of subalterns "couldn't live with the white people" and "had to live with each other." The postcolonial experience was "all around us." She points to segregation as factor in how she grew up, but she recognizes that post-Civil Rights would be a misnomer, "as if there wasn't any [segregation] now!" The coloniality of elsewhere, moreover, migrates to within the U.S., in uncanny ways.

Despite the subaltern status of colored people, Shange grows up with a cultural richness from which America at large is somewhat deprived because of an encoded segregation. In her childhood, figures like W. E. B. Du Bois and Cesar Chavez visited the family's home (Lyons and Shange 1987), and Shange was "part of the first Afro-American generation educated in a de-segregated environment" (Anderlini 1991: 85). As she conveys in the 1991 interview with Anderlini, her childhood encounters gave her first-hand impressions of these subaltern experiences, as is evident in her mention of "people from Togo, Jamaica, Panama, Costa Rica, East India, the Philippines and Japan." Alongside her own Gullah-Geechee heritage, these cultures texture her poetic language. She is "a child of the new world," sensitive to a Black diaspora and the porousness of "national boundaries" (Anderlini 1991: 88). Like Baldwin, she widens her purview well beyond Black American experiences, putting the Black subaltern in its imperial context.

At the same time, the Black Arts Movement "was fundamental" to Shange's poetics, but she adds to it a more deeply performative dimension. On the one hand, she cites Baraka as an important influence. In her words, "I've built my work on my understanding of his work" (Shange and Ross 2014: 487). Reflecting from the 1990s, she sees her aim in the 1970s as that of crafting poetry that did what Baraka accomplished, but inclusive of women. On the other hand, she describes male beatnik poets as men standing still at their microphones reciting their work, hands steadily at their sides. She wanted something more fully embodied, poetry that "reached out ... flowed...that was female" (Shange and McIntyre 2013). Through poetry, she was interested in embodying the "collective effort" of feminist writers in San Francisco (Anderlini 1991: 89), where she did graduate studies after completing Barnard College in 1970. Shange was a wordsmith, but her medium was always performance. As she puts it, "if I didn't go to dance class I didn't have a poem." Dance, music, and poetry are all synchronous to Shange because they are "all controlled by the breath" (Shange and McIntyre 2013).

It is notable that a dancer and choreographer, Camille A. Brown, directed the 2022 revival of *for colored girls*. The movement of the women onstage never stops. In the wake of George Floyd's murder and the "BIPOC Demands," the Broadway theater district in New York City and beyond that, the League of Resident Theatres (LORT), committed to diversity and change in a host of ways, including the increased production of plays written by Black playwrights. The revival of Ntozake Shange's 1976 *for colored girls* opened on April 20, 2022. I attended on April 23rd, and I was immediately struck by two scenes, images, or epiphanies from the play. Each has to do with Shange's power of language and the evocative idiom of gesture which Camille Brown's direction and choreography captured. The first is a story, told by a member of the ensemble, of her own fascination as a little girl with the Haitian Revolution. She was taken with books as a child and had learned about Toussaint L'Ouverture on one of her many visits to the library. When she met a boy, she was stunned to learn that his name was Toussaint and thought she was trapped in a fantasy.

This, however, was a boy named Toussaint Brown. The flattening of identity onto this name is telling. It speaks, first, to a dissolution of the self. What does it mean, if the Haitian revolutionary and a little Black boy can have the same name. The girl identifies the boy as the same as her phantasy, although her idealized image can also be transferred onto another person. What's in a name? The answer: possibility. The little boy as Toussaint [L'Ouverture] raises the question of what might be possible for Toussaint Brown, what greatness might be available to him, given his name? The phantasy projection of the girl becomes the disappointment of the woman, but in that moment, two selves, two "I"s, become the collective "we" of an imminent revolution, a self-transformation, as well as a cultural one.

The second image comes from the story of an ensemble member whom a partner has incessantly abused. She has had children with him, but his violent shifts in personality owing to substance abuse leads her to distance herself from him, which further arouses his anger. He alternately proposes marriage to her and threatens violence. In an incident she recounts, he dangles their little boy out of a window and threatens to drop him. *for colored girls* has likely never been discussed in the context of Greek tragedy, but the scene echoes Euripides' *Trojan Women*, where the women of the captive city of Troy are distributed among the Greeks to serve as their slaves.[52] Andromache, widow of the Trojan warrior Hector, is to go with Achilles, but before their departure, she learns that the Greeks have tossed her son, Astyanax, from the walls of Troy. He must be killed to prevent any possible retribution for the destruction of his city. Although the proximate cause of the violence is different, *for colored girls* and *Trojan Women* share in the common plight of women suffering at the hands of men, specifically, but more broadly, within a violent culture. *for colored girls* transforms the "we" of the ancient chorus of women into the mothers in the U.S. whose sons are at risk of violence. This is the Bacchic chorus of women.

The images from Brown's production had as much to do with gesture as with language. For Shange, breath is as important as poem, a sentiment that resonates with Schechner's postulation that the primal epiphany is gesture, not language (see Leczner 2020). In *Environmental Theater*, Schechner elaborates on the performative process. Primarily through the repetitive cycle of rehearsal, "the rhythmic music and singing, and later the dancing of the shaman," the performance comes to "involve every participant more and more in collective action" (Schechner 2000: 183). This is the promise of a Bacchic epiphany.

By Broadway standards, *for colored girls* was a resounding success in the late 1970s, even if it failed to bring the cultural revolution Baraka wanted for the American theater. Its success came in notable contrast to the mainstream rejection of Baraka's work. Papp, who produced the play at his Public Theater before it moved to Broadway, describes *for colored girls* as "all poetry, exquisite writing, very rich and full of the black vernacular" (Turan and Papp 2009: 422). He saw Shange as "a real picture of a young black revolutionary-type woman," but she was not "hostile" (422). As Papp saw it, *for colored girls* came across as "political in the deepest sense," without the "grinding of false mythic axes" (415). Trazana Beverley, who became the first black woman to win a Tony Award for her role in the play as a "Featured Actress," concurred with Papp that *for colored girls* had avoided the "obvious trap" of anger (420). Echoing King's declaration that he criticized the U.S. because he loved the country, Beverley opined that "you don't have great hurt unless you have great love" (420). *for colored girls* expressed that hurt in a way that broad American audiences could recognize. In addition to Beverley's Tony, the play won an Obie Award in 1977. Like Gordone's *No Place to Be Somebody*, Shange's *for colored girls* featured the plights of others, the subalterns that white audience members like Papp could observe and for whom feel sympathy. The play, however, did not ask anything of them beyond sympathy. Thus, it was not "hostile," in contrast to Baraka's "Revolutionary Theatre." It is left to imagine what Papp might have meant by deeming the play "political."

for colored girls who have considered suicide / when the rainbow is enuf was revolutionary in bringing new voices and embodiments—new epiphanies—to the American stage. The performative turn could only effect Dionysiac revolution, however, if broader white audiences in the U.S. could also consume the epiphanies as their own. As has been argued throughout this chapter, performance is the possibility of a ghost dancer, a possession through the shaman, a role that Schechner argues the actor can embody. By usurping the norms of affiliation, the ghost dance offers the potential of a different future. The ghost dance, or the shaman, demonstrates, as Shange saw it, "the role of the enlightened individual protagonist, like the artist, is to raise the consciousness of his society" (Weyenberg 2013: 65). By dictionary definition, the shaman is "a priest or priestess who uses magic for the purpose of curing the sick, divining the hidden, and controlling events."[53] The shaman removes us from organized society to "divin[e] the hidden." For Schechner, a good actor can stand in the role of shaman, transforming the experience of performance from stale commercial theater to original, ritual, and social drama. Schechner posits that "when a society develops institutions to replace the shaman, then the performer as we know him arises" (Schechner 2000: 190).

Any inability to recognize the artist's intervention lies in the audience, not the shaman. From the perspective of cross-viewing, the responses of some white and Black men to *for colored girls* were peculiar, notable, for example, in Papp's description of Shange as a kind of "revolutionary-type woman." In a similar fashion, Baraka rejected *for colored girls*, notwithstanding Shange's consistent praise of him. In his eyes, the Black men talked about in *for colored girls* were "insistently caricatures." They were "pasteboards or beasts" (Lester 1988: 81). These responses to Shange's work exemplify Susan Best's idea that in the performative turn there would be "no larger political agenda that orients actions" for groups (Best 2021: 124). Rather than a "convivial 'we'" (129), who bear some responsibility toward one another, the performative turn had produced increasingly individuated subjects. As we have seen, Shange mitigates this movement in the choral "we" of her Baccants, but such performances were fast becoming identarian and atomized. Such onstage epiphanic encoding manifested in the cultural move (perhaps also postcolonial) of a shape-shifting diversity no longer anchored in the past, whether through history or memory.[54]

Returning by way of conclusion to the "Boy Breaking Glass," recognition would mean seeing the boy in more than sympathetic terms, and as more than a victim or thug—more than *another*. The phantasy of Dionysus was available in the U.S. as an epiphany encoded in various ways—as Nixon, as the sexual revolution, as the chorus of Bacchic celebrants themselves. Dionysus, however, would not be broadly encoded as the boy breaking glass, although as Gwendolyn Brooks knew, this was the god's most urgent manifestation in the 1960s. Throughout the 1960s and 1970s, Dionysus for many artists and authors epitomized the urgency of the subaltern situation in the U.S., the home-grown stranger. The Bacchic proposition is to make of this stranger the host, the body broken as a sacrificial rite for all.[55] Through ritual remembrance, or epiphanic encoding, Pentheus too will become Dionysus, one way or another.

When Trayvon Martin was killed in the winter of 2012, U.S. President Barack Obama said sympathetically that if he had a son, he would look like Trayvon. Epiphanic encoding takes the identification one step further. Through the phantasy and the ghost dance with the past, epiphanic encoding urges a reconstitution of the body, the self, or the community. The Bacchic rite asks the entire culture to say, if even momentarily, "I am Trayvon Martin."

CHAPTER FOUR

BREUER AND TELSON'S *THE GOSPEL AT COLONUS* (1986), DOVE'S *THE DARKER FACE OF THE EARTH* (1996), AND THE ESCAPE FROM BLACK PATHOLOGY

In this chapter, I want to imagine a specific epiphany, that of Oedipus, who would encode (for the broader culture) Black youth growing up in the U.S. as part of a family, perhaps at some point exposed, but reintegrated in some way. From as early as James Baldwin's *Blues for Mister Charlie* (1995 [1964]), we have seen race relations imagined in terms of kinship. "Family values" reaches its apogee as a popular political slogan by the 1980s and 1990s.[1] The family of the phantasy projection never existed; kinship is a fiction to be untangled.[2] The family of these celebrated "values" exposed and cast out members of the body politic, as we will see, the Black thugs and "Welfare Queens" who haunted the popular imagination.

Despite the reality of disinheritance, giving the Black protagonist a familial—and in fact, regal—lineage is what artist Jean-Michel Basquiat (1960–1988) did whenever he would paint the crown on his canvas alongside his subjects. Basquiat was a celebrated artist by the 1980s, viewed as a protégé to Andy Warhol. In fact, he was reportedly with Warhol in 1983 when he heard the news of the police killing of Michael Stewart, a 25-year-old Black artist whom officers brutally beat on the night of September 15th, in New York City.[3] The officers accused Stewart, who died in police custody on September 28th, of spray painting, or "tagging," a subway car. None of Stewart's friends or anyone from the community of graffiti artists in the City knew him as a tagger. Although Basquiat's paintings are known for the ubiquitous crown, a sign of kinship through royal lineage, a scrawled halo replaces this symbol in "Defacement," the impromptu piece that Basquiat drew with a marker on drywall.[4] At the center of "Defacement," Stewart's life is snuffed out, black lines draping the body, a shroud that suppresses any possibility of redemption. Ripped from regal lineage, Stewart as haloed martyr eternally awaits further violence. A police officer is positioned on either side of the central figure, not fatherly embodiments repressing a possible rival but voracious animals, pigs that would devour their meat. There, too, are the batons, the phallic extension of an Oedipal drive, foreshadowing in 1983 what would transpire with Abner Louima in 1997. Stewart's defacement, as it were, is not an isolated event. The actions of representatives of the American family, namely the state, would be repeated in the brutality of the treatment of Louima, the Haitian American man who accused NYC police officers of sodomizing him with their batons.[5] Stewart's outrageous murder and Louima's disgraceful treatment were the *fin de siècle* reminder that the Black subaltern subject is not kin. Rather, he is a subhuman miasma to be treated lethally, no chance of survival risked.

Given the realities for Black youth during the 1980s and 1990s, alongside the simultaneous proliferation of Oedipus storylines on the American stage, I argue that representation of Black subalterns as Oedipus amount to an evasion, an instance of epiphanic encoding that represses or completely shuts out Black kinship as a possibility. I will recount some of the realities of the period throughout this chapter, which include the urban unrest and ongoing War on Crime; the HIV/AIDS crisis, infecting African Americans at disproportionate rates to white people, and the myth of the Welfare Queen, who like her male counterparts, was in no way part of the American family.

Ironically, the 1980s and 1990s were a period that saw an increase in adaptations of Sophocles' *Oedipus* onstage in Europe and the United States, and some of these adaptations were in African American settings. These include, for example, Lee Breuer and Bob Telson's *Gospel at Colonus* (1993) and Rita Dove's *Darker Face of the Earth* (1994). These plays, though very different from each other, betray a similar evasion of the realities of Black life during the period. Whereas *Gospel*'s escapism is toward an ecstatic, religious experience familiar to attendants of the Black church, *Darker Face* retreats to the antebellum South, where Oedipus embodies a revolutionary potentiality realized only once in the history of the New World: the Haitian Revolution of 1791. The impossibility of a broader cultural encoding of Greek myth that could meet the realities of the time in part helps to explain August Wilson's intervention, his 1996 keynote address for the Theatre Communications Group, *The Ground on Which I Stand*, in which he decried colorblind casting and called for Black artists to create their own stories, for their own balm and edification (see Wilson 1997). It is no accident that the stories in Wilson's Century Cycle plays focus on Black families, so urgent was the political and moral repair necessary to reconcile Black life to the broader American public.

The power of a subaltern Oedipus that does not seek to escape the realities of life for Black and Hispanic young people living in the U.S. is realized in Luís Alfaro's *Oedipus el Rey* (Alfaro 2020), which I will discuss at the end of this chapter. That play was staged in the 2010s, decades after the peak of the family values phantasy. The play is instructive when we consider the connections between art and political life, or what political movement makes possible in art. Politics paved the way for the artistic realization of Alfaro under Attorney General Eric Holder. After its electoral victory in 2008, the Obama administration had undertaken a series of criminal justice reforms, including challenges to the school-to-prison pipeline.[6] Recall Obama's intervention after the shooting death of Trayvon Martin in 2012: "If I had a son, he'd look like Trayvon." Epiphanic encoding and therapeutic interventions point to the cyclical, mnemonic nature of collective experience; culture operates on the register of ritual, not history.

INTRA- AND INTERRACIAL OEDIPUS

James Baldwin, who assimilated Sophocles' story of Oedipus into his own biography, imagined himself as symbolically murdering a literary father, in this case Richard Wright. For Baldwin, Wright was "a roadblock in my road, the sphinx, really, whose riddles I had to answer before I could become myself" (see Chapter 1). Ever attuned to the artificiality of kinship, Baldwin knew that Wright was, as we have seen, as appropriate a relationship as any to which he might ascribe ties of blood. From early in his life, young Jimmy already understood surrogacy through David Baldwin, who was not his biological father, the latter having disappeared after James' conception. Each paternal relationship, whether by blood or affiliation, promised to displace the previous, more troubled one. It is worth noting the extent to which the Oedipal model is based on constructions of masculinity that Baldwin understood, even if he queered them.[7] As a man who talked about queerness before it was a concept in wide currency, Baldwin's deployment of the Oedipus figure is oddly normative.

Baldwin's biographical imagination is not the only place in his writing where Oedipal fantasies surface. In addition to Black kinship relationships and their substitutes, Baldwin could also craft Oedipal desire through a white character like Jesse in "Going to Meet the Man" (Baldwin 1965) Here was "psychoracial" desire, where the son's libido, his rivalry with father, is displaced not only onto mother, but even directed toward the queer figure of the lynched Black victim (Kim 2017). Psychoracial desire produces violence in white people, such as in Jesse's twisted recollection of the lynching of a Black man that he witnessed as a child alongside his own father. The remembrance produces libidinal desire in Jesse. The psychoracial imagination results in countless real-life Black victims, unable to mature, and even emasculated, such that the victim's sexual potency is transferred to the perpetrator of the violence. Crossing a racial divide, Baldwin casts Oedipal fantasy in reverse, or perhaps an incipient Oedipal story where the exposed child does not survive, as the mature father-figure continuously murders the son, whether real, or the son's substitute, e.g., the Black boy.

In foundational American fantasies, the Black adolescent figure prevented from maturing is embodied not only in Thomas Jefferson's Black children vis-à-vis his broader rejection of Black people as kin, murders real and symbolic, but also in George Washington's purported son, West Ford, whom he disavows.[8] These victims, these exposed children, are ever demonized, the Biggers (Bad Niggers) who deserve their fate.[9] By virtue of his nature, which manifests in behavior, Bigger cannot be kin and therefore is never Oedipus, who at least gets to survive and tell his tale, however ill-fated or, in Freud's estimation, guilt-ridden it might be. If the exposed child *does* mature, sublimated desire can also produce a projection of the infantilized elder, the infamous figure of Uncle Tom.[10] There will be more to say about Uncle Tom later, who has more sympathetic origins than what popular imagination remembers. Although Baldwin would deem himself Oedipus in intra-racial kinship ties, Oedipus is vexing as a figure for Baldwin's relationship to the broader culture. As Oedipus in the U.S., Baldwin himself can never truly mature. Oedipus could never serve as an interracial figure for Black maturity as American, as Baldwin's "Going to Meet the Man" suggests.

As we have seen, Baldwin imagined racial affiliation in terms of ties of kinship, and the taboos that keep the myth of kinship intact haunt the story of Oedipus: the unconditional love of offspring that infant exposure upends (preventing infanticide), the rejection of incest (which is non-heteronormative sexual intimacy within the family), and the reverence for—awe of—parents that prevents patricide or matricide. Imagined in terms of kinship, interracial ties would have to observe these taboos. As we have seen, however, the Black revenant in the U.S. produces ambivalence, the Bacchic push-and-pull that simultaneously engenders association and induces repulsion. As an interracial phenomenon, Oedipal desire has constructed the lynched victim, the hypersexualized other-than-human, whether male or female, the emasculated elder, etc., each a neutralization of Black vitality. Tellingly, kinship as a fantasy evokes the same ambivalence, this desiring and regretting (see Butler 2017). The Black presence as kindred in the U.S. has always been problematic, producing efforts to expose and abandon, or as Ralph Ellison put it in an essay, the persistent effort to "get shut" of Black people (Ellison 1970). Barack Obama's declaration that if he had a son, that child would resemble Trayvon Martin was reaching to draw Black youth back into kinship, but the incantation would always have had the inverse effect, that of breaking whatever temporary spell ever allowed a foreigner—someone outside of the family—to be an American President.[11] Even as late as 2012, citizens of the U.S. seemed unable to imagine Trayvon as kin (much less could they *be* Trayvon Martin). The reality is that of an Oedipal figure not merely abandoned but hanged in indefinite suspension, unable to be incorporated into an adoptive family. Such a specter could never return to claim his disturbing birthright.

MYTHS OF BLACKNESS AS PRODUCTIVE PHANTASIES

Oedipus is ubiquitously encoded across modern and contemporary life, thanks in no small part to Sigmund Freud, but Oedipus is also a productive phantasy for imagining the various pathways toward racial reckoning, especially as were possible from the early 1980s to late 1990s. For Oedipus to be a productive phantasy, we would have to imagine the various roads not taken during these years, a period rife with a plethora of troubling racial projections: the specter of ongoing urban unrest, HIV/AIDS among Black Americans, the Welfare Queen, and phantasmagorias like Willie Horton, a furloughed inmate at Northeastern Correctional Center in Massachusetts, whom George H. W. Bush used to derail Michael Dukakis' 1988 presidential campaign.[12] The proliferation of racial projections during the period with which this chapter is concerned threatens to disintegrate the imagined nuclear family. Already by 1965, Daniel Patrick Moynihan had pointed to the disintegration of the Black family as a problem for American society. His report of absent Black fathers and single-mothers (matriarchs) doing their best with Black boys, who resort to gangs for familial love, still reverberates well into the twenty-first century (Moynihan 1965).[13] The useful fiction of family values was concomitant with the production of racial projections that fall outside of kinship. In other words, there was a pristine, white Christian nuclear family everywhere under threat of dissolution.[14] Oedipus is a foundational symbol within the nuclear family, but the fiction of the heteronormative family has encountered several important challenges, including Gilles Deleuze and Félix Guattari's *Anti-Oedipus: Capitalism and Schizophrenia*, originally published in 1972 (Deleuze and Guattari 2009 [1972]). Their idea of "anti-Oedipus" is useful for its decentering of received ideas about the individual, privacy, and the family. In place of this familial phantasy, Deleuze and Guattari present various disembodied desires. Anti-Oedipus, because of the ways that such a figuration dissolves the kinship structure and projects human desire and emotions onto a larger, public matrix, is a fitting trope for the fragmentation and proliferation of the racial subject within the American body politic.

In place of the fiction and narrative resolution of the Oedipus story—violators of family bonds and incest taboos will be aptly punished—Deleuze and Guattari offer that what we observe all around us are "producing machines," which result in the totalizing control of a master narrative supporting an established order. In political terms, this totalizing effect (the Nietzschean "will to power") is fascism. Within the context of the U.S. during the 1980s and 1990s, we might consider such fascism as manifest in national mantras such as the War on Crime, the War on Drugs, Family Values, and so on.[15] These political platforms (wars) contend with various problems in the society: the urban violence of Black youth, Welfare Queens, and the various colored and queer bodies that are imagined as sites of HIV/AIDS infection, to name only a few. The narrative resolution (the producing machine) eradicates these intrusions, which do not belong. Although Oedipus is punished for his wrongdoing, the racial projections within the U.S. are not sons and daughters within the proverbial family, and thus their punishment happens in other ways from familial reconciliation. Race is produced, and racial subjects are contained or eradicated. Within such a structure (a producing machine), the Oedipal construct, as one potential narrative with resolution, faces various challenges. For example, who is the Welfare Queen within the Sophoclean/Freudian fantasy? Is she Jocasta? Antigone? Certainly not Ismene. Deleuze and Guattari best characterize the impasse to which I am referring: "It is often thought that Oedipus is an easy subject to deal with, something perfectly obvious, a 'given' that is there from the very beginning. But this is not so at all: Oedipus presupposes a fantastic repression of desiring-machines" (2009 [1972]: 3). Desiring machines are not family members (brothers, sisters, fathers, mothers), and they threaten to destroy the well-crafted fictions of the family.

For Deleuze and Guattari, desire is everywhere, as if itself a machine, and the family is the site where a repressive hypothesis is enacted, in such mechanisms as the Oedipal complex, where the son displaces free-floating desire (a will to power) onto the mother. Repressed desire is actualized as incest, which would destroy the fiction of the family. For Deleuze and Guattari, the hyperproduction of desire that capitalism encourages leads to various forms of psychosis, where unreality prevails over consensus. Within the U.S., "schizoanalysis" is fundamentally destructive to the myth of kinship, revealing race as one of the most persistent forms of psychosis. Eugene W. Holland defines schizophrenia, in the way that Deleuze and Guattari use it, as follows: "the term will in their hands designate one pole of the economic, cultural, and libidinal dynamics of capital (the other pole being designated by the term 'paranoia')" (1999: 7).[16] Although primarily locating the analysis in "the capitalist economy," what schizophrenia produces, collectively, pertains to culture and libidinal drives. The schizoid, as it were, resists at every turn the narrative impositions (the reality) that surrounds, projecting different fantasies into public space. Although teasing out the full complexity and difficulty of Deleuze and Guattari's analysis is beyond the scope of this chapter, it is worth working through a few of the projections within this chapter's period of concern. As we have seen, periodization falsely delineates phenomena that continue in the culture, returning cyclically. Nevertheless, the 1980s and 1990s manifest the schizophrenia of racial fantasies in ways that are apropos of Deleuze and Guattari's analysis. What is more, these projections linger in the culture beyond this period.

URBAN UNREST

The ongoing narrative of urban unrest, the HIV/AIDS crisis, and the myth of the Welfare Queen are three of the many productive racial fantasies of the period. By racial fantasies, I am not suggesting anything about the veracity of these stories, although as will become clear, such projections as that of a Black woman outside of familial structures exploiting the government was an egregious fiction. By focusing on fantasy, I return to the narrative and "imaginal" power of the stories, their production value, and how they shaped (racial) realities.[17] By the 1980s, for example, the recurring incidents of urban unrest in the U.S. meet a "system," a producing machine for their suppression, as Elizabeth Hinton argues in *America on Fire* (2021). Hinton analyzes the urban unrest from the 1960s to the present as uprisings, not uncoordinated and merely destructive riots, but rather a form of political action. Even before the assassination of Dr. Martin Luther King, Jr. in 1968, a cycle of violence was occurring across the U.S. Although the flare-ups in major cities hold the national attention, Hinton focuses on the manifestations of the cycle in smaller cities, such as Fort Lauderdale, Florida; Fort Wayne, Indiana, or Akron, Ohio. Put in terms of desiring machines, we might discuss these moments in terms of disembodied, free-floating emotions, such as fear, anxiety, and anger. Doing so helps in grappling with the disproportionate responses embodied on both sides of what became enemy combatants, the police and Black youth, otherwise the state and the citizen it should protect. How does an incident of children throwing stones at police cars, such as occurred in Fort Wayne, Indiana in 1968, result in large-scale riots and unrest? Psychosis is evident on either side. As it pertains to the children, one wonders what disconnection from reality would allow them to believe it would be appropriate—or even survivable—to throw stones at armed police officers? For the officers, a failure to recognize that these children posed no real threat reveals a hyper-vigilance, what we find by the 2020s in the analysis of an "excited delirium"[18] existing in Black men, itself a psychotic, unsupported diagnosis, a medical condition only (or primarily) manifest in victims of police action (see, e.g., Jouvenal 2015). We might ask, to what extent does the cyclical repetition of these incidents forebode their future repetition?

Rather than a narrative of children playing, to which a response might be a proportionate scolding, the producing machine creates a story of Black criminality and the need for its control. Michael Steward's death in 1983, his murder at the hands of police officers cited at the beginning of this chapter, was a case in point, but it is only one of a tragically repetitive cycle. Alternatives to violence, such as youth centers and programs (or spending on public schools), are (somewhat understandably from the perspective of treating a symptom) secondary to increased surveillance and control.[19] This is also psychotic. Even when the details do not conform to the metanarrative, such as in the case of Stewart's killing, the recurrences are made to fit—Stewart recast as a criminal, defacing public property. The producing machine encodes each individual instance as a repetition of the design. The paradigm is not only one of familial desire, i.e., the child within a family that might need redirection. Rather, the child is rendered criminal, monstrous, given to excited delirium.

Hinton recounts the details of instances of urban unrest in microscopic detail. Other historians, such as Michelle Alexander (2020) and Isabel Wilkerson (2020), join her in unveiling the cyclical nature of these incidents, as well as their ties to the prison industrial complex and the educational system. As a habit of their disciplines, however, they do not tend to discuss their evidence in symbolic terms, although they certainly draw hypotheses regarding the patterns they see. Were Hinton to speak of urban unrest in epiphanic terms, Oedipus would be a fitting figure. As it pertains to the role of young people in many of these rebellions, for example, pubescent drives often motivate their activity. The number of times a parental paradigm appears—e.g., the police acting in the role of father in their effort to repress youthful activity—is uncanny. As the Moynihan Report of 1965 had it, the absence of the father in the nuclear family led to the cycles of poverty and urban unrest. As a symbol, the Oedipal complex has the advantage of sketching the activity of Black youth in normative, universal terms, rather than in the language of deviance and criminality. Such a normative frame also raises important questions. What do we do with queer Jimmy (James Baldwin), for example? The frame would at least have inscribed Black youth within the family. Rather than as a juvenile delinquent, a Black pubescent boy could have been viewed as an Oedipus at the crossroads, whose bravado and unknowingness usurps the authority of the father. Within the terms of the Oedipus complex, such usurpation happens as a rule. No such epiphany manifested, however. The police elide the role of the father with that of the state, which becomes fascist in its insistence on a particular narrative structure. As we have seen, this structure, or drama, designates protagonists and antagonists, friends and foes, family and its destroyers.

Many of the provocations of urban unrest conform to this Oedipal pattern, although in her assessment of youth rebellions of the 1960s and 1970s, Hinton never uses this symbolic language. She is careful to assert, moreover, that by the 1980s, older Black protagonists (who were not necessarily young men) would join young people in their frustration with the cycle that had emerged in the 1960s. In addition to her examples from regions across the U.S., Hinton could easily have added the infamous example of Rodney King from 1991, which again emblematizes the metanarrative of paternal imposition sanctioned by the state and arrested Oedipal development. Viewers have come to know the Rodney King video in a partial, fragmented state, but there was more to the beating as a scene of the police state that had amassed to repress urban unrest. In "Witnessing Race in the New Digital Cinema,", Peter McMurray (2019) restores the sonic dimension of the videotaped beating of King at the hands of police officers. McMurray argues that during 1991, news broadcasters routinely dubbed out the audio with their own commentary. When the audio is restored, however, the police helicopters of the surveillance state could be heard in the background. By the 1980s, urban police forces had become domestic armies, deploying weaponry—heavy artillery, tear gas, aerial surveillance—that had been deployed during the Vietnam War (Hinton 2021: 11). As Hinton argues, by the 1980s, the cycle of violence led to a system wherein roles were fixed within the broader cultural production. Were we to apply the Oedipal figure to these events, he would point not to the regal intellect and steel will of the Theban father-killer but rather to his arrested development, to the impossibility of Oedipal maturation within a producing (repressive) regime that seeks not even to abandon him, but rather to eradicate him entirely.

HIV/AIDS

Given this ongoing tension between state and federal governments, on the one side, and Black communities, on the other (the "cycle," in Hinton's language), it is no wonder that some Black people who suffered during the HIV/AIDS pandemic of the 1980s and 1990s would suspect a government plot to enact genocide. The conspiracy was of course untrue, but myth crystallizes phantasies that speak to deeper truths. The year 1981 saw the first reported case of AIDS in the U.S. The Center for Disease Control reported that during 1981–1987, 92 percent of new HIV infections were among men, a category of "men who have sex with men" (MSM).[20] Of all infections, 59.7 percent were white, 25.5 percent and 14 percent Black non-Hispanic and Hispanic, respectively. By 1996–2000, the overall number of infections in men, by percentage, had dropped to 77.4 percent, as HIV became an infection that impacted heterosexual communities. Overall infections were now minority white (34 percent), with the plurality of cases impacting Black communities at 44.9 percent. By these numbers, infections among Black people had increased 76 percent in just over a decade, not to mention the growing impact of HIV/AIDS within Hispanic communities. Infections among Hispanic people had increased to 19.7 percent. A 1999 peer-reviewed article in Preventive Medicine found that of 520 Black adults sampled, "twenty-seven percent ... held

AIDS-conspiracy views and an additional 23% were undecided."[21] The authors found that "endorsing AIDS-conspiracy beliefs was not related to blacks' age or income." Perhaps somewhat contrary to expectation, "Blacks who agreed that AIDS is a conspiracy against them tended to be culturally traditional, college-educated men who had experienced considerable racial discrimination." The producing machine had created Black deviance, but it also engendered an oppositional, conspiratorial response in its subject. Many Black men held the view that HIV/AIDS was a genocidal, government conspiracy. They could not imagine themselves within the majority culture as regal sons within a family structure, even if the exposed and rejected Oedipus.

Although the conspiracy theory around HIV/AIDS might seem an extreme response to the pandemic, a "schizoanalysis" pushes what might seem delusional or psychotic responses to the center. From the perspective of Black men, who were most likely to believe conspiratorial origins of HIV/AIDS, there was already ample evidence of state-sanctioned terror. The producing machine generates Black deviance, on the one side, and efforts either to eradicate it or to protect the broader population from its harm. The War on Crime, which targeted Black communities and exponentially increased the number of Black and Hispanic prison inmates from the mid-1960s through the 1980s, had been in effect for twenty years by 1987. When he took office in 1981, Ronald Reagan reinvigorated Richard Nixon's War on Drugs, which had begun in 1969 with the influx of heroin into the U.S. during the Vietnam War.[22] Prison sentences for possession of small amounts of "crack" cocaine led to the boom in sentences for Black and Hispanic men, which corresponded to the increase in emergency room visits from cocaine overdoses. The arrest and conviction of five young Black men in New York City in 1989 for the brutal assault rape of a white woman who had been jogging in Central Park met a bivalent response.[23] For the broader population, justice had been served; Donald Trump had taken out a full-page advertisement in the *New York Daily News* calling for the arrest and conviction of the murderers.[24] For the young Black men, it was open season. The prison sentences of the Central Park Five were vacated in 2002, but they already collectively served almost a century in prison. If the state produces this kind of exposure of young Black men, it should be no wonder that forms of paranoia persist. The desiring machine, as Deleuze and Guattari see, ultimately epitomizes hopes, fears, and other passions. These emotions find coherence, however, only through existing cultural production.

THE WELFARE QUEEN

One additional figure that gained prominence in the 1980s is worth mentioning in considering how the desiring machine mapped free-floating passions onto existing and newly manufactured epiphanies of the family. This is the figure of the Welfare Queen. A symbolic backlash against the social programs of the Great Society, which can be traced to the post-Civil Rights era of the late 1960s through the 1970s, the Welfare Queen was a fiction that Ronald Reagan began to popularize during his 1976 campaign, described by Franklin D. Gilliam, Jr. as a "narrative script," that turned public sentiment against Black women. As Gilliam, Jr. put it, "the welfare queen script has two key components—welfare recipients are disproportionately women, and women on welfare are disproportionately African-American" (Gilliam 1999).

During his 1976 presidential campaign, Ronald Reagan created the "Welfare Queen," painting a fantastic picture of a woman having "80 names, 30 addresses, 12 Social Security cards and is collecting welfare under each of her names."[25] Although this woman was a figure of mythology, she was part of the material cultural production of the period. That is, she was produced as a problem that needed to be addressed: "among white subjects, exposure to these script elements reduced support for various welfare programs, increased stereotyping of African-Americans, and heightened support for maintaining traditional gender roles" (Gilliam 1999). Once he deployed the narrative script of the Welfare Queen, Reagan could later resort to simple asides about welfare in his speeches. During his April 23, 1980 debate at the Albert Thomas Convention Center with George Bush, Reagan did not need to mention race. When Bush advocated for government resources to states rather than broad federal programs (like the Great Society), his reference to the Fifth Ward of Houston clearly indexed a predominantly Black and Hispanic community. (George Floyd was from the Third Ward of the same city.) Bush's position of states' rights was in keeping with Republican practice, but Reagan would go even further, questioning social programs even at the state level. He roots his analysis in the 1950s, saying that if Americans, rather than undergoing heavy taxation for government programs, "had been able to save and invest, if our economy had only grown one and a half percent more a year, our incomes would be 50 percent higher; jobs would be plentiful; we'd have a balanced budget; lower payroll taxes" (Reagan 1980a). Reagan's prosperous outlook included both economic and "military superiority" over the Soviet Union.

In Reagan's September 21, 1980 debate with John Anderson, he directly calls out "inner cities," where there is "a higher percentage of people on welfare," although there is no mention of race in this speech. Reagan argues that a tax moratorium would incentivize business in those districts. The government, whether federal or local, does not collect taxes from "individuals who are on welfare rather than working" (Reagan 1980b). By his October 28 debate with Jimmy Carter, Reagan directly cites deception in the welfare system, providing a figure of "$7 billion" worth of "fraud and waste" (Reagan 1980c) At his election eve address in November, Reagan had long mastered the script:

> We brought into California government the best leaders from the private and public sectors. We cut the rate of government spending and provided billions in tax relief to our citizens. We brought

> the state back from bankruptcy by working closely with the legislature in constructing a welfare program that put cheaters off the rolls, reducing them by 350,000, while it increased benefits to the truly needy. The Urban Institute, a Washington non-profit scholarly foundation, recently referred to this program as a major policy success.
>
> Reagan 1980d

Reagan inscribes himself into the group of "best leaders" who seeks good outcomes for "citizens," an in-group designation akin to family. Outside of the familial structure are "cheaters," extraneous people who steal from the "truly needy." Having already constructed the Welfare Queen, Reagan would not need to repeat in polite company her role in fraud, waste, and cheating. She was not truly needy; she was a criminal. When he won the election the next day, Reagan could begin to implement the tactics he used in California at the federal level.

The Welfare Queen was a fiction, part of a producing machine that needed a "scapegoat," a word that Clarence Page used in his 1991 editorial about Clarence Thomas' fabrication of his sister's reliance on welfare, a case in point that gives the lie to Reagan's representation. The number of people Reagan presents as fraudsters is not necessarily incorrect. By homing in on this problem, however, Reagan was focusing on an extremely small subset of the California population—1.4 percent, to be exact—in 1980. Nevertheless, the fantasy of the Welfare Queen was etched in the imagination. The future Justice Thomas could call upon this myth in his discussion—betrayal, from a kinship perspective—of his sister. As Thomas famously put it in a 1980 speech, "she gets mad when the mailman is late with her welfare check. That's how dependent she is." Thomas went on to cite the generational impact, the myth of the broken Black family, as "her kids feel entitled to the check too." As Page writes, however, "Thomas' stunning story wasn't true." Rather than a Welfare Queen, his sister, Emma Mae

Martin, was part of a hardworking family, the third generation out of enslavement. She "worked two minimum-wage jobs while her brother attended law school" and only succumbed to unemployment when she began caring for an elderly family member. Although Emma Mae did spend several years on public assistance, she began working again at a job to which she reported daily at 3 a.m., as Page wrote. Emma Mae's fastidiousness was likely more the rule than was the folly of her fictional counterpart. A striking aspect of the myth is the degree to which Black people like Thomas are part of the producing machine. Page opens the same article about Emma Mae with the story of Janet Leslie Cooke, a journalist who won a Pulitzer Prize for a piece she wrote about a 7-year-old heroin addict, an embodied antithesis to a child living within a loving family. Cooke happened to be Black. The story was untrue, and Cooke was later stripped of her Pulitzer (Page 1991).

It is self-evident that these tropes—those of wayward youth involved in urban unrest, the Black relationship to HIV/AIDS, and the figure of the Welfare Queen—rely on broader cultural narratives, a producing machine that valorizes a certain kind of family, in which Freud's Oedipal complex operates. By universalizing Sophocles' interpretation of the myth, Freud created a repeatable framework for birth, rivalry, usurpation, and ultimate self-realization. The male figure is at the center of the paradigm.[26] The anti-Oedipus is a fitting theoretical rejoinder because it reveals the extent to which the myth of the nuclear family was always already a fabrication. The familial trope of kinship bonds, moreover, became a means of pathologizing Black experience. Whatever the behavior of specific Black actors, they were never truly part of the American family.[27] In contrast, the anti-Oedipus embraces the emotions and parts that fall outside of the familial cultural production. Oedipus could not represent Black male coming-of-age in the U.S. as a cross-racial epiphany of familial maturation, because the Black man was not kin. This is not to say that there were not Black Oedipuses onstage, but they would by and large fail to be effective epiphanies for the issues at hand during the 1980s and 1990s, such as the HIV/AIDS crisis or the other plagues which beset the culture and Black people in disproportionate ways vis-à-vis the broader population.

ESCAPING BLACK PATHOLOGY: *THE GOSPEL AT COLONUS* AND *THE DARKER FACE OF THE EARTH*

As it pertains the impossibility of the proverbial return home of Black kindred as Oedipus, three iterations of Black Oedipuses onstage are especially noteworthy: Lee Breuer and Bob Telson's *Gospel at Colonus* (1986), Rita Dove's *Darker Face of the Earth* (1994), and Luís Alfaro's *Oedipus el Rey* (2020). I discuss this last example at the end of the chapter. Each of these plays presents a different kind of subaltern Oedipus, but only Alfaro's play embodies Oedipus in terms that do not ghost the realities of the twentieth-century *fin de siècle* for the Black protagonist. Whereas throughout this book, I have used "ghosting" primarily as haunting, the ghost here is an absence. The escapism of representations of Oedipus onstage during the period is especially noticeable given the simultaneously ubiquitous pathology of Black life in the American public sphere. The figure of Oedipus in the 1980s and 1990s conceals (ghosts) the everyday realities of Black life. Oedipus is an epiphany from another time and place in the first two plays (a ghost), but he also obscures or conceals the problem of a cross-racial, familial public discourse in the U.S. Dove's Oedipus, named Augustus, might be said to haunt from the antebellum-period American enslavement. Whereas Breuer's Oedipus is an escapism of an emotional or religious sort, by casting Oedipus as a fugitive enslaved by his white mother, also his rapist, Dove brings the revolutionary zeal of the Haitian Revolutionary Toussaint L'Ouverture to the stage. The play, however, ghosts Augustus' descendants living in the contemporary 1990s of its production, except in so far as the cultural myth of fugitivity might be thought empowering.[28] In its temporal evasion, *Darker Face* is akin to *Gospel*, where the otherworldly, transportive power of Christian ecstatic worship allows escape from the realities of the period. In this case as well, the cultural resources of Christianity, alongside classical myth, are presented as liberating, harbingers of peace and, as Breuer has it, a catharsis of emotions like fear and pity leading to "joy."[29]

In "Oedipus in the East End: From Freud to Berkoff," Fiona Macintosh (2004) argues that Oedipus broke onto the European and American stage in the 1980s, a late embodiment of the character, notwithstanding the significance that Freud gave to Sophocles' *Oedipus Tyrannus*. Macintosh's comments about the factors that influence representations of Oedipus are striking and relevant. She underscores the idea that before Berkoff's production Oedipus had become comedy. While *Orestes* and *Electra* "lend themselves more obviously to contemporary social and political concerns" (314), Oedipus relied on a star system of actors—and thus rare performances—that attracted audiences but was becoming increasingly outmoded.[30] By the mid-twentieth century, however, there were new adaptations that "challenged the hero-centered plays in the traditional repertoire" (317). Modern and contemporary Oedipus had two compelling features: he was a psychological being, a creation of Freudian analysis; and he was a Promethean worker, dominating the material world with his brain and brawn. Macintosh describes Steven Berkoff's 1980 adaptation of Sophocles' *Oedipus Tyrannus*, called *Greek*, as a psychoanalytic work in which Oedipus/Eddy is "narrator and participant in his own drama" (321). Anthony Turnage adapted the play to opera in 1988.[31] A psychological and brawny Oedipus worked well in the context of twentieth-century London—and in the later twenty-first century revival at the Brooklyn Academy of Music (BAM), New York City—in no small part because of a low-end aesthetics: the play's interest in Eddy's working-class situation.[32] Turnage's *Greek* might have grand theatrical ambitions, but it is a "beer and pizza" opera (Sulcas 2018), "tak[ing] aim at the 1980s greed-is-good government of Margaret

Thatcher."[33] Not only does *Greek* give us a broader sense of Oedipal adaption in the late twentieth century, but it also demonstrates that those adaptations can be political. They can present ghosts that haunt the contemporary scene with an ethical reckoning.[34]

Whereas Aristotle's tragic hero is a regal entity from the great aristocratic families, in the contemporary U.S., as opposed to the aristocratic class in Athens of the fifth or fourth centuries BCE, these blood ties are between everyday citizens. In the modern context Oedipus can be an everyman, a consideration that Ellen McLaughlin notes in her discussion of her 2005 adaptation of *Oedipus the King* for the Guthrie Theater in Minneapolis, Minnesota. As Ellen McLaughlin sees it, "tragedy is the recognition of blood ties." McLaughlin's statement that "the Athenians ... would have recognized themselves in Oedipus" says as much—if not more—about her hope in Oedipus for contemporary audiences as it does for Athens (McLaughlin 2004: 463). As a blood relative, Oedipus has something to say to McLaughlin's audience. She writes that "we must ... understand our kinship with Oedipus at the end of his cruel story" (456). Oedipus as a cultural epiphany in the U.S. was primed for a racial inflection. Even McLaughlin deploys racial tropes in her understanding of the staging of her multicultural play. As she sees it, the chorus of *Oedipus* had to be "a group of people who look as if they might be members of the audience, representatives of the local community, mostly middle-aged, but ethnically and physically diverse" (468). At the same time, she adds her own "Pan-African[ism]," to paraphrase her, namely, "the trickster, a figure who is always linked to the crossroads." A parallel to Oedipus at the crossroads, "there's something archetypal about this that I want to explore."

Wavering somewhere between a modern everyman and an otherworldly incarnation, the Oedipus epiphany of Breuer and Telson's *Gospel* was undeniably inspired. It would be impossible for American adaptations of any of Sophocles' Theban plays—or even Aeschylus' *Seven Against Thebes*—to ignore the manifestation of Oedipus in *Gospel*. For McLaughlin, *Gospel* was "a magnificent interpretation of Sophocles' *Oedipus at Colonus*, which struck me then, as it still does, as the best modern adaptation of a classical Greek text every done." She adds that she admired *Gospel*'s "unapologetically religious bent" (321). The play was part of Harvey Lichtenstein's launch of the Next Wave Festival for BAM.[35] It was born, however, in the Black church. Writing for *The New York Times* in 1983, Jon Pareles recounts Breuer's visit to La Gree Baptist Church on 125th Street, in Harlem, where he heard the gospel group the Five Blind Boys. When Telson asks Breuer what he thought of the music, Breuer responds, "They're playing Oedipus." Interpreting Sophocles' *Oedipus at Colonus* as "a whole new idea ... not following a tragic form" but "an ecstatic form," Breuer speaks of "theological mythology." In particular, he focuses on Oedipus' apotheosis, "the idea of dying without dying, of being lifted directly to Heaven or taken directly into the bosom of God." He reads Sophocles' play as a "sermon," and because of this he sees the gospel setting as a fitting one for its adaptation (Pareles 1983). As Justine McConnell notes (in Bosher et al. 2015), Breuer strongly positions the play as an adaptation of Sophocles' Theban tragedies, possibly relying on Robert Fitzgerald's 1941 translation. Mel Gussow (1988), the reviewer for the play's Broadway debut in 1988, affirms Breuer's use of Fitzgerald and Dudley Fitts' translation, describing the play as "faithful to the original." Whatever Breuer calls the "ecstatic form" of the play, its re-rooting on American soil would alter its context and its tropes, even if in subtle ways.

In a departure from the original, *Gospel* folds many Oedipuses into the drama, as Morgan Freeman, Clarence Fountain, and the Five Blind Boys all double as Oedipus. This doubling of each actor as himself and the character in the drama has more in common with Richard Schechner's *Dionysus in '69* than with the adaptations' Greek counterparts. Breuer's company, Mabou Mines, was part of the same avant-garde movement toward the experimental theater.

Gospel is effective as a transportive experience, but despite its evident American bloodlines, it ghosts any social concerns in the here-and-now. Breuer entrusts the Black protagonists to a cathartic, spiritual experience that would lead to joy, ultimately gesturing toward the "love and community" (as Woolfe 2018 put the case) of *Greek*. In doing so, however, for similar reasons to the ghosting of catastrophes of the 1980s and 1990s that spiritual transport performs, Breuer reintroduces a dimension of Sophocles' interpretation that Freud disliked. In *Civilization and its Discontents* (first published in 1930), Freud (2017) asserts that "life as we find it is too hard for us; it entails too much pain, too many disappointments, impossible tasks"[36] Human beings, he offers, "cannot do without palliative remedies," of which he offers three: diversion, substitute gratification, and intoxication. He goes on to write that through phantasies, which are "illusions in contrast to reality," art provides one type of substitute gratification.[37] For a palliative remedy to life, Freud finds art "none the less satisfying" than drugs or other diversions.[38] Sophocles' *Oedipus* is to Freud "a fundamentally immoral play" not because the protagonist commits incest with his mother. Rather, the drama's immorality, its unbearability to rational, European man, is that it "dispenses with the moral responsibility of men, it portrays godlike powers as instigators of guilt, and shows the helplessness of the moral impulses of men which contend against sin."[39] Recognition in oneself of the Oedipus-complex as a "sublime disguise of his own unconscious" is reasonable in whoever reads the drama, and this recognition of the fantasy results in the "consciousness of guilt." Rational man, however, can break free from this guilt, whereas the "neurotic" fixates on the fantasy. For Freud, grappling with the material realities of the here-and-now would make for a better Oedipus. In its catastrophe of World War One, Europe had evaded its material responsibility. In a similar way, Breuer and Telson's Oedipus retreats, in this case not to the guilt of his actions, but to his salvation from them.

In *The Gospel*, the pastor (doubling as Oedipus) provides Freud's substitute gratification through religion. He preaches from the text of his sermon, the "Book of Oedipus," in which Oedipus (Clarence Fountain from the musical ensemble Five Blind Boys) comes to the end of his life at Colonus, after a cursed existence of killing his father and having children with his own mother. It is a story of human struggle and strife, drawing from the Ode to Man in Sophocles' *Antigone* as much as from the other two plays of the Theban cycle, *Oedipus Tyrannus* and *Oedipus at Colonus*. Whereas the Sophoclean ode ultimately affirms human ingenuity, urging the listener—Antigone, first and foremost—to obey the laws of the city, in *Gospel* the ode ends a verse early, focusing on death as the only phenomenon that human beings cannot master.[40] Stage directions signal for "a clap of thunder" as "God's lightning opens up the ground" (Breuer and Telson 1986: 44).[41] Breuer draws on a projection of otherworldly belief, but in doing so he falls into a pattern of treatment of the Black subject's spiritual transport. Such transport, at-one-ness with death, requires a retreat from any confrontation with the harsh realities of this world, forgiveness and forgetfulness conspiring to absolve the modern Oedipus not only of his guilt, but even of the need any longer to act.

The mode of ecstatic transport of *The Gospel at Colonus* is consistent with a strain of American Christianity. In *Black Messiahs and Uncle Toms: Social and Literary Manipulations of a Religious Myth,* Wilson Jeremiah Moses describes the symbolism as follows: "The qualities of kindliness, patience, humility, and great-hearted altruism, even in the face of abuse, were the very Christian virtues that were needed to redeem the world" (Moses 1993: 49). Moses recognizes a "romantic racialism" across American myth, where Black Americans possess "a redemptive destiny" (50). During the antebellum period, even Black writers "chose to emphasize slave loyalty because lynching was on the rise and the supposed black propensity to rape was the most commonly supplied excuse for mob violence" (53). No figure embodied the projection of the ennobled Black actor more than Uncle Tom, whom Moses argues was modeled after a historical figure, Josiah Henson, "guilty of cooperating with the slaveholder by returning a cargo of slaves to Kentucky soil after inadvertently freeing them in Ohio" (52–3). Although Uncle Tom has come to be a much-derided figure, in Harriet Beecher Stowe's novel (where the character originates), he was noble, meeting the sadism of the slaveholder with Christ-like masochism. The Black protagonist was to be Christ-like, and Breuer's Oedipus resembles the Christian Messiah as much as he does his ancient Greek namesake. Oedipus as Uncle Tom is not a characterization that has previously been advanced of Breuer's *Gospel*, but the play's escapism is curious considering the realities of the 1980s. By refusing to encounter the truths of the period, this Oedipus fails to be an epiphany that could enrapture an integrated American audience into its necessary recognition of surrounding circumstances, the catharsis that precedes joy.

Moses aligns the myth of Uncle Tom with that of more revolutionary figures like Nat Turner. Christianity, as Moses astutely and counterintuitively argues, can also imply militancy. Although Rita Dove's Oedipus, Augustus Newcastle, is a militant whom West African ancestral worship drives more than Christianity, the link between the ennobled, passive figure of Christ and the revolutionary one more consistent with the Old Testament prophets (and the Yoruba revolutionary) each highlights the escapism of the mythic deployment.

Conceived in 1979 and published in 1994, Rita Dove's *Darker Face* was not staged until 1996 at the Oregon Shakespeare Festival, by the Crossroads Theatre Company.[42] The play is set in the antebellum South. It contends with the plight of a Black revolutionary within an ostensibly rational order. Augustus is the enslaved offspring of a white slaveholder, Amalia Jennings LaFarge (Jocasta), and another of her enslaved men, Hector. Louis LaFarge (or Laius) is Amalia's husband but not Augustus' biological father. When he realizes that his wife has had a child with another man, to wit, a slave, he sends the child away to perish, placing horse's spurs in his crib to disfigure him. The scars become the identifying mark, the "swollen feet" of Sophocles' protagonist. Augustus is raised in the Caribbean and as such has an education beyond what the laws of the U.S. allow. Counterintuitively, through this education Augustus knows that the idea of a rational order is a paradox in the context of human chattel. He is the worldliest character onstage, an avid reader, although an enslaved person. His intelligence and erudition put his white counterparts to shame, including his mother/owner/sexual violator, whose tidy sense of the order of things he disrupts.

A play celebrating Black revolutionary zeal was not unsurprising, given the mission of Crossroads Theatre Company to "celebrate the culture, artistry and voices of the African Diaspora," which includes "providing a nurturing, professional working environment for writers and artists in the development of plays created and interpreted through the lens of the Black experience."[43] The company "present[s] authentic portrayals of people of color." In *Darker Face*, Oedipus is akin to Toussaint L'Ouverture, the Haitian general of the 1791 uprising, the only revolt of enslaved people in the New World to result in a free, independent Black nation. As with the Haitian Revolution, religion plays a critical role in Augustus' planned revolt in *Darker Face*.[44] The practice of prayer among the enslaved people is mentioned in various stage directions, and in one scene the character Scylla (pronounced "Skilla") prays in (what appears to be) Yoruba to Eshu Elewa, the god of crossroads and mischief. Through religious and other cultural practices, the enslaved people form a close-knit community capable of revolution, a feature prominent across productions of the play.[45] As Moses has it, however, the revolutionary enslaved is also a myth, even if rebellion and fugitivity bring their own benefits, as modes of existing in the world. The figure of the revolutionary enslaved belies the realities of slavery, which genealogically haunts the modern and contemporary scene but can also be a site of impotent escape from it.

Dove takes a great deal of artistic license with the Greek plays, as Breuer does with his classical material. In *Aristotle and Black Drama: A Theater of Civil Disobedience* (2013), I argued that the story that Dove takes from Sophocles—the *mythos* as a formal structure—moves closer to the original as Dove continues to adapt the play. In the 1996 play, for example, Augustus is shot rather than blinding himself, and it is unclear whether he survives to continue his revolution. Quite apart from Oedipus' self-blinding, which returns in later staging of Dove's drama, the initial production of *Darker Face* leaves open the question of Oedipus' existential plight.[46] The self-blinding is closer to Sophocles' version. In that earlier publication, however, I did not discuss the degree to which this *mythos* is also, ultimately, problematic from the standpoint of Black kinship. That is, when Oedipus is cast as a Black enslaved offspring of a master, his existential question cannot be one of guilt. Incest is a cultural taboo, not a spiritual catastrophe. Incest, moreover, presupposes kinship, and the enslaved cannot be kin.

Put as a question, can master also be mother? The master of the enslaved has total domination, as Orlando Patterson (2018) puts it, including the right to govern the body. Amelia's corporeal use of another enslaved man, Hector, leads to Augustus' birth. Her activity is a matter of domination, not kinship once we realize kinship, itself as a fiction and not the reality of immutable bloodlines. As enslaved, Oedipus' fate is no longer intertwined with blood heritage. Rape is only another manifestation of the master's domination over the body of the enslaved.[47] The child as mother's property (and not even the offspring of her husband) creates the possibility of the guiltless Oedipus about whom Freud speculated. *Darker Face* roots the issue of Oedipus as a Black epiphany in the original soil of the U.S., namely the enslavement of African people in the New World, but in doing so, it problematizes its resolution. Oedipus has nothing about which to feel guilt, as he has violated no taboos. It makes sense, therefore, that he should be shot because self-blinding for Augustus is nonsensical. The real question is whether Augustus, like L'Ouverture, can lead a successful revolution. As such, Dove's revolutionary Oedipus, in one iteration, comes close to self-mastery.[48] As it pertains to the social context of performance, Augustus can be a distant, ghostly forebear of Black revolutionaries of the 1970s. In the 1990s, however, the radical moment had passed, and something more subtly transformative, perhaps even separatist, was transpiring. Unable to flourish in their own soil, Black protagonists in the U.S. either shriveled or turned inward for sustenance.

THE OEDIPAL BIND AND THE COLORBLIND: AUGUST WILSON'S THERAPEUTIC INTERVENTION

The Gospel at Colonus and *The Darker Face of the Earth* demonstrate the difficulty of embodying disparate experiences in such a way as for myth to represent, or ground, all of them. This is not to say that American theater practitioners needed to stage an Oedipus that was in some ways authentically Black (and contemporary), as if racial authenticity were an unproblematic concept in and of itself. That said, if myth has the power to convey some collective reality, to ground a group in significant narratives (Bottici 2007), and to serve as an epiphany that encodes in memory, the adaptations of Oedipus during the 1980s and 1990s in the U.S. are telling. The group in question, in this case the American public, endorsed escapist interpretations of Greek myth that ghosted the surrounding realities of a good portion of the collective, namely Black Americans. When these ancient myths merged with Black radical expression, such as in Dove's Augustus, they were still set in a past distant enough to evoke feeling without disturbing the status quo.

A counter to the line of thinking that the foregoing pages have advanced is the well-known claim that there is no requirement for art to represent the world as it is. Art and reality—or truth—has had a long and contentious relationship. The staging of a play that represents characters from the ancient past, moreover, expressly distances itself from the contemporary subject. The plays that have been discussed in this chapter call broader audiences in the U.S. and beyond to bear witness to Black forgiveness, or to the potential destructiveness of Black militancy. They do not imagine the pain and turmoil of the Black subaltern as familial, that of a native child coming into its own.

The Black protagonist as a Western projection is fraught. There were practitioners who challenged this approach to art and representation. August Wilson for one, like James Baldwin before him, was not pleased with what he saw on the contemporary American stage and sought to intervene through his famous 1996 keynote address for the Theatre Communications Group, "The Ground On Which I Stand" (Wilson 1997).

To fully appreciate the vein in which Wilson was writing, the question of the purpose of art—and theater specifically—needs to be viewed in the broadest possible light. Universalist claims about art are not historically removed but illuminate debates within the culture during the 1980s and 1990s. It is no coincidence that Allan Bloom, who in 1987 published the bestseller, *The Closing of the American Mind: How Higher Education Has Failed Democracy and Impoverished the Souls of Today's Students* (Bloom 2012 [1987]), had translated an edition of Jean-Jacques Rousseau's 1758 *Letter to d'Alembert on Theater in Politics and Art* in 1968 (Rousseau 1968 [1758], and Bloom 2004). For Bloom, Greek and Roman texts represented a high point in Western literary, aesthetic, and political traditions. Bloom thought that America would do well to return to the high principles that he saw in those works, which continue from Greece and Rome into the treatise of the French Enlightenment writer.

Regarding *Closing*, Bloom took on intellectual and aesthetic discussions of the day through a descent into the past. His was an "anti-democratic" approach to American society,[49] presenting a worldview in which "the destruction of the aristocratic university was a failure for — not merely of — democracy" (Bloom 2012 [1987]: 36). Bloom traced America's educational decline to the 1960s, when protestors had "now become virtual agents of democratic form and democratic purpose all over the place—especially (but not peculiarly) in the nightmare of Cornell" (34). For Bloom, academic decline, which is a sign of broader disarray across the culture, results from "the redirection of the university toward various forms of social engineering. The most prominent have been in the field of racial and social 'justice.' The best-known mechanisms have been quotas" (35). From Bloom's perspective, the university should not be attached to "the social." Race is the most apparent evidence of the pernicious attachment. Higher education cultivated the individual. The separation of the individual from the group, moreover, enables Bloom's easy dismissal of race as a serious social problem that could be addressed in higher education. Race exists somewhere in the political realm, and by "engaging in the political," intellectual elites "surrender their detachment" (36). Bloom is concerned with how the culture was continuing an impure miscegenation. As he puts it, students "will assiduously study economics or the professions and the Michael Jackson costume will slip off to reveal a Brooks Brothers suit beneath" (Bloom 2012: 81).[50] No incidental reference, Jackson represented for Bloom the failure of aristocratic leaders to rebuke the indiscriminate mixing, the miscegenation, that democracy occasions.[51] America's ruler was failing the youth: "When they turn on the television, they will see President Reagan warmly grasping the daintily proffered gloved hand of Michael Jackson and praising him enthusiastically" (76).

Bloom's bestselling book became an emblem of the debates of the period, but more fundamentally he was advancing a principled position about art and contemporary politics. Was the expectation, for example, that theatrical art (as a parallel to Bloom's rendering of the university) should engage with real-world troubles, or is theater a place where audiences should be able to escape these, at least to think apart from them? Regarding the broader question, Rousseau's letter was the most immediately relevant in the long history of art criticism. Bloom had translated the letter when a professor at Cornell. In it, Rousseau opposes Jean Le Rond d'Alembert's (one of the editors of the modern encyclopedia) plan to establish a public theater in Geneva. The letter is in dialogue with Plato's *Republic* and Aristotle's *Poetics* about theater's politics, the question of whether theater is a corrupting force in civic life. That such a work would concern Bloom, alongside publications like *Closing* and his translation and commentary of Plato's *Republic* (Bloom 2016), is telling.

Rousseau's letter evinces the claim, as David Osipovich puts it, that "of all the arts, the one with the *richest* history of conflict with the defenders of morality, both theological and philosophical, is the theater" (Osipovich 2004: 355). Rousseau argues that theater operates on three levels. First, a play is an independent work as art, whether the text or literary work, a product within a given society. The work of art exists autonomously from the broader society or from moral considerations. On a second level, that of performance, the work of art interacts with a public. As such, it is of moral value, promoting or discouraging types of character and behavior. Autonomists (the first level) would argue that Oedipus is apart from the society in which the character is being performed, whereas moralists see him as representing something imitable among the viewers, something of character, although what this is would be open to interpretation. Thirdly, theater is as an institution, where a range of influences impact which plays are chosen to be performed and which are not.[52] The theater as company, a corporate body, is notable on this level.

These arguments manifestly concern the possibility of representing the social concerns discussed in this chapter. As Osipovich argues, "with respect to theater as literature, Rousseau is a moralist. He sees a clear connection between the worth of a play and the morals of the community for whom the play is written" (Osipovich

2004: 357).[53] In this case, theater that has moral value is written by moral people. Playwrights can do their writing without being didactic, which is to say, without *moralizing*. Nevertheless, as it pertains to social and institutional structures, Rousseau in his time proposed what Osipovich sees as "a nascent theory of *autonomism*" (358), namely that theater would simply reflect the surrounding society. There would not be enough moralist playwrights or self-reflective theater companies to engender positive change in society, and therefore the theater in Geneva would not yield good results.

Although Wilson might not have seen himself in direct dialogue with Rousseau (if even through Bloom), his position on theater represents a moralist current during the time. Wilson responds to the arguments about colorblindness and merit—an autonomous view of art *and* politics—that were pervasive in the culture, within and beyond the theater. In their book, *The Bell Curve: Intelligence and Class Structure in American Life*, Richard J. Herrnstein and Charles Murray (1996) locate "the sources of human differences and their consequences for social policy" in IQ.[54] *The Bell Curve* argues that the relatively new field of psychometrics, more specifically the IQ test, was revelatory to why certain groups were advancing in the society, others languishing. Like *Closing*, the impact of *The Bell Curve* when it was first published was staggering. A 1996 review in *The American Sociologist* summarized the book as "a major socio-historical event" (Kaye 1996: 79).[55] The reviewer for *The Journal of Blacks in Higher Education* notes that the book "debuted as number five on the Publishers Weekly" and was only "knocked off" twelve weeks later, on February 12, 1995, with O. J. Simpson's publication of *I Want to Tell You* (The JBHE Foundation 2000: 32). The catalogue of what the reading public was devouring at the time conveys the zeitgeist. Readers in the United States "hunger for intellectual confirmation of their racial views that blacks are not only inferior biological beings but that blacks are also responsible for most of our crime and other social problems" (32).

The polemic regarding theater that Wilson raised can be read in light of Bloomian aesthetic theory and his translation of Rousseau. There is no doubt that Wilson was frustrated with plays like *Gospel* and *Darker Face*, although he does not name these plays directly in the 1996 keynote address. These were plays in which European emblems were Black(ened).[56] They at least imbued characters with some semblance of Black experience, but worse in Wilson's thinking were those plays in which the race of the character might not seem to matter at all, i.e., colorblind casting. The practice of colorblind casting in theater was institutionalized in 1986, when the Actors' Equity Association co-founded the Non-Traditional Casting Project (NTCP).[57] The purpose of the project was "to address and seek solutions to the problems of racism and exclusion in theatre, film and television." At the core of the project's statement is an articulation of the *individual* as artistic potential: "The ultimate aim of NTCP is for all artists to be *considered as individuals* and to achieve within the profession, as well as the public, a better understanding of and respect for racial, cultural, and physical difference" (my italics).[58] What could Wilson see to attack in such a lofty and estimable goal? He might well have alarmed many in the audience when he asserted that "colorblind casting is an aberrant idea that has never had any validity other than as a tool of the Cultural Imperialist who views their American Culture, rooted in the icons of European Culture, as beyond reproach in its perfection" (Wilson 1997: 498).

Where Wilson was taking his listeners on this digression about colorblind casting was a sharp detour from the journey on which he embarked in his opening affirmation, his homage to the "pioneer[ing]" contributions of the ancient Greeks and their European successors. By 1996, Wilson had arrived on solid ground alongside these great European and American playwrights. He had staged seven of the ten plays in his Century Cycle, which told stories of formerly enslaved African people in the United States, their migration to Northern cities, fight for Civil Rights, and struggles to arrive at full citizenship in the late twentieth century. It is impossible to overstate how decorated a playwright Wilson had become, but here is a sample of some notable awards: *Ma Rainey's Black Bottom*, 1985, Tony Award for Best Play; *Fences* in 1987, four Tony Awards, including Best Play and Best Director, as well as a Pulitzer Prize for Drama; *Joe Turner's Come and Gone*, 1988, New York Drama Critics' Circle Award for Best Play; *The Piano Lesson*, 1990, Pulitzer Prize for Drama; in 1991, *Two Trains Running*, 1992 Tony Award for Best Actor (Laurence Fishburne); and in 1996, *Seven Guitars*, New York Drama Critics' Circle Award for Best Play. These are only the highlights, without mentioning the various nominations, other accolades bestowed upon Wilson for these plays, and the awards that he would go on win after 1996, in revivals during his life and after his death in 2005.

The pace that Wilson set in "The Ground on Which I Stand" and the dilemma to which he arrived abbreviate the path toward racial recognition on the American stage. Wilson's plays were interested in African American subjects, but he had also cited Aristotle and had aimed at making his characters a new kind of Aristotelian hero.[59] His homage to European forebears in "Ground" and previous interviews would seem a far cry from his indictment of "Cultural Imperialists" and his mocking tone regarding "European Culture" in the address. From Wilson's established pedigree, "Ground" takes an unexpected turn. Wilson moves from philosophical ruminations to practical application when he lambasts the practice of "colorblind casting." If Wilson stood on solid ground, some members of his audience would feel the earth shake beneath them. To those theater practitioners who assert that they do not see color, Wilson retorts, "We want you to see us." He "reject[s]" the idea that white people "carry that much spiritual weight" that all other people can be grouped together in contrast, as if "one white person balances out the rest of humanity lumped together as nondescript 'People of Color'" (Wilson 1997: 500). If the law courts and educational institutions refused to see color and its attendant histories, Wilson calls upon theater not to be colorblind, but indeed to recognize the long-standing racial problems in the U.S. In Rousseau's terms, Wilson was a moralist.

Wilson's provocative remarks led to serious debate within theater circles, certainly in New York City. In fact, for Broadway theater in the 1980s and 1990s, Wilson *was* the debate. Wilson's detour from the Greek playwrights and the European and American greats—who were, incidentally, all men—to "the Black Power movement of the 1960s" (495), which he calls "the kiln in which I was fired," would no doubt jar some of his critics who might have been along for the ride, such as Robert Brustein, who had already lambasted Baldwin in 1964 as being angry (see Menand 2021). Brustein debated Wilson in New York City (at Town Hall) on January 27, 1997. The playwright Anna Deavere Smith moderated. Brustein was the one-time Dean of the Yale School of Drama (1966–1979) and founder of the Yale Repertory Theatre, who in his debate with Wilson in 1997 states that "art doesn't change anything."[60] In Rousseauan terms, Brustein's response to Wilson's opposition to colorblind casting was an autonomist position. Wilson would have already read this argument in Brustein's 1993 article for *The New Republic*, "On Theater: Unity from Diversity." In the article, Brustein argued that "sociological criteria" were overriding "aesthetic criteria" in the funding of theater. In Brustein's opinion, this attention to the collective, social plight of a community was lowering the standards rather than broadening perspectives. Brustein had no time for Wilson or his Black Power influences. In keeping with his incendiary remarks about Baldwin, he would describe Wilson as angry during their debate, although later conceding that "I was not prepared to meet a man of such quality."[61]

Brustein's language of producing theater of "proven quality" during the 1997 debate parallels the language of merit, standards of excellence, and colorblindness in the wider public discourse of the time. As we have seen, Bloom had called upon quotas as an ill of the period. Brustein would argue that "aesthetic considerations" should override sociology. High-quality Black actors had their chance to play any role they chose, through colorblind casting. This practice allowed for the "best possible actor in the role regardless of race."[62] Brustein's position, however, was not as autonomous from contemporary blind spots as he might have thought. Of course, Brustein evades uncomfortable truth, such as the fact that the estates of some playwrights would resist the casting of their characters as anything but their original (often white) racial identity (see Harris 2018).

The audience during the debate was audibly taken aback when Wilson condemned colorblind casting. He chided Black actors who took roles in prominent white productions. These actors would "create an illusion rather than face the harsh and uncompromising truth about ourselves." The moderator, Smith, was a black woman whose 1992 one-woman documentary play, *Fires in the Mirror: Crown Heights, Brooklyn, and Other Identities*, had won numerous awards and had been nominated for a Pulitzer Prize (see Smith 1993). The play was about the death of Gavin Cato, a black boy who was struck and killed by a Jewish driver a year earlier, a death that incited riots and exposed the fault lines between two communities in Brooklyn, New York, the Hasidim and their black neighbors.[63] Even Smith is noticeably aghast, asking Wilson whether there might be "another position." For Wilson, there was no other position. As a moralist, he argued that the "politics of art is camouflaged. It's hidden." He advocates for a theater that would be more reparative of Black experiences in the United States. Such a theater would have to contend with slavery, Jim Crow segregation, exploitative practices in Northern cities during the Great Migration, and damaging policies such as the War on Drugs and the governmental endorsement of the criminal industrial complex (see Alexander 2020). As Smith herself does in 2019, such theater would have to contend with the school-to-prison pipeline for young Black and Brown men. Theater that dealt with these topics with depth and integrity would be reparative, even if this reparation operated more on a psychological than material level.

Turning back to the 1996 speech "Ground on Which I Stand," we see that Wilson moves to an institutional perspective from the moralist position. Rather than making room for the stories of people of color, Wilson points to the funding given to the "66 LORT theaters" (League of Resident Theaters) and the "tremendous outpouring of plays by white playwrights" (498), which in no way helps to tell new stories that would expand the aesthetic and psychological scope of theater audiences. His point of departure, the "kiln in which he was fired," includes his Western forebears: "In one guise the ground I stand on has been pioneered by the Greek dramatists, by Euripides, Aeschylus and Sophocles, by William Shakespeare, by Shaw and Ibsen, and by the American dramatists Eugene O'Neill, Arthur Miller and Tennessee Williams" (494). In another sense, however, Wilson points to an epiphany not yet realized. In *Aristotle and Black Drama*, I argued for an interpretation of Wilson's use of Aristotle's notion of *opsis* as an insight into understanding the "spectacle character" in the Black playwrights Century Cycle plays. Focused on spectacle, the playwright homes in on a feature of Aristotelian drama. There is another way of viewing Wilson's language, however, or at least another focal point. In speaking of the spectacle character, Wilson appeases interviewers who were asking him to address Western tradition in his plays. In his particular deployment of Aristotle, he slyly moves beyond any European perspective. Beyond coining the idea of a spectacle character, which I viewed as an homage to Aristotle, Wilson makes space for a mode of theater that has not yet been realized, one that centers the subaltern experience.

PERIODIZATION AND CYCLICAL RETURNS

As we have seen, Rousseau's idea in his treatise on theater was that audiences bring their whole selves to the viewing experiences, as do writers, directors, and playwrights. As such, a play is always already moral—always already political, as Bottici would put it—in that even if set in distant times and places, its storymaking touches on some aspect of lived experience. This is not to say that theater must be didactic, but for Rousseau, there can be no sincerely autonomist position. As we have also seen, Wilson's rejection of colorblind casting can be read in a moralist light; the broader social concerns of the 1980s and 1990s belied the widening of access to roles for underrepresented actors through such practices as colorblind casting. Plays that put traditional characters, like Oedipus but not limited to him, within Black cultural settings for Wilson fell in the same category. That is, these plays were not telling stories of significance to Black experience. Outside of the adaptations discussed thus far, there were attempts to close the distance between fantasy and reality, but those too are curious specimen. In 2001, for example, Jonathan Wilson staged an adaptation of *Oedipus the King* in Hartford, Connecticut (see Wilson 2001). Playwright Adrienne Kennedy, who had staged *Orestes* and *Electra*, is cited as a consultant for the play. Although the play itself is traditional, in its framing it foregrounds HIV/AIDS as the plague besetting the modern-day Thebes, someplace not in the United States, but in South Africa.[64]

Although nothing within Wilson's play announces HIV/AIDS as the sickness, an actor directs comments to the audience that they are in a "community health clinic." Information about HIV/AIDS was distributed at the performances, and proceeds went to local efforts to educate the public and combat the epidemic. The staging has illuminating moments. The production foregrounds the equation of the political state *in loco parentis* as father, a theme discussed throughout this chapter. As such, the role of

Teiresias, who "serve[s] no king but Apollo," is remarkable. The only actor to maintain a consistent and convincing South African accent, Wilson's Teiresias is reminiscent of Desmond Tutu, who throughout the 1980s maintained a measured and sustained critique of the Apartheid state through his Anglican, moral resolve. Given this framing, Teiresias' words to Oedipus seem a prophetic Jeremiad not only to his morally blind nemesis, but also to the pervasive and fantastic blindness that can beset a society. Creon's reluctance to govern, his declaration that doing so would be to "exchange ease for anxiety," evoked laughter from the audience that can be heard on the videotape of the performance. Like *Gospel*, Wilson's adaptation relies on the Fitzgerald and Fitts translation of Sophocles' play. As such, Creon's last words to Oedipus in the 2001 production echo the lines with which the preacher opens *Gospel*: "Think no longer that you are in command here, but rather think how when you were, you served your own destruction" (1522–23).

Notwithstanding its purported setting, Wilson's adaptation avoids the local concerns that surround the Black subject in the United States at the end of the twentieth century. In contrast to this, Luís Alfaro's *Oedipus el Rey* is the only adaptation not to evade (consciously or otherwise) the contemporaneous realities of Black and Hispanic young people in the U.S. (Alfaro 2020). Considering the periodization throughout this book, it is telling that the production does not begin to gain traction until 2008, well after the period with which this chapter has been concerned. The time of the play is "now," and the script includes the specific, global-positioning satellite identifiable location: "California State Prison | 2737 W. Cecil Aven, North Kern State, Delano, CA, 93215 | Highway 99." Although the play falls outside of the chronological constraints of this chapter, it merits consideration by way of conclusion, as one possible epiphany of Oedipus that addresses the contemporary moment directly. In framing the constraints on the individual as Oedipal, Alfaro surprised some viewers, but the generational inheritance that haunts the play's "now" was undeniable. In a 2008 review of the developing play, Michael Sedano puts the case as follows:

> Chicano culture [since the 1960s and '70s] has reached a kind of maturity today, and there's less, if any, requirement to lionize our criminals. Pintos are not heroes, and they're certainly not gods. Yet jail is where Luis Alfaro starts off his work-in-progress Oedipus el Rey, and pintos form his Chorus. It's a strangely inappropriate starting point that Alfaro explains in the program like this: "the more versions (of Sophocles) I read, the deeper the themes of the play started to take root inside my head. I began to obsess about the notion of destiny."
>
> (Sedano 2008)

In her introduction to the 2020 edition of Alfaro's script, Rosa Andújar echoes the focus on the "inappropriate[ness]" of the character, the idea that "pintos are not heroes." She highlights the "cycle of imprisonment" that Alfaro connects to "the notion of destiny" that he finds in Sophocles. Andújar stresses the "pressing issue of recidivism in twenty-first century America" rather than the underlying causes of poverty, substandard schooling, and the prison industrial complex—the school-to-prison pipeline. Imprisonment becomes a different kind of kinship, the bond a "longer chain of family tragedy" that manifests in the play. The phantasy speaks to the lived conditions of subaltern men living in the U.S. The reception of Oedipus as an epiphany of such tropes as "the legacy of the absent black father" reinforces the myth of family. As we have seen, the Oedipal complex universalizes a particular kind kinship, one that lionizes the father-figure and reduces other relationships, such as that of mother and daughter. Andújar's introduction, however, is a separate issue from Alfaro's play, as is that of Sedano. In fact, my preceding analysis in this chapter should help to redeem an aspect of Alfaro's achievement that Sedano and Andújar miss: Alfaro's Oedipus engages with the implications of a subaltern Oedipus in the United States in ways that, I believe, heed the therapeutic intervention of August Wilson. Alfaro is out of time (in terms of the chronological frame I have offered), but unfortunately the Oedipal plight of subaltern youth in America seems timeless, the "now" of *Oedipus el Rey*.

CHAPTER FIVE

THE WAGES OF WHITENESS, THE QUEERNESS OF RACIAL REGRESSION

The Laramie Project Cycle, *2000–2014*

In the last two chapters, I have argued that the anticipated Dionysian cultural revolution of the 1960s and 1970s gave way to a structural, familial, or Oedipal crisis in the 1980s and 1990s. Whereas the postcolonial mood of the earlier period promised a society free from the constraints of the past, such as racial segregation, there was a subsequent impasse when it came to recognizing Bacchic elements of the culture, embodied in the Black subaltern, as autochthonous. Despite the rhetoric of family values that saturated the public sphere in the 1980s–1990s, there was no place for the figure of Black kin (remember President Barack Obama's later declaration that "if I had a son, he would look like Trayvon Martin"), except in fantasies of a haunting past full of potentiality. As we have seen, Emmett Till is the spectacular figure from this past, one that belies broader narratives of racial progress or a historicism that places him and his gruesome lynching in the past.[1]

In this chapter, I show again how myth and storytelling work in American memory and forgetfulness, this time at the turn of the century. I propose that the theatrical productions of the first decade of the twentieth century and the conversations that surround them illustrated a continued repression of racial memory in the culture and its consequences. If identity is comprised of "lies that bind" (Appiah 2018), theater practitioners, including writers, directors, and critics, chose to promote some lies over others. Rather than ushering in a post-racial period in America, with the election of Barack Obama as President of the United States in 2008 as the closing proof of full integration, the 2000s brought a series of regressions, a collective forgetfulness, well beyond theater. Because queer bodies were among those late to be fully recognized in Civil Rights legislation, and theorists have been particularly adept at recognizing and exposing the entanglements that others might miss, I propose in this chapter that the regression in the culture evident in the first two decades of the twenty-first century was a queer phenomenon.

In the late twentieth century, James Baldwin was already prescient in noting the entanglements between race and gender as American social categories. In one of the instances where Baldwin speaks about his own queerness, he asserts that "all of the American categories of male and female, straight or not, black or white, were shattered, thank heaven, very early in my life" (Baldwin 2021: 689). This shattering was the result of several experiences, including one in which an adult male propositioned young Jimmy in an alleyway (see Introduction). In this case once again, the father-figure—Laius—fails to protect his kin, surrogate or otherwise, and this kind of failure haunted the Oedipal Jimmy. Although Baldwin recounts these as painful experiences, they meant that he was estranged from normativity, from early in his life: "Once you have discerned the meaning of a label, it may seem to define you for others, but it does not have the power to define you to yourself" (Baldwin 2021: 689). Existing somewhere between those social categories of male and female, Baldwin uses the term "queer" to describe his interstitial existence: "It wasn't only that I didn't wish to seem or sound like a woman, for it was this detail that most harshly first struck my eye and ear. I am sure that I was afraid that I had already seemed and sounded too much like a woman" (693). Baldwin's self-presentation as queer, as a body that does not conform to established social categories, can be extended to the intersections of gender, sexuality, and Blackness. A central focus of this chapter, the representation of the gay Matthew Shepard in *The Laramie Cycle*, reasserts categories of "male and female, straight or not, black or white." The *Cycle* falls short of the queerness that Baldwin defines because it re-inscribes rather than "shatter[ing]" gender and racial categories. There is no transgression or transfiguration. This is not a wholesale failure, however, as *The Cycle*'s enormous success across the culture shows. In Baldwin's imagination, queer is after all a category of dreams, a Protean unconscious that has the power of the ghost dance, able to transform society, but hard to attain in reality.

Matthew ("Matt") Shepard passed away at the UCHealth Poudre Valley Hospital in Fort Collins, Colorado on October 12, 1998. Twenty-one years old at the time of his death, Matt, an openly gay University of Colorado student who was also HIV+, had been brutally beaten six days earlier.[2] His assailants, Aaron McKinney and Russell Henderson, cited Matt's sexuality as a provoking factor, whatever the subsequent revisions regarding the reason for their violent and fatal actions. Matt's death created a watershed, the overflow of a teeming collective opinion about gay and queer young people in the United States. Although a theme would emerge about the shock felt in Laramie, Wyoming—namely that such a crime could not possibly happen there—a Time/CNN poll conducted in the days following Matt's death "found that 68 percent of the 1,036 adults questioned" reported that "a similar attack could happen in their community." An even stronger majority of those polled (three-quarters) "think the problem of violence against homosexuals is serious across the country."[3] Matt's murder activated a movement toward the recognition of a particular kind of violence that was occurring in the United States.

A decade after the 1999 trial of McKinney (Henderson pleaded guilty and therefore was not tried), U.S. President Barack Obama signed into law in 2009 the Matthew Shepard and James Byrd, Jr. Hate Crimes Prevention Act, which created a federal law criminalizing willful bodily harm under the following conditions:

> (1) the crime was committed because of the actual or perceived race, color, religion, national origin of any person or (2) the crime was committed because of the actual or perceived religion, national origin, gender, sexual orientation, gender identity, or disability of any person and the crime affected interstate or foreign commerce or occurred within federal special maritime and territorial jurisdiction.[4]

The Act affirmed federal protections based on race, color, religion, and national origin, extending these to the oversight of "actual or perceived" gender, sexual orientation, gender identity, or disability. It captured the countervailing forces of legal and historical programs and culture, which can be regressive or backward, to borrow a term from the queer theorist of international politics, Rahul Rao (2020).[5]

By 2022, there would be even further action to shut the door on the racial animus of the past through the Emmett Till Anti-lynching Act. Emphasizing the importance of the moment in 2022, Illinois representative Bobby Rush named lynching "a uniquely American act of terrorism that is motivated by hated" (Cineas 2022). Passed during the same year that the two killers, George McMichael and Travis McMichael (father and son, respectively), were sentenced to life in prison without parole for the murder of Ahmaud Arbery, a Black jogger they cornered with a pickup truck in Glynn County, Georgia, the Till Act "sends a message that America will no longer continue to ignore this shameful chapter of our history," when such acts went unpunished (Cineas 2022). The Act is evidence not only of legal and historical progress but also of the ritual cycle resulting in inevitable regressions. Whether or not the arc of history bends toward justice, the collective memory reshuffles and realigns in its modifications to changes in the environment.

As it pertains to the slow ritual cycle that manifests in myth, we have seen, for example, that Till's mother used language that likened her son to Christ. (See also Figure 2.) Lynching as akin to Jesus' ritual sacrifice was a motif as early as Harlem Renaissance writer Claude McKay announced the "awful sin" that "remained still unforgiven,"[6] despite the victim's plea, an allusion to the words of the dying Christ recounted in Luke: "Forgive them, Father, for they know not what they do" (Luke 23:34). An epiphany that galvanized a portion of the broader American culture through the first half of the twentieth century, Till's lynched body as the Christian host was a dormant figure in the early 2000s. Manifestation of his Black kin as Oedipal, the prodigal son in the American vernacular, were also absent, as we saw in the last chapter. The filial ties that James Baldwin imagined Till to have had with his white assailants are widely missed, even as much as a half-century after his murder. Given the segregated world in which McKay wrote his poem, the pessimist might argue that broad cultural compassion and recognition were never operative. That is, Black sacrificial and epiphanic death had once been encoded in the culture as worthy of compassion. In artistic and theatrical representation broadly, outside of these topics there was by the early 2000s a tendency that Susan Best (2016), referring specifically to photography, calls a "reparative aesthetics." For Best, reparative aesthetics utilize "affect as a component of the work of art rather than an expression of the artist's feelings" to engage—rather than "shame"—the viewer (7). Such art "confront[s] shameful events in national histories" (1).

In this chapter, I borrow Best's idea of reparative aesthetics to expand upon documentary or verbatim theater. I argue that something like reparative aesthetics is operative in the Tectonic Theater Project's plays, *The Laramie Project Cycle*, which revisit the murder of Matthew Shepard.[7] *The Cycle* is the most successful work of American documentary theater to date. The first of the plays, *The Laramie Project*, which the Tectonic Theater Project produced, is cast in Laramie, Wyoming in the aftermath of Matt's brutal murder in 1998. Founded in 1991, the company's vision includes the utilization of space, movement, and deep research to accomplish its shared goals for production. The company cast its inaugural production exclusively around female characters in the plays of Samuel Beckett.[8] The company was the brainchild of Moisés Kaufman and his partner Jeffrey LaHoste (inspired by Arthur Bartow). In *The Laramie Project*, these men, who happen to be gay, created a play that calibrates the hatred and ugliness surrounding Matt's murder. Like *Angels in America*, the play brought the HIV/AIDS crisis center stage and helped to normalize homosexuality within the broader culture across the U.S.[9] What is not evident in the play, however, is a reparative move extending beyond the gay white male as host toward the Black victim as well, which would be something like a trans* figuration, which I amplify below. When referring to the first play, I use *The Laramie Project*; the second play, *Ten Years Later*, and for both plays, *The Laramie Cycle*.

The *Laramie Project Cycle* plays were originally staged from 2000 to 2013 and published as a volume in 2014. The trans* entanglement of race and sexuality across the culture was traceable in the HIV crisis and the contestation over hate crimes legislation, yet the solidarity between and among impacted groups that would constitute a reparative aesthetics was not fully forged. By the 2000s, formerly marginalized social groups, including Black and gay people, would seem to have arrived, and yet another reality was at play, one bound up in historical entanglements not easily unraveled. Thus, in this chapter I mean through Matt to queer—i.e., to see otherwise, to restore repressed collective memories that were everywhere recurring across the culture. Building on Baldwin's comments on his queer body, I follow Rao's use of "queer ... as an analytic" in relation to LGBTQI rights, but beyond this, as an analytic for the culture at large (Rao 2020: 9). I ask the same question of America in the 2000s that Rao asks of gay, queer, and trans* rights in postcolonial Uganda and India of roughly the same period: What happens when we get what we want?[10] Rao's study shows culture as a lagging indicator vis-à-vis laws or juridical acts. Rao's model of a trans* critique uncovers the hidden cultural ties that entangle seemingly separate social phenomena.

ELLEN MCLAUGHLIN'S *HELEN* AND THE DEMOCRATIC WORK OF THEATER

Throughout this book, I have presented theater, commercial or otherwise, as a pro-social space and activity. Theoretical reflections on theater throughout the century provide therapeutic intervention for society, whether the institution or its public heeds the redirection. Throughout the preceding chapters, these interventions began with Baldwin's comments on the avoidance of important social topics on the American commercial stage. Amiri Baraka repeats Baldwin's warnings in his call for "The Revolutionary Theatre," which would do the culture's Dionysian work, and August Wilson helps to clarify why theater should even be concerned with social issues. As a place where images—or even epiphanies—are projected, theater has an ongoing role to play in cultural transformation or transfiguration (Baldwin's dreamscape). That is, theater is a place where a certain degree of encoding takes place.

Oskar Eustis, who took over the role of artistic director at Public Theater in 2005, defines the work of theater in democratic terms, an important intervention into its contemporary import (Eustis 2018). A director, dramaturg, and artistic director who had commissioned *Angels in America* for the Eureka Theater Company in San Francisco, California in the 1990s, he would be at the helm of Public when it premièred *Hamilton* in 2008. His 2018 TedTalk conveys his essentially classical approach, his sense of theater as an essentially democratizing institution. Looking back, he proclaims that during the 1990s and early 2000s "theater was doing its part to change what it meant to be gay in the United States." In the talk, which had been viewed over 74,000 times by the spring of 2023, Eustis declares that "theater is essential to democracy." The principle that he upholds is one inscribed in the stichomythia of classical drama, through which interlocutors voice opposing viewpoints. Channeling what he believes is the function of the stichomythia, Eustis declares that "if you believe in democracy, you have to believe that [hearing these contrasting perspectives on truth is a necessity]." Indeed, several theater companies in New York City and across the country were welcoming progressive storylines like those of *The Laramie Project* and *Head Over Heels*, which featured the first openly trans actor in 2018.[11] Production of these plays and many others like them surely had a role in the opening of the culture to alternative ways of being in the world, as they mobilized the experiences from the margins of American society by staging them in the mainstream.

Eustis has ample evidence that the vision that he brought to Public Theater was impactful. Following Joseph Papp would not have been an easy assignment for George C. Wolfe, and then Eustis. Hearkening to Papp's creation of Shakespeare in the Park, Eustis lauds it as the "best theater we can provide, for free," flattening access to great works. Eustis makes a distinction between theater as "commodity" and theater as a "set of relationships between people." He believes that the broader American culture has turned its back on most people living their realities. His example of a different kind of production—theater as a set of relationships—is Lynn Nottage's *Sweat*, a play about the deindustrialization of Reading, Pennsylvania that opened in 2015. Like *The Laramie Cycle*, the play confronts history, documenting the memories and assumed norms of another middle-American community. Striking and salient in Eustis' telling are the disjuncture between the progressive storylines brought to the American stage and the regressive realities, or the backwardness, across the broader American society.

Eustis' comments strike at the heart of notions of progress and an expanding democratic inclusivity, but he also betrays the possibility of backward steps. Viewing the idea of backwardness in theoretical terms, Rao identifies a "Western anxiety about backwardness and savagery" (2020: 39). He exposes a link "over time in the imagination of the nation itself" between gender identity and backwardness (179), given the desire for normative social relations, for which gender is representative.[12] Backwardness, as a trope that uncovers the underlying messiness of democracy, is a challenge to Eustis' utopian view of theater. Nottage herself, the black female director of *Sweat* whom Eustis names, took to the streets in 2011 to protest with others during Occupy Wall Street. Other signs linger that reveal Eustis' hopefulness as dream more than reality.[13] Narratives of progress run the risk of crystallizing viewpoints. They prevent openings for the recurrent stories that disrupt history and memory, or center and periphery. The contrasting positions that Eustis asserts are essential to democracy can be subsumed by history or state-sanctioned narratives. As we have seen throughout *Theater and Crisis*, history and memory are not simultaneous or identical phenomena. Polarization was an evident possibility in the personal voices of the performative turn that I have discussed earlier. Democracy does not lie in discrete identities unrelated to each other, but in mythic possibilities, the community ultimately working its way toward a grounded and significant set of shared epiphanies. August Wilson's position of promoting the representation of minority or subaltern experiences onstage gains some support from Eustis' arguments, and yet classicizing theater can so often amplify heteronormative—or even homonormative—whiteness.

In this process toward shared meaning, it is noteworthy that under the artistic direction of George C. Wolfe in 2002, Public

Theater would stage Ellen McLaughlin's *Helen*, her adaptation of Euripides' play from 412 BCE. The reception of classical characters, myths, and narratives on the American stage is a persistent reality, and yet for turn-of-the-century progress toward cultural hybridity in America, *Helen* curiously foregrounds whiteness and heteronormativity.[14] McLaughlin's adaptation is worth a brief digression for how its regressive currents, its demonstration of how dominant phantasies can remain in the culture despite efforts toward different grounding narratives.

Euripides' *Helen* was in some ways a curious play for McLaughlin to adapt, and critics questioned the choice and its success. Having acted in *Angels in America*, McLaughlin had already staged Greek plays during the 1990s, most notably *Iphigeneia and Other Daughters*, which the Actors' Gang in Los Angeles, California commissioned in 1995. It was perhaps second nature, then, that in the aftermath of 9/11 and America's rush to invade Iraq and Afghanistan, McLaughlin would turn again to Greek tragedy as a site of memory, tapping into a deeper fount than the newborn millennium could offer. In 2003, she would direct Aristophanes' *Lysistrata* for the Brooklyn Academy of Music and Aeschylus' *Persians* for the National Actors Theater, which, she writes, was "a direct response to the American invasion of Iraq in March" (McLaughlin 2004: 254). By 2004, she had staged an adaptation of Sophocles' *Oedipus*, which Lisa Peterson, her "old friend and collaborator," directed for the Guthrie Theater in Minneapolis, Minnesota. McLaughlin's choice of Euripides' *Helen* for her 2002 production gestures toward the idea of marginal stories, and even the revision of dramatic standards in unexpected ways.

Within the context of queering norms, Euripides was an ideal choice for McLaughlin.[15] Building on an alternative narrative already in the culture, Euripides disrupts the legend of Helen's travel to Troy with Paris after leaving her husband Menelaus. In the alternate version, Helen is not at Troy but rather her ghost. The real Helen has been in Egypt during the ten years of war resulting from Paris' abduction of her. In Euripides' play, Helen has spent seven more years in Egypt waiting for Menelaus' return. Euripides' Helen is holed up at a burial site for protection against the Egyptian king Theoclymenus, who wants to marry her. Taking her cues from Euripides, but moving in a more secular direction, McLaughlin's Helen is tucked away in a luxury Egyptian hotel room swatting flies and watching television. McLaughlin does away with Helen's foreign suitor, Theoclymenus, the reason she needs ancestral protection in Euripides' play. As it pertains to gender, Helen says that she had been "doing the wife-of-the-great-man bit for, like, *years*" (139). She has renounced this social role for the margins, now stuck in this hotel, while her "copy" conforms to cultural and marital expectations. Personality and personal memory exist in these margins, not the image in magazines and movies that others see, the "splitting of image from being" wherein "copy spews forth copy" (155).

Particularly in her changeability as she passes through different artistic and cultural passageways, Helen for McLaughlin, by performing against her expected role, names the silences that history creates. As McLaughlin puts it, "we are, most of us, ostensibly marginal to history, witnesses at the best of times, but often not even that" (McLaughlin 2004: 129).

Although focused on those who are "marginal to history," McLaughlin curiously writes (and casts) a white, heteronormative Helen. McLaughlin writes that her gift to Helen (as much, perhaps, to the traditional, legendary narrative) "is to give her the opportunity, not to reenter the myth that outstripped her individual self so long ago, but to step outside of it and take her place in the margins, where writers stand" (129). This idea of the "individual self" is a focal point of the play. As a legendary or mythological figure, Helen might step outside of history, but she does not exist apart from historical contingencies, the culture that she brings with her to Egypt (as it were). The play attempts to press against heteronormative, gender performativity, but it retains an unspoken association with the Greek myths as emblems of whiteness.

Like Helen, Menelaus disrupts history (the narrative or story as it has been handed down as authoritative) when he arrives on the scene. In keeping with the Euripidean precedent, McLaughlin represents ideas of war and its relationship to masculinity through his character. When Menelaus enters onstage, he expresses weariness of his masculinity. The realization that Helen was a copy means that the war was fought for no good reason, like the Iraq War and the weapons of mass destruction that never materialized. Nevertheless, the lie must persist, even if "all those boys" died for nothing (186). Menelaus as warmonger (albeit reluctant and perhaps somewhat repentant) would have recalled the martial lie of the period, the post-9/11 mirage that justified the first of many deployments ostensibly to save America from its enemies.

The critical response to McLaughlin's *Helen* gives a sense of the theatrical state of play during the early 2000s. Charles Isherwood reviewed *Helen* for *Variety Magazine* on April 8, 2002,[16] noting that Public Theater was "newly hot" with its "strongest season in years" under Wolfe's direction. Wolfe had just won a Pulitzer Prize for directing and producing Lori-Parks' *Topdog/Underdog*, a play that fully tackles the "subterranean" American myths of Abraham Lincoln and slavery, which Lori-Parks calls the country's "Oedipus" and other such myths.[17] In McLaughlin's production of *Helen*, Phylicia Rashad played the character Io, and she had "a ball with this diva's sassy impertinence" (Isherwood 2002). This role would be the only hint at race, with the actress who played the deracinated Claire Huxtable (Rashad as the mother in *The Cosby Show* from 1984–1992). Critics unanimously note that Rashad brings the only colorfulness to the drama with her Io, who is not in Euripides' play.[18] Intimating an association of this brilliance with racial identity, Isherwood notes Io's reference to the globe as "just another hide stretched on pain, no different from my own tortured landscape of whiteness pocketed by countless welts and weals, every one of them a site of misery." The whiteness of skin, the "welts and weals" that themselves provoke memory through the misery they cause, is a telling sign, an irrepressible slippage. The passing—even marginal—indications of a racial indicator belie the haunting silence on race notable in the production of *Helen*.

Isherwood's notice of Wolfe's "strongest season" calls attention to the Public Theater's artistic producer, who happened to be gay and Black. Wolfe's productions of *Topdog/Underdog* and *Helen* might seem separate matters. A Public Theater staple, Lori-Parks' notice of Greek myth as a "subterranean thing" in American society is revelatory. Even when not stated, race is also inevitably mixed into the strata of cultural experience, as critic Ben Brantley further suggests (Brantley 2002). While silent on McLaughlin's *Helen* as a matter either of gender or racial identity, Brantley's review does convey a sense of the play's ennui, not only the weariness of its main character, but the out-of-time nature of the entire production. As he puts it, "the biggest problem ... is that you feel you've read or heard almost everything that's said here, and the play keeps saying it over and over." If the play is post-, whether post-feminist, post-classical, or postmodern,[19] its presence is spectral, "a taking-off point for speculation on things more cosmic than cosmetic." Brantley looks to Donna Murphy, a "two-time Tony winner" whose performance "become[s] more labored" after the first five minutes of the play, this through no fault of her own but owing to "Ms. McLaughlin's not terribly original content."[20] Murphy's stature as an actress of over nine plays across four decades, over two dozen films and over three dozen television productions, reifies *Helen*'s interrogation of real and fantasy, copy and original. Given her status and stature, Murphy's presence begs the question of marginalization.

I offer McLaughlin's *Helen* as a counterpoint to *The Laramie Project*. Whereas the former depends on heteronormativity, the latter establishes a homonormativity that is similar in its whiteness. Reflecting on *The Laramie Project Cycle* in 2013, Isherwood concludes that "some stories — painful though they may be to hear — gain in meaning and stature in the retelling." History, myth, and legend are modes of these retellings, and the stage is a site of memory. There is something to be noted in why the legend of Matthew Shepard, like the subterranean classical epiphanies continuously reencoded in the culture, evokes emotion in *The Laramie Project Cycle* while McLaughlin's *Helen* seems as empty as her copy, which might well have been the point of McLauglin's adaptation. Matt's "stature" only increased in the decade after his 1998 murder, his formerly reclusive mother becoming "a dogged champion of the cause of gay rights and hate-crimes legislation" (Isherwood 2013). Attempts at revision only buttress the indelibility of the story; *Ten Years Later*, the second installation of the *Cycle* plays, reenforces Matt's mythic significance to the culture. By the late 2000s, Matt had become an epiphany for gay rights, as is evident in Obama's signing of Civil Rights legislation named after Matt. Matthew's killer McKinney, with his *20/20* interview on the American Broadcast Company in 2004, "makes glaringly clear his continuing hatred of homosexuals," even ten years on.[21] However insistent the attempts to revise Matt's death as ordinary—the result of a drug deal gone bad—his iconic place in cultural memory could not be erased. By his 2013 review of *Ten Years Later*, Isherwood charts "895 productions since 2008" of *The Laramie Project* itself. Theater on this scale must certainly be impactful on the culture. Such a play normalizes its subject matter so that revisions to the story of Matthew Shepard could not easily stand. Still, there was something during the decade even queerer than the homonormative representation of Matthew Shepard, and this queerness is apparent in McLaughlin's *Helen*, if we trans*- our reading.

Rather than a period of post-ness, 2000–2014 revealed the inability of American theater to fully apprehend the powerful entanglement among people, places, and causes that lay beneath the democratic surface. If *The Laramie Project Cycle* held something of the zeitgeist, McLaughlin's *Helen* was also a notable specter, a haunting presence that spoke to the emptiness of official stories. It was certainly McLaughlin's purpose to haunt, which is why she chose Euripides' most ghostly play, a performance itself about ghosts, appearances, absences, copies, and shadows. But whiteness, as a normativity, in this case homonormative, is as much the open secret of *The Laramie Project Cycle* as it is of *Helen*. Voices from the margins are present, but the play's point of view overwhelms several other concerns during the period. I turn now to one of those concerns, namely the potential queerness underlying even homonormativity. Murdered in 1993, Brandon Teena embodied the trans* perspective I offer as an important rereading of the period.

BRANDON TEENA

The murder of Matthew Shepard was not the first such high-profile killing from the late twentieth century to the early twenty-first ostensibly based on sexuality or gender expression. The rape and subsequent murder of Brandon Teena in 1993 in Humboldt, Nebraska had become a national conversation piece by the end of the millennium. Hilary Swank won an Academy Award for playing the role of Brandon in the film, *Boys Don't Cry* (Pierce 1999). Brandon, assigned a sex of female at birth in 1972, was only 21 when two men, John L. Lotter and Marvin Thomas Nissen, stripped him naked to challenge his gender representation.[22] Abducting him by car, each abused him in turn. The audiotape of Sheriff Charles B. Laux's interrogation of Brandon is itself an all-out assault on human sensibilities. Rather than focus on Lotter and Nissen's brutality or the culture that produced it, Laux is fixated on genitalia and sexual acts, almost as if he is salaciously reliving the events himself, placing himself at the scene of the crime, perpetrating the violent actions once again in their reiteration. Brandon Teena's shame is evident. In the audiotape, he wonders why it should matter what his sex is, what genitalia he has, and other curiosities that move from the violent acts against him to speculation about function, pleasure, and enjoyment.[23] The issue at hand should have been the brutal crime, not Brandon's sex, gender, or sexuality.

Laux's behavior was not new to Brandon. In the years leading up to his rape and murder, he struggled with heteronormative sexuality. Although born with female genitalia, he was attracted to women and presented as a man. Brandon Teena's 21-year-old reality of struggling with his identity and the shame of it (which the norms of society generate) is evident in his voice, demeanor, and responses to Laux. Even Brandon's mother did not accept his reality until years after his murder. Brandon's pain is palpable, but its recall is critical to understanding the broader situation it exposes.[24] Histories of progress or post- (i.e., after the Defense of Marriage Act or DOMA, post-gay rights) assert that these stories of violence are in the past.[25] One of my aims here is to queer such a normative conclusion.

It is also worth noting the racial entanglements entwined with the Brandon Teena story. Not only was there shame tied to Brandon's expression of gender and sexuality, but racial shame is also evident in the story. Lana Tisdel, a woman Brandon had been dating at the time of his murder, sued the producers of *Boys Don't Cry* for the depiction of her in the movie. She balks at the suggestion that she knew Brandon had female genitalia. She also protested that the film depicted her as "white trash."[26] Despite the historical context of this story in a post-Civil Rights America, the waywardness—the backwardness, to borrow Rao's language—of racial identification in the United States, even at the turn of the century, is notable. This idea of whiteness is a relevant though repressed feature of *The Brandon Teena Story* (Muska and Olafsdóttir 1998). It is discernible in Tisdel's resistance to what she purportedly saw as her depiction as white trash.

The documentary released in 1998 (a year before *Boys Don't Cry*) opens with scenes from Lincoln, Nebraska, Brandon Teena's birthplace, and moves to Humboldt, Nebraska, where fearing that he would report their rape of him to the police, Lotter and Nissen co-conspired to kill him. Brandon had in fact reported the rape, but as we have seen, Sheriff Laux was more concerned with genitalia than solving the crime. Along with sex and gender expression, whiteness passes as the standard: heterosexual and white are the invisible norms. The testimony of JoAnn Brandon, the mother of the person born Teena Brandon, and others interviewed, characterize what they call a "white," Midwestern reality. Whiteness here reads as the ordinary, and everyone was "normal" except Teena. Normalcy and whiteness are conjoined in this narrative, inextricably entangled. Within this framework, the writers and other commentators can present the behavior of Lotter and Nissen as egregious, abnormal, or pathological.

Normalcy, as heterosexuality and whiteness, allows a transferral of guilt onto Lotter and Nissen, who in the narrative are the wayward, backward element of society. Recall that as Rao argues, backwardness is the counter to progressive, official narratives of the state. Backwardness is a characteristic that describes individuals and communities who fail to make progress. Communities, moreover, escape the charge of backwardness when they charge individuals with any resistance to their norms. Communities at large, whether the local ones or the broader American community, do not bear guilt. Rather, these individuals do.

In the case of Brandon Teena's murder, the ostensibly straight white men—white trash no less—become incarnations of "evil;" something in their nature prevents them from making progress.[27] In pointing to the transferral of responsibility from the community to the individual, I do not mean to absolve Lotter and Nissen of their heinous crimes. They indeed perpetrated acts of hate and—rightly—remained incarcerated as late as 2021 for their brutality, their unspeakable behavior. I do want, however, to problematize the normalcy that sees Lotter and Nissen as somehow aberrant, individuals capable of egregious crimes, rather than embedded members of communities, which themselves act out scripted norms. These communities—white, middle-American—are sites of nostalgia, whether as capable of utopian futures or as longing for a pristineness that never existed. Such purity is in fact the promise of whiteness. Such a place is the Whitestown of *Blues for Mister Charlie*, the Eden, to which the sinner, now "whiter than snow," can return; Baldwin exposes this locale as Plaguestown (see Chapters 2 and 3). The Brandon Teena case, like the Matthew Shepard one to follow, reveals sexuality and gender expression as aspects either of ostensible progress or backwardness.

Society cared for Brandon Teena's murderers no more than it did him. They evidence signs of backwardness in the U.S. Although in their case, race manifests as whiteness rather than as the situation of Black, racial minorities, their existence is part of America's racial reckoning. They manifest the myth of race and act out their own neglect in violent ways. There is ample evidence of my claim of social neglect, wherein white trash is adjacent to Blackness. In 2017, for example, "an expert's evaluation" showed that Lotter, who had been sentenced to death for his 1993 murder, had a functional IQ of 67 "and deficits in adaptive behavior that have been present since childhood" (see Pilger 2021). Further troubling the neat and tidy narrative of normalcy, on the one side, and manifest evil, on the other, in 2007 Nissen recanted the original testimony that put Lotter on death row, claiming to have himself pulled the trigger of the gun that killed Brandon Teena (see Duggan 2007). He, too, was a product of an environment that concealed its deviance under the cover of whiteness. Notwithstanding claims to normativity, hetero- and otherwise, communities remember crimes. Reminders of these seemingly egregious events are everywhere, called to memory even when the culture and history seem to have moved on.

I return to the scene of the crime of Brandon Teena's murder. What motivated Lotter and Nissen's first act of rape was their desire to see who Brandon was, mistaking his genitalia for the truth they were seeking. Rather than the truth of otherness, however, what these men see is a reflection of themselves, much like the reality that the exposed body of Emmett Till reveals to the (progressive) citizens of the U.S. In the face of their heinous crime, their community turns the gaze back on them, claiming a normative whiteness that shuns their actions. Queering the story of these men's individual deviance revisits the scene of the crime but not to interrogate Brandon Teena any longer. He should have been accepted for what he said he was. Rather, the scrutiny turns toward the interwoven identities within broader cultural fabric, the myths of who and what we say we are. To queer the story of Brandon Teena, moreover, is to recall the silent presence at the scene of the crime of another victim, Phillip LeVine, who happened to be a Black man. Nissen and Lotter killed him too, on that fatal night. LeVine had at the time been dating the sister of Lisa Lambert, the third person murdered along with Brandon and LeVine. On that night, Lambert's home became a bloody site, one characteristic of the bloodlines and entanglements across American society. These entanglements are the transecting realities missed in the myth of whiteness. As we will see in *The Laramie Cycle*, this myth can even subsume sexual normativities.

MATTHEW SHEPARD AND *THE LARAMIE CYCLE*

If Emmett Till is the ghostly haunting that occasions *Blues for Mister Charlie*, every scene of which the fictional Richard, Emmett's double, discomfits, Matthew Shepard is the spectral presence across *The Laramie Cycle*. Matt's death figures as sacrificial—the body of Christ—across the culture, just like Emmett's. Each person becomes a mythic icon for a cause: in Emmett's case, that of racial justice; in Matt's, the extension of civil rights to include sex and gender. *The Laramie Cycle* manifests a movement toward gay rights as normative, whether it is the cause or effect of such an arrival. Insofar as *The Laramie Project* collects documentary evidence to distill and retell Matt's story, it does the work of myth (see Preface and Chapter 1). As theater, the *Cycle* does not claim to be history, but the interviews it recreates and real persons it embodies onstage purports to a kind of authenticity. What is more, the retelling is not necessarily re-traumatizing because it presents the story in terms of progress. To do so, however, *The Laramie Cycle* whitens—in the sense of distilling, whitewashing, or purifying—the queerer aspects of Matt's story. It ties together any loose fabric surrounding Matt's death, and it also represents HIV/AIDS, the ubiquitous pandemic that became a public health emergency in the 1990s, as a disease impacting gay white men. In the play, Reggie Fluty, the real-life patrol officer who found Matt fighting for his life, speaks about having to take the medication AZT as a prophylactic because she already had open wounds from carpentry and handled Matt's bloodied bodied with her bare hands. The audience learns early in the play that "Matthew had HIV," potentially infecting Fluty.[28] The HIV/AIDS crisis is conspicuous in *The Laramie Project*, but what is not evident are the entanglements of HIV/AIDS, race, and its representation (which I discuss in Chapter 4). For *The Laramie Project* and its audiences, gayness might have become acceptable, but this expiated miasma could not mix with other contagions, such as those associated with Blackness. Homonormativity had officially become white and male.

Like the narrative of Brandon Teena, Matt's story is set in *small-town* U.S.A., in this case Laramie, Wyoming. Laramie, Wyoming is "our town,"[29] a normal place where such heinous acts do not occur. Early in the documentary account, the character Sergeant Hinds, a representation of the real-life detective with the Laramie Police Department, describes the town as a "good place to live" with "good people, lots of space."[30] In fact, no one in Laramie was gay prior to Matt, it might be imagined. In such a place, the actions of Aaron McKinney and his accomplice, Russell Henderson, who drove the vehicle and was convicted for his crime of October 6, 1998, are aberrant.

The Laramie Project insists on the brutality of the crime, the abnormality—or backwardness—of its perpetrators, and the extreme nature of the violence that places the murder outside of human norms, relegated to the realm of evil. In the play, Dr. Cantway, the emergency room doctor who first saw Matt, describes the sight of the boy's beaten body:

> Ah, you expect it, you expect this kind of injuries to come from a car going down a hill at eighty miles an hour. You expect to see gross injuries from something like that—this horrendous, terrible thing. Ah, but you don't expect to see that from someone doing this to another person.
>
> (Kaufman et al. 2014: 34)

The pauses, the repeated "ah," conveys unfathomable horror of someone (though used to seeing hurt people) rendered speechless. That is, these acts were outside the norms even for a trauma doctor: "You don't expect to see that from someone doing this to another person." There is no question that the crime was egregious, but I want to call attention to the play's deftness in placing the perpetrators outside of the norm, as the villains of a mythic narrative, even counter-epiphanies to the martyr.

Since "hatred is not a Laramie value,"[31] the actions of the perpetrators are abnormal. The murder upends Laramie, and by extension the norms across the U.S. In considering the brutal beating that put Matt in critical condition, Dr. Cantway says that the thought of something like this happening in Laramie "offends us" (35). Such a heinous anti-gay crime as the murder of Matt would offend theater audiences across the U.S. The writers craft the drama to create appropriate degrees of fear, pity, and grief for the victim. The gay white male becomes an appropriate site for human affection. Whereas Emmett Till's open casket was to disturb American viewers and incite them to action, *The Laramie*

Project reconfigures Matt's body through narrative, making mythic memory of the historical event.

My reading of *The Laramie Project* in terms of a kind of regression into a false myth of whiteness is not to deny the play's gestures toward racial inclusion. The play betrays a degree of self-consciousness about the reality it presents, a knowingness regarding its various gestures. For example, the character who disturbs the idea that "Laramie is not this kind of town" is Zubaida Ula, a Muslim woman living in town:

> If it wasn't this kind of a town why did this happen here? I mean you know what I mean, like—that's a lie. Because it happened here. So how could it not be a town where this kind of thing happens? Like, that's just totally—like, looking at an Escher painting and getting all confused, like, it's just totally like circular logic like how can you even say that?
>
> (Kaufman et al. 2014: 57)

Zubaida's reference to M. C. Escher is one instance of a gesture that connects to a certain kind of listener, one who may know the 1953 lithograph *Relativity*, with its slanted staircases and distorted perspective. In her insistence that "we have to mourn this," Zubaida Ula helps to assimilate the community's denial, toward an acceptance of the reality of hate against certain communities as somewhat normal but unacceptable. The murder of a gay man did "happen here," and therefore it *can*. In light of the events of September 11, 2000, which would occur after *The Laramie Project*'s first run at New York's Union Square Theater from May 18 to September 2, 2000, Zubaida Ula's words are eerie.

The writers of *The Laramie Project* do not knowingly present whiteness as normative. Its grounding and significance, however, come from its identification with certain kinds of people within society.[32] As we have seen, from the narrative perspective that the play presents, Laramie is transformed from its particularity to "our town," an American anyplace, itself, nowhere and everywhere at the same time.[33] This identification makes possible catharsis, the recognition of emotions as simultaneously in the characters onstage and in the audience. This recognition is to bring about identification and healing. And yet nonwhites are by and large outside of the human norms that the play represents. The entanglements between Matthew Shepard's death and Emmett Till's 44 years earlier would be missed, even though both were called lynchings (and even though that identification would be made years in the future). The *Project*'s mythmaking becomes most evident in the second play, *Ten Years Later*, where I see a rejoinder to the revisionist story that emerged by the end of the 2000s.

In later accounts of Matt's story, the killing might not have been a hate crime but rather a drug deal gone bad. Within a historical or forensic context, Matt's murder could have been both an anti-gay crime and a drug deal gone bad. Myth, however, resists this kind of complexity, if it is to be a grounding narrative for a group, like gay white men, their families, and their supporters. *The Laramie Project* meticulously constructs Matt in sacrificial terms, and sacrifices require from its objects of transferral a certain degree of innocence. In *The Laramie Project*, Matt was an out, gay man in the 1990s, in a city that "doesn't have a gay bar ... and for that matter neither does Wyoming" (Kaufman et al. 2014: 17), although a local limousine driver Doc O'Connor asserts that "there's more gay people in Wyoming than meets the eye" (19). Doc "know[s] a lot of gay people in Wyoming" and does not think that "Wyoming people give a damn one way or another if you're gay or straight" (19). As such, the fact that Matt was well-liked aligns with the representation of the town. Matt is a "blunt little shit" but also has an "incredible beaming smile" (17). He is kind and considerate, tipping the waiter Matt Galloway when others treat him to "dimes and quarters." Shepard joins an LGBTQ group on campus and was "getting ready for Pride Week ... totally stoked" (18). Even before the revisionist process of the 2000s, Rebecca Hilliker, the head of the theater department at the university, expresses concern that "in the trial they were going to try and say that it was a robbery, or it was about drugs" (89). According to a waiter Matt Galloway, however, "money meant nothing to Matt, because he came from a lot of it" (28).

Although the documentary theater process makes space for individual memories over official stories or historical narratives, *The Laramie Project Cycle* advances a persistent point of view, that of the move toward normalcy for gay rights. McKinney gives the motive for his brutal act on Matt as what would later be legislated a hate crime:

> We drove him out past Wal-Mart. We got over there, and he starts grabbing my leg and grabbing my genitals. I was like, "Look, I'm not a fuckin' faggot. If you touch me again you're gonna get it." I don't know what the hell he was trying to do but I beat him up pretty bad. I think I killed him.
>
> (Kaufman et al. 2014: 88)

In McKinney's telling, resorting to violence was a response to Matt's sexual transgression. His defense was "gay panic," or the "Twinkie" legal defense.[34] Popularized during the trial of Dan White for his 1978 murder of Harvey Milk, California's first openly gay elected official, the defense was that a diet of Twinkies, consumed because of his distress over such aberrations as gay lifestyles, led White to have a diminished mental capacity. To some extent, the defense worked at the time, as White was acquitted of first-degree murder on May 21, 1979. Although he was found guilty of manslaughter, he only served five years in prison for two killings. In 2009, one year after Sean Penn won an Academy Award for playing the gay rights activist and politician in the movie *Milk*, Barack Obama awarded Milk a posthumous Presidential Medal of Freedom. Gay rights would seem to have come a long way. As another potential sign of progress, the Twinkie defense had not worked in the case of Matthew Shepard's murderer and his accomplice.

As a mythic figure that grounds a community, Matt's significance should be clearcut. His good character, juxtaposed to McKinney's villainous behavior, sanctifies him for the purpose of progress. Homosexuality is the miasma that McKinney is afraid will spread to him, should he be "touch[ed] again." The fear of contagion, the concern that the performance of gender and sexuality will overtake McKinney, becoming the sex act itself, is the narrative within which Matt performs his role. In this narrative, the villains are two evil killers, McKinney and Henderson, as well as a certain strain of the Christian Church. In *The Laramie Project*, Stephen Mead Johnson, a progressive, Unitarian minister "so far left I'm probably sitting by myself" is enough outside of an orthodox Christian framework to be able to speak to the problem while still being within the Church (22). He puts the case as follows:

> Conservative Christians use the Bible to show the rest of the world, It says here in the Bible. And most Americans believe, and they do, that the Bible is the word of God, and how are you gonna fight that.
>
> (Kaufman et al. 2014: 23)

As a Christian, Johnson can authoritatively reject the idea that "homosexuality is a sin" (83). *The Laramie Project* brings to the American stage the narratives of what it might mean to be gay in Laramie, Wyoming, at the end of the twentieth century, and the positive theatrical reception of the play speaks to the resonance these stories had with broader audiences.

The persistence of the narrative perspective as a grounding myth that brings significance to a community is evident in the Tectonic Theater Project's return to Laramie, Wyoming, in the 2013 staging of *The Laramie Project Cycle* at the Brooklyn Academy of Music, which includes the second play, *Ten Years Later*. The second play opens with the revisionist potential by incorporating actual dialogue from the 2004 American Broadcast Company (ABC) *20/20* story by Elizabeth Vargas, a journalist and 14-year veteran of the show at the time:

> *20/20* NARRATOR: November twenty-sixth, two thousand and four—Good evening and welcome to *20/20*.
>
> The killing of Matthew Shepard was widely perceived as a hate crime, because Matthew was gay, but over the next hour, you will hear a very different account from the killers themselves and from new sources that have come forward for the first time. A *20/20* investigation uncovers stunning new information about one of the country's most infamous murders.
>
> You may think you know what happened next, but you haven't heard the whole story.
>
> (Kaufman et al. 2014: 133)

Mounting a "different account" stemming from "stunning new information," closure is certainly not the posture of the 2004 revision. Rather, even as the broader American culture seems to be moving toward acceptance of the LGBTQ community, another narrative point of view emerges different from the story that you "think you know."

As was the case with my analysis of the Brandon Teena case, by problematizing the treatment of Matthew Shepard onstage I do not mean to diminish the crime or challenge the importance of *The Laramie Cycle*. Rather, I want to show the plays in the process of myth, as a narrative that grounds a group, in this case primarily white Americans coming to terms with gay rights. The story told of Matthew Shepard, as a myth, is of significance to this group. Its mythic importance is clear in the Tectonic Theater Project's rejection of any alternative narrative, or any other memories, which is evident in *Ten Years Later*. From this second play's point of view, it hardly matters whether the killing was a hate crime, or a drug deal gone bad, although it argues the former. The production focuses on the collective impact of the murder, the work of the mythic figure, the epiphany (of Matt as a Christ figure), in the formation of community. Matt was gay, and a man whose sexuality killed him. As Deb Thomsen, an editor with local newspaper the *Laramie Boomerang*, puts it in the second play, "I think everything is a hate crime. You have to have some kind of hatred in you to do that to another person" (123). More important than retrying the case in the court of public opinion is the reification of the cause. By 2014, Matt has become an emblem of the struggle for LGBTQ rights. As his friend Jim Osborne says in the play, "before Matt's murder, nobody talked much about gay and lesbian people or issues in Wyoming" (124). Outside of legislative processes, the community comes to include "the conversations that go on in our locker rooms, in the hallways at schools, on the playgrounds, in our living rooms, and places of worship. That to me is progress" (125). The Tectonic Theater Project retains this triumphalist narrative through the 2013 staging of *The Laramie Project Cycle*.

TRANS*-ING *THE LARAMIE CYCLE*: QUEER AND BLACK ENTANGLEMENTS

By way of conclusion, it is worth returning to the meta- or para-theatrical, therapeutic interventions outside of theater that reveal its relationship to the broader culture. These therapeutic occasions confirm racial reckoning to be the work of myth and memory rather than matters of history or progress. Beyond *The Laramie Cycle*, a further document that inadvertently betrays the trans* entanglements within the culture is Moisés Kaufman's 2019 article, commemorating the fiftieth anniversary of the Stonewall raid, when "gay men and allies took to the streets in an uprising that lasted six days." On June 28, 1969 police raid of the Stonewall Inn, a gay bar in Greenwich Village, New York City. Kaufman describes the uprising as the beginning of "a radical redefinition of the character of the L.G.B.T.Q. person in the popular imagination," one that showed the world "a new image of our community." It is noteworthy that Kaufman's essay has only a single explicit reference to race. In it, Kaufman warns gay communities against the kind of historical regress that others have seen: "Look at the progress made by African Americans during Reconstruction, which was undone during the Jim Crow era." By analogy, the LGBTQ community would do well to learn from the black struggle: "We know wins can be reversed."

Kaufman's analogical reasoning represses the hidden entanglements between black struggles and gay rights, the trans* nature of Civil Rights, the truth that rights cross or transect groups. Stonewall, moreover, is a particularly queer reference, an event that has been "whitewash[ed]," most notably in the 2015 film that Roland Emmerich directed. The uprising, as researcher Sam Stageman argues, was "actually started by trans women of color, not a cisgender white male" (2017). Although Stageman concludes that most protestors at Stonewall were indeed white, the film's creation of a fictitious cisgender white male disentangles from the event the "number of people of color who had a major role in starting the riot."[35] In queer time rather than the historical time of the nation's progress, LGBTQ rights and Black and brown struggles are entangled, not analogical. Collective and individual memory resist historical narratives, the norming of the story, calling into question the nature of progress itself as a narrative device.

Progress assumes chronological time and one-directional travel through it. Memory, however, disrupts time, occurring when it will, out of order, crossing societal, spatial, and personal boundaries. In the context of a purportedly post-racial America of the early twenty-first century, it is noteworthy that President Obama could state in 2004 that "marriage is between a man and a woman" (see Steinmetz 2015). His reversal in 2013 in time for *United States v. Windsor* (the rejection of DOMA) would seem a sign of progress, a flagship for the country to follow. The transgressive reality, however, is that as early as 1996, Obama had already been on the record as saying, "I favor legalizing same-sex marriage," strikingly different from his official, state-sanctioned position (Steinmetz 2015). Twelve years after this early statement, Obama's election to the United States presidency was a transformative enough experience (Coates 2012), even without exposing his more progressive ideas. He would have to think, and speak, like the state.[36] His 2004 statement was the official position at the time, not his own, but memory belies history. Normativity, like any regulated behavior, charts time in historical terms of progress rather than as cyclical recurrences of collective and individual memory. Memories, however, are trans*, i.e., they transgress, crossing over from repressed realities into conscious expression seemingly at their own will.

Returning to *The Laramie Project*, Brantley in his 2000 review of the play's opening at New York's Union Square Theater is himself curiously unable to repress the entanglements between race and sexuality, although he also makes a passing analogy rather than delving into analysis. He discerns the entanglements between *The Laramie Project*'s documentary method and that of Anna Deavere Smith, "especially in her study of racial conflict in Brooklyn, 'Fires in the Mirror'" (see Brantley 2000). Brantley does not, however, move beyond, never trans*-ing or transgressing beyond gender and sexuality. He does not comment on what was truly being documented, namely repressed memories of violence in the United States impacting several interconnected communities.

In addition to his passing notice of the entanglements between race and sexuality, Brantley seems to push against the teleological, martyr narrative that *The Laramie Project* adopts, referring to Matthew Shepard, perhaps somewhat glibly, as "a poster boy for the casualties of anti-gay violence." As he puts it, "the central players in the tragedy of 'Laramie' are essentially presented as what they have come to stand for." The play pushes toward "a 'correct' representation of Laramie," although the characters lack the "authentic" voice that Smith gives her embodiments. Nevertheless,

Brantley concedes that as theater can, the play conveys the idea that "what has happened is beyond humanity," an "unconditional physical reality that cannot be ignored." The language of *The Laramie Project* conjures "the feelings of horrified astonishment that certain acts of brutality can still elicit." In normative time, Matt remains the ideal subject, perfectly relatable. The elements of a deeper analysis along the lines of race and class are present at the surface of Brantley's reading, but he stops at the threshold, unable to transgress.

In queer time, the 2000s were a period of racial regression, so it would have been reasonable for Brantley to note the entanglements not mentioned in *The Laramie Project*. Matthew Shepard's HIV+ status was a bridge. The Center for Disease Control reported that of the 125,800 people diagnosed in 32 states with HIV/AIDS in 2000–2003, non-Hispanic Black people "accounted for more than half (64,532 [51.3%])" of these cases, although this group "constituted 13% of the population of the 32 states during these 4 years."[37] Non-queer audience members watching *The Laramie Project* and hearing about Matt's HIV+ status would likely undergo cognitive dissonance to repress the reality of HIV/AIDS as, at the time, a disease of others—gay men, women and especially non-white people. Assimilating the violence of the crime meant the suppression of other associations, Matt slipping into normalcy. The whiteness of the Matthew Shepard narrative belies more colorful, simultaneous realities, the entanglements between Matt and non-white people, or those between Laramie and the broader American population, even as it pertained to the War on Drugs. While Matt's drug use and associations were overlooked in the official narrative, the War on Drugs led to an over 500 percent increase in the number of incarcerated people in the United States, mostly Black men: "According to the Sentencing Project's website, the rate of incarceration for white Connecticut residents in 2005 was 211 per 100,000 people; for black residents it was 2,532 per 100,000" (Alexander 2020). Black people suffered from all violent crimes at higher rates than all other Americans in just about every category except those like "attempted to take property."[38] During the same period, the New York theater critics might well have had a diversity problem, as so many theater critics and commentators of the time note, but an onlooker might not realize that the theater companies themselves had the same problem, at least judging from the prominent faces leading a few theater companies, like George C. Wolfe at New York's Public Theater. More than superficial skin, this diversity problem had to do with the repression of the experiences of a significant segment of the American population and their stories, their memories, and mythmaking. The 2020 reckoning would unleash these stories, returning the unresolved repressed.

CHAPTER SIX

ANTOINETTE NWANDU'S *PASS OVER* (2017–2021)

Black Moses and the Promised Land

I have proposed that epiphanic encoding happens by virtue of a community embodying myth the way that an individual has memories. As a theoretical framework, epiphanic encoding helps us to understand some of the difficulties involved in the project of racial reconciliation. Race itself is an overarching myth, a story that a community tells about itself that grounds it in memories surrounding objects, events, and people (see Preface and Chapter 1). I have used a chronological approach to highlight the prominence of certain stories at distinct moments across a 56-year span, but the "work on myth" means that these epiphanies are not fixed in place for one time.[1] Mythic phantasies manifest as ghostly recurrences, such that, for example, the figure of the Christ-like, sacrificial victim is as formative for the memory of Matthew Shepard as it was for Emmett Till.[2] The encoding of the epiphany is strongest when there is enough therapeutic intervention for considering new possibilities of seeing and being in the world. In the case of Matthew Shepard, Moisés Kaufman's Tectonic Theater Project provided an important intervention through *The Laramie Cycle* plays, and

Kaufman's meta- or paratheatrical comments reinforce the work of Shepard's story in progress toward gay rights, which became a kind of homonormativity. James Baldwin was part of a similar process for Emmett Till's memory. Across the last half-century, theatrical, therapeutic interventions ranged from Baldwin's own comments on *Blues for Mister Charlie*, found in his introduction to the play; Amiri Baraka's "The Revolutionary Theatre," with its Bacchic call (see Chapter 3); August Wilson's "The Ground on Which I Stand," which demanded new phantasies outside of the Western canon of myth (Chapter 4); and most recently, the "BIPOC Demands" (Chapter 1).

The metatheatrical, therapeutic interventions discussed throughout *Theater and Crisis* are only some examples that could have also included Suzan-Lori Parks' "New Black Math" (2005), a rejoinder (if explicit she does not say) to Wilson's insistence on what a Black play must be,[3] but each example only reinforces the work on myth, the search for meaning within the community through stories and the phantasies surrounding it. Myth is a powerful source for intervention because of the way that, through it, stories and images encode fantasy projections into memory. Myth transforms lived experience into memory, and memory operates both at the individual and cultural levels. In ancient times, the mnemonic process might include a pilgrimage to a sacred site of spectacle.[4] At the beginning of Plato's *Republic*, for example, Socrates is returning from the port, where he has gone to pay honors to the goddess Bendis, when he encounters Polemarchus, who invites him to his home. Socrates' activity, his pilgrimage to Bendis, is a *theoria*, a sighting of the visual representation of the goddess. Pilgrimage remains a mainstay of religious communities, whether it is the journey to Mecca, the Wailing Wall, or the church service on any given Sunday. For secular communities, *theoria* is more spontaneous and improvised, but a makeshift memorial is no less impactful for the faithful. Three years after the murder of George Floyd, visitors were still leaving flowers at the impromptu shrine across from Cup Foods, where he took his last breath.

If the murder of George Floyd proved an opportunity for community grounding around a significant event, becoming a kind of religious epiphany of *theoria* and its theorization, the "BIPOC Demands" (2020) document was a therapeutic intervention, an opportunity for deeper interpretation and sense-making of the event within a context of preceding phantasies and their narratives. Collective memory presumes the existence of a community. Encoding within the community occurs through ritual remembrance and the incorporation of new epiphanies. Within the United States, for example, Emmett Till might figure later as Trayvon Martin. These men are incorporated into a broader narrative about Black life because of their murders. They might even transcend their immediate group to be of significance to broader populations in the U.S. and beyond. In 2020, the American community readily recognized George Floyd as an instantiation of the abjection of Black people within the country, however short-lived the moment of recognition might have been. Floyd relatively quickly becomes a larger-than-life, mythic figure. Epiphanies from the past haunt the present, folding onto the new encoding, so that the community incorporates Floyd in a pantheon of Black sufferers. Individuals can (and do) resist the memorialization, or question its meaning. Not all members of a community necessarily agree with the meaning made of an event, and backlash to the veneration of George Floyd was discernible.[5] Resistance is a reality of group identity because the community forms the "I" or "we" from the inside out. Groups defend against the outside in the same way that the individual balances oppositional pulls and ambivalent desires about potential outcomes. The work on myth presumes ongoing adaptation.

As a theoretical framework, epiphanic encoding is process-oriented; it describes how a community encounters events and mythologizes them. Myth is at the center of epiphanic encoding because it is one of the ways that a community encounters, accounts for, reckons with, and/or encodes its past. Myths are metaphors that continue to generate meaning centuries—or even millennia—after their initial iteration. Myth transcends the contemporary moment, allowing new epiphanies, which are psychic fantasies, to be encoded meaningfully.

In this final chapter, I explore the potential of hope already theorized within Black communities through the Passover story. Passover is a memory, a myth, defined as a narrative that gives a community grounding in a significant event. Passover is oriented toward the future, and the recurring phantasy manifests again in 2017 through Antoinette Nwandu's *Pass Over* (published in 2019). This is not to say that the decadal turn, the advent of the twenty-first century, was itself any more hopeful than previous times, but the recurrence of the Passover story onstage in 2017 and 2021 is noteworthy. Although the Passover story is the province of Jewish and then Black subalterns as an adaptation of the Christianized myth, it is a narrative that has animated American society for centuries. I will go into some detail about its source and reception later in the chapter because of its significance to Nwandu's play. Given the potentially transformative role that myth can play in society, the Passover story, which is recorded in the Biblical Book of Exodus from the sixth century BCE, is a quintessential narrative of the transport of a community from one reality—with all its pretense of factuality, permanence, or fixity—to a better place, a land "flowing with milk and honey" (Exodus 3:17). The idea of Passover, as a fantasy projection in psychological terms (see Preface), forecasts a future that takes flight from the bleak realities of the present. A figure for diasporic groups within the U.S., in particular, Jewish and African American communities, the Passover story is future-oriented, as interested in the movement *whither* the people are going as *whence* they come.

Nwandu's *Pass Over* is significant for several reasons. The play premiered at the Steppenwolf Theatre in Chicago, Illinois, in 2017. Spike Lee filmed the drama, and the result is more than a documentation of the theater play.[6] I argue that Lee's movie heightens the stakes of the play by focusing on the subjects most impacted by the violence it features, namely young Black children. *Pass Over* could easily be—and has been—interpreted as didactic theater,[7] a provocation to white theatergoers to consider the structural or systemic reasons why the drama's protagonists find themselves at the periphery of American society. By 2021, however, *Pass Over* had become something else. As I argue, Nwandu's rewriting of the play's ending for Broadway's post-pandemic reopening expands its mythic scope, allowing it to operate not explicitly as moralizing drama, but as an instance of epiphanic encoding for a broad community of theatergoers. Rather than fixating on a material past of problemed interracial interaction, Nwandu's fantasy-filled manifestation of the Passover story generates energy toward a promising future. Through theater, Nwandu offers a different mode of meaning-making from how Martin Luther King, Jr.'s "mountaintop" speech has come to represent a shared future. Like King's Mosaic intervention, which falls within the therapeutic mode discussed throughout this book, Nwandu works through memory, encoding, and the work on myth. In the context of the events of 2020, which include the murder of George Floyd, the pandemic, and the "BIPOC Demands," *Pass Over* was momentous, becoming the flagship post-pandemic play revisited not only on Broadway but also in regional theater.[8] *Pass Over* presents the future not simply in post-racial, temporal terms, where the teleology of history has its end in narrative resolution,[9] but rather through the encoded temporality of memory and myth, which is cyclical (even regressive at times), unending, and constantly at work.

MATERIAL REALITY AND GHOSTS

By the time of its 2017 premiere at Chicago's Steppenwolf Theatre, *Pass Over* had already received some critical acclaim as a new play. It was a contender for the Ruby Prize, which is awarded to female playwrights of color, and made the Kilroys' List of plays by women playwrights.[10] It had an afterlife post-Steppenwolf, including a run at the Kiln Theatre in London, England, which the 2020 pandemic interrupted.[11] In the play, Moses is one of two Black men within the materiality of broader experiences in the United States: the street corner where they pass the time, their meager provisions of daily bread, and their lyrical and creative play on the English language, through which they make meaning of their struggles. Kitch is Moses' counterpart. On the street corner, they encounter two passers-by played by the same actor who doubles, first, as a lost traveler, himself drawn from the mythic tropes of Edenic promise,[12] or the American dream, and then as a police officer. In 2017, Nwandu presents the police officer in didactic terms as the embodiment of evil. The officer as Ossifer (Lucifer) is a role that she revises in the 2021 production.[13]

Critics have compared Nwandu's play to Samuel Beckett's *Waiting for Godot*, given its characters, setting, and structure. As with *Godot*, very little happens in *Pass Over*. Moses and Kitch banter throughout the drama, their exchange interrupted only when the white men arrive and depart. The first white passerby is dressed in a "light-colored suit and a baseball cap," according to the stage directions. Although he evokes the Old South, particularly with his name, Mister, which later morphs into Master, "he cannot speak with a Southern accent." That is, his character should not allow a disaffecting localization. He is broadly American. His attire, song, and red-and-white checkered tablecloth, which he pulls from a basket of food he is bringing to his mother's house, are evocative of fantasy and fairy tale.[14] These items ground Mister in a local, American materiality. His gestures and language are extremely formal, evident in the greeting, "why salutations and good evening to you, fellas!" These narratological features call to mind the structure of mythic storytelling. The material symbols are of a kind of American innocence: at once emasculate, cautious of Moses and Kitch, and yet unmasked in time as the main perpetrator of violence, Mister as "Master," the officer as Lucifer.[15]

Although *Pass Over* is not a work of realism, it is grounded in the materiality of race, class, and masculinity in the United States. The historical passing over of Black life is well-documented in history and has been one of the underlying crises named in this book's title. As early as the beginnings of the United States, the Founding Fathers considered what to do with the multiplying but unassimilable mass of Black enslaved people. The word *mass* is appropriate because of the relationship of masses of people to the realization of a material burden, a mass to be discarded, or a cancerous tumor on the nation. Thomas Jefferson might well have repudiated slavery, but there was the problem of mass accumulation (the leftover presence of formerly enslaved people and their descendants, eventually). For Jefferson, Black people were in every way inferior beings, by nature something distinct from whites. The intermingling of the races through miscegenation was not an option he desired, whatever his personal predilections.[16] Thus, the end of slavery was both inevitable and problematic, and Black people would haunt America. Jefferson put the case as follows:

> It will probably be asked, Why not retain and incorporate the blacks into the state, and thus save the expence [*sic*] of supplying, by importation of white settlers, the vacancies they will leave? Deep rooted prejudices entertained by the whites; ten thousand recollections, by the blacks, of the injuries they have sustained; new provocations; the real distinctions which nature has made; and many other circumstances, will divide us into parties, and produce convulsions which will probably never end but in the extermination of the one or the other race.[17]

The future of racial reckoning that Jefferson imagines is not hopeful. He foresees resentments on both sides: the "deep rooted prejudice" of whites, and the "recollections" of Black people. Even as the "Great Emancipator," Lincoln saw no future for Black people within the nation, speculating that some offshoring of their bodies (to Africa, or perhaps to the Caribbean) might be a solution to their mass presence in the United States.[18]

The twentieth century saw the mass movement of Black people from enslavement in the South to urban centers across the industrial northeast, the wayward lives who sometimes traveled en masse, as Saidiya Hartman recounts, with "dogs, goats, and chickens" (Hartman 2019: 47). Akin to these animals, Black people at times faced the prospect of mass sterilization. The Tuskegee experiment is a preface to the fantasy among Black people that HIV/AIDS might be an effort at genocide.[19] By 2020, this fear helps to understand the initial reluctance within some communities to accept the COVID-19 vaccine. To be a mass is to be a burden. Jefferson and Lincoln are representative of the American commentators who saw no immediate solution to the presence of Black people, who in turn develop a paranoia about their imperiled situation. Hartman captures the mood well. Like the passed over persons of "fast women, petty thieves, itinerant preachers, hawkers and elevator boys, cooks and domestics, painters, writers, socialists, and black nationalists" that lined Harlem's Lenox Avenue in the early twentieth century (Hartman 2019: 300), Moses and Kitch of *Pass Over* are incidental Black city dwellers, part of an indistinct chorus, a mass choir singing cacophonous notes to an American society wanting to shut its ears.

Whatever the imagined distance between nineteenth-century repatriation schemes and the twenty-first-century American city, the materiality of life in the U.S. is a result of accretion and accrual. Spike Lee's 2018 film of *Pass Over* conveys this materiality.[20] Lee's cinematography strengthens the visual and emotional ties between the fictive world of the play and the lived experiences of the teenagers who attended the Steppenwolf production in 2017. The film emphasizes the consequences of the past though the camera's gaze upon the substance of Black life in the U.S., in this case Chicago.

Rather than human refuse, Lee's subject is ennobled. Lee's film opens with images of these teenagers boarding their buses to the theater. Their Black and Brown faces appear as portrait shots over Howard Drossin's bluesy musical composition. Images of their locked hair, tattoos, and AirPods accompany camera shots of alcohol bottles, concrete walls crowned with barbed wire, and hub caps and discarded tires. This is the material reality, the scene against which the young people's heroic action will take place, as they fight against the hand of fate they were dealt. Put otherwise, Lee's film mythologizes lived experience, i.e., gives it grounding and significance, just as lived experience is staged in plays like *Pass Over*. The set design of the play reproduces the detritus of Chicago's streets on the stage (see Figure 4). As the play begins, Lee's film splices the intersection of Martin Luther King Drive and East 64th Street on Chicago's Southside with the play's first scene, set on the same corner.[21] As gunshots resound onstage, Lee cuts to the startled faces

Figure 4: Jon Michael Hill and Julian Parker in Steppenwolf Theatre's 2017 production of Antoinette Nwandu's *Pass Over*. Photograph by Michael Brosilow.

of the teenagers in the audience, who like Moses and Kitch, experience the threat of violence daily (and yet are understandably still alarmed at the sound of gunshots). Rather than the passed over, the children in the audience are to Lee the elect. By extension, Kitch and Moses (like his Biblical counterpart) are the Chosen. Like Nwandu, Lee becomes mythmaker (or Creator), not only naming these personages, but also setting the stage on which they act.

Notwithstanding the materiality to which the film draws attention, *Pass Over* is not a drama in the mode of realism. It is based in the substance of Black experiences in the U.S. but renders these realities symbolic, through its appeal to myth. By naming the character who succumbs to violence Moses, Nwandu encodes reality in a way that renders the personality as an epiphany. Moses signals the deeper significance of his name early in the play when he and Kitch run through their "promised land top ten," a wish list of fantasies that includes everything from Ferraris and collard greens to world peace and a luxury hotel, where they order room service (caviar, of course). Although "plans to get my black ass off this block" do not materialize, the promised land stands in for the more hopeful future that would heal Moses and Kitch's current conditions. Freezing time in an eternal present of expectation, *Pass Over* raises the issue of temporality through a corporeality that overdetermines the characters' potential actions.[22] The promised land is a fantasy set against these realities. It is as if the future, like the past, can haunt, when it tantalizes with an expectation that will never be met. This haunting is distinct from the immanence of the ghost dance discussed in Chapter 3, where the potential future is at hand and observable in the fates of others who are like you. Black Americans in the 1960s could look to the emancipation of African countries from their colonial powers and see themselves akin to these movements. Such hope languishes, however, when it is met with repeated disappointment, an infinite regress that disrupts received temporality, creating something like a future-past, past-future, past-future-present.

Pass Over achieves its disruption of time through mythical recurrence, which scales events for a longue durée, Moses as simultaneously a figure from the ancient past of Biblical narrative, and a Black American in the twenty-first century marking the quotidian, slow passage of a day. For these Black protagonists in the present, the past and future can be equally haunt. Moses and Kitch are trapped in a time warp, each day passing by as they slowly pass the time. The material weight of the past haunts their existence, the violence to which they will inevitably succumb, even as their existence haunts the stage. To consider these characters as ghosts would be to raise the question of the "something to be done," the ethical problem that America has produced in its realities (see Chapter 1). Moses and Kitch figure for millions of others like them, the real-life young men and women Lee represents in his film, the theatergoers who make their pilgrimage to see the *theoria*.

As a place where ghosts move freely, theater has been a site for the exhuming of historical realities. Like the memories that a person struggles to cast aside, the past makes its appearance when one might least expect it, in this case onstage. By presenting Moses and Kitch as ghostly embodiments, projections of racial myth and memory, *Pass Over* has a great deal in common with Branden Jacob-Jenkins' *Appropriate* (2019). In that play, an Arkansas family, the Lafayettes, gather at the home in which they grew up in the wake of their father's death. They uncover photographs and relics from the past that reveal the patriarch's relationship to slavery. The characters wrestle with this haunting. This twenty-first-century, white American family, seemingly removed from racial concerns, cannot rid themselves of the material and psychological remnants of the past. Moses and Kitch are likewise exorcising the past in their relationship to the white passers-by.

There are several linguistic signs of indelible ties of the present condition to an American past. Stage directions reveal that Mister is "earnest. wholesome. terrified but also a plantation owner." In something of a Freudian slip, Mister corrects Moses' initial greeting of "yo mister yo—" with "master." Mister, or "master" as he wants to be called, haunts and is haunted by the past. As "Master," his name evokes this past: "it's just a name | a family name | so | you know | pass it down | and pass it down ... | it's just a name | it doesn't mean a thing." Kitch's overture that Moses should "know his place" is met with the idea that this is a "plantation" mentality. With his "pass[ed] down" (as opposed to passed over) name and authority (or mastery), Mister reinforces the idea that the city street they are on is a plantation three additional times. Nwandu's play on language belies Mister's notion that the name is meaningless. Heritage is passed down, while the refused mass is passed over. As it pertains to language, the passed over are forgotten, and yet Passover is a ritual of remembrance. Like *Appropriate*, *Pass Over* raises the Faulknerian question of whether the past is really the past. In this case, the drama enacts the relational implications of haunting. How are Moses and Kitch supposed to relate to the asymmetrical relationship between themselves and the white passers-by, one of whom is the haunt of a plantation owner, the other a police officer, a warden of the state? Can there be a future where the antagonistic relationship between and among races in the U.S. no longer figures? As we have seen, Jefferson wrote that the breach between the races in the U.S. was so profound that the conflict would have to end in the obliteration of one or the other.

Nwandu signals that in *Pass Over* the dilemma of interracial conflict will be expressed through language, which generates meaning, even playful banter. Linguistic play is a temporal loop, a way that the drama conveys its time warp. Language is power, but it is also the signification of the powerless. For example, I count 20 uses of the word "nigga" in Moses and Kitch's staccato banter, sometimes as an anti-heroic epithet accompanying their names. They emphasize their meager power to deploy this word in their insistence that Mister/Ossifer not use it.

For its parallel time warp and its similar questioning of purportedly asymmetrical power relations, in this case romantic ones that are ostensibly equal, Jeremy O. Harris' 2018 drama *Slave Play* merits some attention here (2020). The play presents different scenarios of Black and white people in enslaved and master relationships. In the first of these, a slave master sexually exploits his Black female slave. Another enacts a bedroom scene between a white female slaveholder and a Black male slave. Harris even broaches the probability of same-sex erotic relationships in the antebellum South. A Black male slave and a white male worker tryst in between their labors. As the play unfolds, the audience learns that these personae are not in fact from the antebellum American South. Rather, they are contemporary, twenty-first-century couples in a peculiar form of relationship therapy, in which biracial pairs enact these dynamics between masters and their enslaved people to peel back layers of psychic trauma. Harris suggests that even in private romantic relationships, the past haunts, and phantasies of group signification ground these interactions as well. That is, myth imposes itself on time and power, such that each interpenetrates the other. There is no person or personality outside of the truth of myth. By this analysis, if whiteness is an operative myth, a Black lover will ever embody the fantasy of the enslaved. Harris' play presses audiences to raise this mythic idea or unconscious phantasy to the level of consciousness.

The reception of *Slave Play* speaks to the potentially unresolved (dis)affection that Jefferson anticipated would be inevitable. If there were any doubt about the affective power of race, a video recording has captured in real time the potentiality of *Slave Play* and other contemporary dramas to unearth deep-seeded emotions. During one post-performance discussion, a white woman suggested that *Slave Play* was "racist against white people" (Knowles 2019). In the video, the woman's anger is palpable. On the other side, some petitioners against the play saw it as anti-Black. Language is power; it can haunt. Language can evoke the past in disturbing ways.

Like *Slave Play*, *Pass Over* presents the eternal return of racial discourse, which has a certain stability within the pervasive narrative of American exceptionalism. As we saw in Chapter 4, Ronald Reagan popularized the myth of the Welfare Queen. He also emblematized exceptionalism, the idea of the U.S. as the "shining city on a hill."[23] In *Pass Over*, Mister/Master embodies the Reaganesque fantasy, the language of "morning in America." In fact, the character sings the lyrics of Rodgers and Hammerstein's "Oh, What a Beautiful Mornin'." Mister's utterance that "this country is ours again" repeats a hearkening to a pristine past. The rhetoric of "mak[ing] America great again" would certainly have influenced Nwandu's 2017 version of the play. Through the relationship between Mister and the passed-over, Black protagonists, Nwandu draws attention to the distance between America's hopeful promise and the reality for many people. Through a process of memory and reflection, audience members could well also recognize this distance when they encounter Moses and Kitch, in the same way that the specter of Matthew Shepard connected groups concerned about gay rights (see Chapter 5). This is not theater as didactic but rather as a memory machine (see Introduction).

As has been suggested, where Nwandu (and Harris through *Slave Play*) represents the neuroses and psychoses of interracial relationships, whether civic or romantic, some audience members have perceived preachiness, victim-blaming, or reverse racism in their writing. This is evident in the reception to Nwandu's resolution of the 2017 play, just as it was with *Slave Play*. In *Pass Over*, after Mister/Master comes and goes, leaving some item of food for the hungry Moses and Kitch, the actor returns as Ossifer (Lucifer/Police Officer), the second passer-by, "white, male, late twenties/early thirties. an enforcer of the law." Master and Ossifer personify veiled and explicit forms of violence, the threat of which always hovers in the background for the Black characters. Representing this threat as a haunt of a plantation owner and then a police officer who acts with hostility toward the Black men did not sit well with Chicago theater critic Heidi Weiss, who condemned

Nwandu's treatment of state-sanctioned violence against Black people. Weiss' words are worth requoting here:

> To be sure, no one can argue with the fact that this city [Chicago] (and many others throughout the country) has a problem with the use of deadly police force against African-Americans. But, for all the many and varied causes we know so well, much of the lion's share of the violence is perpetrated within the community itself. Nwandu's simplistic, wholly generic characterization of a racist white cop (clearly meant to indict all white cops) is wrong-headed and self-defeating. Just look at news reports about recent shootings (on the lakefront, on the new River Walk, in Woodlawn) and you will see the look of relief when the police arrive on the scene. (Weiss 2017)

More than the response of a single critic, Weiss was reflecting one of the many kinds of responses to the "problem" that she readily acknowledges. Nwandu's approach is "wrong-headed and self-defeating" because the evidence of violence is in Black communities. By citing "the lakefront, the new River Walk, in Woodlawn," Weiss points to white- or white-adjacent neighborhoods, where "the look of relief" is visible "when the police arrive on the scene." Even before the backlash against Abolish the Police and the surge in crime during 2021, Weiss' response is suggestive of the potential localization of violence as a Black problem, to be dealt within this subgroup.

From the perspective of Weiss' critics, she was demonstrating the very collective psychosis that Nwandu was trying to address. In her reflections on the 2017 play (considering the 2021 revival), Nwandu called the drama "chemotherapy for the white community," a phrase that recalls Baldwin's Plaguestown as well as the context of global pandemic in the aftermath of 2020 (see Tillet 2021). Nwandu reports that she "'was writing to white people specifically' to wake them up to the increasing regularity and tragic reality of white police officers and everyday citizens killing African American men and women." As we have seen, however, the process of theater is more like psychotherapy than chemotherapy. As with the former, the challenge is not to poison the patient but to guide an analysand toward the self-recognition of a crisis. In the latter analogy, the audience inevitably reacts angrily as opposed to coming to accept an unexpected epiphany.

The theatrical approach that Nwandu likens to chemotherapy deserves one additional parallel. Jackie Sibblies Drury's 2018 Pulitzer Prize-winning, three-act play, *Fairview* (published in 2019), which begins with the setting and tropes of a Black situation comedy not unlike *The Cosby Show* (centering a Black family, in this case the Frasiers), takes an unexpected turn, shining its proverbial light onto the audience (Drury 2019).[24] The play shifts in the second act, where White characters are watching the action of the first act (*reenacted*) once again. This time, they replay and critique the actions of the Black characters. One white character, Suze, expresses a phantasy of becoming Black. In the third act, the Suze character directly intrudes on the action of the Black characters. *Fairview* ends in what can best be described as an altar call, in which white people in the audience are physically separated from others, made to come forward, get onstage, and become spectacles for the viewership of those left in the audience. In this way, the objectification shifts, as does the power dynamic, the gaze now given to the subaltern, the minority (in the case of the performance I attended at Woolly Mammoth Theatre in Washington, D.C.) of viewers left in the audience. The approach of *Fairview* can be likened to corporate diversity training, against which a palpable cultural backlash exists.[25] In this kind of training, white people are asked to recognize differing degrees of privilege (the proverbial knapsack of privileges that people carry unknowingly) (see McIntosh 1989). For Nwandu, the approach shifts in the 2021 Broadway production of *Pass Over*, when she says that the promised land is "any place where Black life can flourish" (Tillet

2021). In rewriting the play's ending, Nwandu amplifies the mythic dimension of her play, providing a narrative of significance that grounds the intended audience. Given the critical reaction to the 2021 play, the group that the narrative of *Pass Over* impacts goes well beyond Black people.

THE METAPHOR: THE ANCIENT STORY OF THE HEBREWS IN EGYPT

As might be imagined in a play that draws from the Passover story and has a central character named Moses, the promised land is *Pass Over*'s culminating trope. In her comments in 2021, Nwandu extends this metaphor into unexpected corners of the U.S.: "I need Flint to be a promised land. I need Katrina to be a promised land" (Tillet 2021). Nwandu draws from two of the most notorious instances of the passed over thus far in the twenty-first century (if not in American history). In each case, masses of Black people, the huddled masses in Southern cities and in the North, would seem to be the cancerous mass to be treated with poison. Municipal infrastructures failed Black people. While Nwandu's vision of the promised land might seem consonant with the rhetoric of post-racialism, the post-racial narrative failed to encode conflict and struggle. As she does through her characters, Nwandu's rhetoric enfolds the trauma of these experiences, effecting something like the emotions of King's mountaintop speech, which was also Mosaic. The mountaintop analogy was epiphanic, but King was attuned to its various registers, including the prophetic, moral, and political. As pastor over his proverbial flock, King realizes the therapy that symbolic language could provide. King's mountaintop speech was theater. In the hands of the politician, however, a trope like Katrina as a promised land could easily fall flat. By shifting from the poison to the phantasy, from chemotherapy to the talking cure, Nwandu's 2021 rewriting heightens the metaphors that figure for cultural exchange in the United States.

As early as the 2017 staging of the play at Chicago's Steppenwolf, Nwandu's figurative language made *Pass Over* memorable. Metaphor moves the language of mundane materiality to the sublime and dreamlike stage where therapeutic intervention can occur through encoding rather than by intellectual processing. Operating like memory, the encoding enters a nonlinear sphere where past and present blur. As we have already seen, many features move the play from realism to surrealism: the "promised land top ten," the name Moses, "git[ting] up off of dis block," and ongoing allusions to the Biblical story of Moses conducting the Hebrew people into Canaan, the land "flowing with milk and honey."

It will be worth recalling how aligned to Black experience the themes of the Biblical narrative that make their way into *Pass Over* have become. In the Biblical Book of Exodus, the Egyptians hold the Israelites in slavery. The Egyptian ruler, the Pharaoh, feels that the Hebrew people "had become far too numerous for us" and conspires to "deal shrewdly with them" (Exodus 1:9, 10). The Pharaoh fears insurrection: "If war breaks out, [they] will join our enemies, fight against us and leave the country" (1:10). Despite enslavement, however, the Hebrew people continue to multiply. The Pharaoh orders midwives to kill the male children born to Hebrew women. When this plot fails owing to the women's noncompliance, Pharaoh pronounces that the boys must be thrown into the Nile River. Moses is one such child, born to a Levite woman: "When she saw that he was a fine child, she hid him for three months. But when she could hide him no longer, she got a papyrus basket for him and coated it with tar and pitch. Then she placed the child in it and put it among the reeds along the banks of the Nile" (Exodus 2:2–3). Finding the well-preserved boy, the Pharaoh's daughter takes pity on him, naming him Moses, meaning "I drew him out of the water" (2:10).

Like the Biblical Joseph, Moses is culturally subaltern; he is Hebrew but raised at the center of Egyptian power. Both men experience the social death of slavery but continue to retain some aspects of Hebrew identity despite their condition. Evidence of Moses' commitment to Hebrew people despite his service to the Pharaoh is clear. For example, despite having grown up in the Pharaoh's court, as an adult Moses murders an Egyptian man whom he sees beating enslaved Hebrew people. Through this commitment, Moses is poised to be a leader of the Hebrews, and the Passover story of liberation looks to future time. Having established Moses' ability to toggle between Egyptian society and his Hebrew identity, the narrative shows several signs of cosmic sympathy, including plague, a swarm of flies, swarms of locusts, and water turning into blood. God gives the death of firstborn Egyptian children as the culminating sign of the Hebrew community's eventual transcendence, despite their ongoing oppression.

Instructions are given for a ritual event that will result in the sparing of Hebrew children. Sacrificing a lamb, each Hebrew family is to mark its door with the animal's blood, and God will pass over those homes when devastation is meted out on the Egyptians:

> On that same night I will pass through Egypt and strike down every firstborn of both people and animals, and I will bring judgment on all the gods of Egypt. I am the Lord. The blood will be a sign for you on the houses where you are, and when I see the blood, I will pass over you. No destructive plague will touch you when I strike Egypt.
>
> (Exodus 12:12–13)

There are several salient features of the story. First, it is important that the passing over of the Hebrew houses distinguishes a community from its exterior and from the devastation that will come to others, in this case the Egyptian oppressors. Secondly, there is a meaning-making process whereby this community interprets signs and wonders—the epiphanies—as favorable for their future. Thirdly, the permanence of the mythological narrative is remarkable, despite change over time. The Hebrews pass over, out of captivity in Egypt and into a promised land, but Passover becomes a ritual performed (annually, optimally) thousands of years after the foundational event. Through ancient opposition, pogroms, and the Holocaust, the Jewish people preserve the story of Passover during an annual spring ritual celebrating the passing over of their children, and their passing out of subjugated status in Egypt.

"SOMETHING TO BE DONE:" THE ETHICS OF THEATRICAL GHOSTS

The stability of the Biblical story of Moses and the Hebrew people speaks to the strength of the group it grounds and because of this, to the deep encoding that myth offers. What is more, as myth, the narrative is incomplete, requiring an ongoing imaginative process on the part of people who give the story its significance. That is: without *theoria*, there is no ritual revisitation of the epiphany, no identity. The Biblical narrative hearkens to a past, a time when the Hebrew people were in captivity to the Egyptians. The ritual return through the annual Passover holiday preserves the integrity of a people by looking back from the present, hopefully a time of stability and prosperity. But the myth also futures the past. Its work is to communicate to new observers that they will also enter the promised land, whatever that may mean to them.

It is a mundane yet remarkable reality that the saga of Hebrew enslavement became so identifiable with the hopes of Black people within the United States. In this case, the narrative looks to a future, a potential repetition of the Biblical narrative, this time on behalf of Black people. In this case, Moses is the epiphany, a ghost that haunts the present seeking a future release, a something-to-be-done. As early as Phillis Wheatley's poetry of the 1770s, widely considered the first African American literature in the country (Barnard 2018), Moses figures in the enslavement of Black people in the United States. In a 1773 elegy for her addressee's father, who had passed away, the enslaved Wheatley seems to propose that

God "descended ... to bear our Crimes."[26] In this descent, Moses is a type of Christ. Some of the later practitioners who take up the story of Moses are Christians who, like Wheatley, see in him the future savior. The signs of divine support of the oppressed are "Like MOSES' Serpent in the Desert wild," a reference to the prophet's scepter turning into a serpent, a sign to the Hebrew people that he is a legitimate, God-sent leader. For Wheatley, her addressees fall within a new dispensation of God's favor because they are part of the Christian Church, which incorporates the Moses story as a prefiguration of the redemption to come: "To you his Offspring, and his Church, be given, | A triple Portion of his Thirst for Heaven." In her use of "our," even as an enslaved, Wheatley sees God's promise in the future, whether as freedom from slavery, or liberation in the afterlife.

Unlike the Oedipus trope, where rejected youth who are Black can never come into maturity within the community (and even an adult Oedipus of *Gospel* is an object of pity), the figure of Moses survives and predicts the flourishing of a people, beyond captivity (see Chapter 4). The Black adaptation of Biblical stories to a modern plight that Wheatley inscribes is the spiritual song of the enslaved, like "Go Down, Moses:" "Go down Moses, way down, in Egypt's land. | Tell old Pharaoh: Let my people go." The use of the trope is ubiquitous, as we see in King's mountaintop speech, but what I am offering is its mobility. Nwandu's desire for Katrina and Flint to be the promised land speaks to the story's work over a longue durée, its insinuation into new contexts. This work leaves the impression of an immutability, but the myth is changing over time and thus always doing new work.

Building upon the story's encoding, Nwandu riffs on the language of "pass[ing] over" to come to terms with the murder of Trayvon Martin in 2012 as a new epiphany, a spectacular event that haunts the culture, demanding a reckoning. Martin's senseless murder is a provocation for *Pass Over*, much like the lynching of Emmett Till was for James Baldwin's *Blues for Mister Charlie*.

Trayvon becomes Moses, not the Oedipal passed over. Instead of ignoring George Zimmerman's casual disregard for Black life discernible across the culture (e.g., Katrina, Flint), Nwandu's therapeutic intervention calls American society into witness, i.e., to recognize the horror of the event. After Trayvon Martin's murder, these interventions returned in earnest with Black Lives Matter, which Nwandu cites as an important moment in her development of the play (Tillet 2021). *Pass Over* is consistent with the theatrical interventions of the period recounted above. As theater does, the play evokes the ghosts of these Black epiphanies through its central characters.

As we have begun to anticipate, in the fantasy projection of *Pass Over*, Mister/Master and Ossifer figure for the (Egyptian) oppressor, the Biblical Pharaoh who kills Hebrew offspring. The built-in antagonism of the narrative maps onto expectations about the broader relationship between Black and white people in the United States. We have already seen the response of one critic, Weiss, who rejected the 2017 play's resolution, although in the play it is not Ossifer, the white police officer, but Master who kills Moses. Nevertheless, there is a fantasy sequence in the 2017 script in which Ossifer fully manifests as a devil, red scenic lighting emphasizing the revelation of his true character. In a social context where confrontation between white figures of authority, namely police officer, and protestors, often Black, often results in fatal violence, the fantasy of ridiculing or killing the police is not unusual.[27] From Weiss' point of view, this is a dangerous fantasy, but it is a frustrated response to the real-life hazard that Black people face. The mythological story of Moses does not resolve as it should, and this again creates a time warp. Moses should not die before his actualization, any more than Oedipus can die when Laius and Jocasta expose him. In its earlier iteration in 2017, *Pass Over* asked its American audience, through Moses' confrontation with Ossifer, to get its "house in order" so that the story resolves as it should.[28] Responding to the dehumanization of being a mass, the structural issues attending to race in the United States, Moses declares to Ossifer that "we are not | the people that 'chu | think we are | not stupid |not lazy | not violent |not thug | We Are Men | Two Black Men." Just as the Biblical Moses demands of Pharaoh to "let my people go," the Moses of *Pass Over* confronts the embodiment of state authority in his exercise of power over the oppressed.

Set against the Biblical backdrop, the deployment of the myth in *Pass Over* loops in an endless cycle of hopelessness. Because the future never arrives, Moses and Kitch are left to their hopes and aspirations, which are not inexhaustible. Hints at their fatigue weigh the play down. When there is no threat of violence, the men contemplate suicide. In one scene, the Black protagonists catalogue all the people they know who have died by violence. Their ongoing refrain of "kill me now" is made real when they gesture toward suicide. On Moses' request, Kitch picks up a stone to bash his head. Although set in the twenty-first century, by alluding to the slave past the characters tie their incidental lives to historical narrative in the United States. That is, their situation is not arbitrary but rather is linked to the materiality of Black life in the U.S. While Moses and Kitch's crisis is comprehendible, more troublesome is the role of passers-by—those who, like Master and Ossifer, see the Black men as external to their experiences. They themselves, however, more than incidental. Nwandu represents them as constituent parts of what makes Moses and Kitch themselves. Master materializes the promised land about which they fantasize, his seemingly bottomless basket of food, wine, and treats flowing with Edenic abundance. In contrast, Ossifer polices desire and suppresses hope. He maintains that the world they want is not one they can have. That is, as much as they may seem exterior to Black life, Master and Ossifer are in relationship with Moses and Kitch and, as such, bear some of the weight of their existence, whether they know or acknowledge it or not. In a less schematized way than *Pass Over*, the other plays I have mentioned from this period, such as *Appropriate*, *Slave Play*, and *Fairview*, represent the material and psychic toll of these interracial relationships.

As human relationships, interactions across people designated as different races evolve. The dynamic in 1964 could never be the same as 2021, however haunting or recurring the figure from the past. Change occurs first in the imagination. Barack Obama might not have ushered in a post-racial period, but he was the first. As such, he impacts the imagination about what is possible. For this reason, the image of the little Black boy touching his hair is poignant, as much as white nationalists who feel they have lost their country. The year 2021 is different from 1955. In the conviction of Derek Chauvin in 2021, the broader American community seems to have affirmed that, whatever George Floyd was doing in Cup Foods on May 25, 2021, the white officer had violated his civil rights when he suffocated the Black man under the pressure of his knee. Chauvin in fact plead guilty to Civil Rights violations. As we know, his was not the only such case that represented a change in outcomes. Although they claimed to have been acting on behalf of the state, George McMichael, William Bryan, and Gregory McMichaal, who directly committed the murder, violated Ahmaud Arbery's civil rights when they killed the jogger on February 23, 2020. The shift to this outcome from the verdict of innocence for George Zimmerman can be mapped onto a linear narrative of progress, an arc from Emmett Till's murder, which garnered a similar verdict of innocence, to the present.

Metaphor is the tool of a shifting imaginary. Nwandu's sense of the interchangeability of Ossifer for Mister/Master echoes a reality. As if pointing to the power of metaphor, the character Moses at one point explains to Kitch that he has deployed a "mega-four" when he refers to a parting of a river, the Red Sea, to which Kitch responds that "you ain't got no river." Moses learns from a mentor referred to as Reverend Missus that, like the Biblical Moses, he could "live up to dat name" and "lead deez boys right off deez streets." The question is not one of material reality, but rather how to confront psychosis. As deployed in the 2017 play, the metaphor of passing over inspires Black life, but it renders white Americans the enemy, the Egyptian oppressor to God's chosen people. Kitch recognizes this when he tells Moses that his friend "spoke yo truth" to the white police officer, "like | like blood | up on dem door posts." As I have mentioned, however, the story does not end as the myth should. Mister reawakens from the dream sequence and shoots Moses. This is the psychosis of American life, where the hopeful story of future promise often does not end as it should for Black youth. Mister's words after the shooting are worth citing here:

> golly gee
> did you guys hear
> a fella was killed today
> black fella
> another black fella was killed
> i should say
> well
> because
> well gosh
> it just keeps—
> (*he makes a gesture for "happening"*) which is sad

By having the killer express ignorance about why Black people are killed at such an alarming rate, Nwandu unveils an ironic truth. Mister's position is Weiss'. His "just keeps" is repeated three times, as he expresses how sad this reality is. If madness is doing the same thing repeatedly and expecting different results, Mister is fully psychotic, but so is the society that produces him and his victim. This psychosis is the sickness that Nwandu (and Baldwin before her) could be said to have misdiagnosed as a cancer when in fact it is a behavioral disease. The 2017 play ends with this scene, as Mister breathes "*a big performative sigh; self-conscious without being ironic.*"

POST-APOCALYPTIC FUTURES

If the 2017 script of *Pass Over* ends in despair and an indictment of the majority culture in its relationship to a Black subaltern, the 2021 adaptation expands upon the mythological metaphor that the drama deploys to offer an epiphanic, therapeutic intervention in dark times. Even in the 2017 play, the fantasy of passing over into a better life at times buoys Moses in his crisis of faith. The fantasy imagines a promised land, a condition like Mister's reality, where abundance flows. Although Moses and Kitch want to pass over into a better future, Moses believes that "in these red, white and blue, that river don't part for niggas like us." In the 2017 production, through figurative language (the river, Moses passing over into a promised land), Nwandu had already created the context for the heightening of metaphor evident in the 2021 staging. As we have seen, throughout the script, Moses and Kitch deploy Biblical language and figures, which they learned from "reverend missus" in church. Set against their lyrical but suicidal "kill me now," their hope, often expressed in the "promised land top ten," allows them to riff on the theme of their most wished-for favorite things. Whereas stage directions set the 2017 play in "a ghetto street ... but also a plantation | but also Egypt, a city built by slaves," the 2021 staging adds "the river's edge ... (and also the new world to come ((worlds without end))." These stage directions affirm the out-of-joint time of the play, where past, present, and future collide. Rather than death at the hands of the white character, in 2021 Kitch ostensibly does act on Moses' "kill me now." After a reiteration of the 2017 scene where Kitch holds a rock over Moses' head, a narrative shift occurs in the 2021 sequence. The setting moves to a surreal dreamscape. For narrative continuity, the audience might imagine that Moses has died, and we are in the afterlife. By this interpretation, the promised land is contiguous with the afterlife of the Christian imagination. Seen otherwise, the setting could be a paradise of the American Dream, where Moses and Kitch experience the same kind of abundance as Mister. After all, Mister walks offstage with them, naked, as if sharing the same fantasy. In either case, there is a break in narrative continuity. Fantasy is necessary to appreciate the Edenic landscape that Nwandu has created.

In the world outside of *Pass Over*'s symbolic and even surreal turn, the American Dream is in no way realized. Nevertheless, what is undeniable is that by 2021, the racial realities rendered epiphanic in *Pass Over* had passed through the crucibles of COVID-19 and the murder of George Floyd. The intervention of the "BIPOC Demands" impacts the play's context and, therefore, the fantasy that it projects. For instance, in interviews, the Black actors in the 2021 production speak about such steps as on-set counseling, to deal with the traumatic experiences that they embody onstage, and chauffeured escorts home, so that they would not have to contend with public transportation after each performance.[29] While this may seem a matter separate from the aesthetic experience of the play, as we saw in Chapter 4 in the discussion of Rousseau's idea of theater, the moral context of drama is not necessarily a separate issue from the experience of watching it, or the conditions of the companies that stage the plays. Audience members are citizens as well, related in the artificial kinship of the nation.[30]

The revised play that Nwandu offers is consistent with what I have called epiphanic encoding. Epiphanic encoding does not didactically instruct. Rather, it represents a process whereby a group can experience a fantasy projection, an epiphany, without being directed how to think about it. The group makes meaning together, in the way that a self seeks its integrity out of disparate, sometimes dissonant experiences. As narratives that ground groups in some significant meaning, all myth operates this way, including stories of the American Dream. The new ending of *Pass Over*, set in the fantastic land of milk and honey, is a dreamlike sequence that requires the viewer's participation in the interpretive work. Nwandu revises the drama in such a way as to amplify its fantasy projections. As epiphanic, the play is ultimately interested in the American project. In the 2017 staging of the play,

Moses tells Ossifer, whom the Biblical plagues torment, to get his house in order, a warning for all intents and purposes issued at the playwright's racial-majority audience members. By developing the Biblical myth more fully in the 2021 Broadway reopening, Nwandu offers the possibility of epiphanic encoding and the audience's re-inscription of the past. Whether as a Biblical redemption in death or a fantasy return to Eden, Nwandu's promised land culminates in the nakedness—real and symbolic—of the men in the play, surrounded by the "milk and honey" of Biblical Canaan. The men's nakedness calls attention to corporeality. The COVID-19 pandemic, with social distancing and public lockdown mandates, isolated people, their bodies potential containers of disease and therefore themselves to be quarantined away from other potential hosts. Given this backdrop, the onstage nakedness is a release, a vision of bodies for their own sake: a prelapsarian corporeality preceding the encoding that social experience requires, before the intrusion of cultural narratives about race.

CONCLUSION

The public health crisis of 2020 prompted the exploration that I have provided throughout *Theater and Crisis* of myth, race, and racial reconciliation. I have presented myth as a grounding factor in group identification and therapeutic intervention. Looking back to 1964, I excavated the underlying causes of contemporary race-based violence and found in James Baldwin's *Blues for Mister Charlie* a similar phantasy to that projected in 2020. Baldwin figures race as itself an issue of public health, the U.S. a country full of Plaguestowns mired in miasma. Baldwin's projections draw from fictional, dramatic works, but they represent reality. In *Blues*, the phantasy is figured as a ghost from the past that haunts the present through the character of Richard, whom a white man kills with the defense of protecting his kin. The ghost is Emmett Till, but he is also figured in the mythic terms of Shakespearean ghosts, like those that haunt Macbeth or, even further back, the visitations that move Orestes in Aeschylus' trilogy. As the theory of myth that I have offered affirms, stories and images ground communities and give people a sense of purpose. This is true of the fiction, but in what we imagine as the real world, race is also implicated. As much as intra-group racial identity can bring belonging and joy, interracial interaction has been a steady source of violence and discontent, as epiphanic visitations from Emmett Till to George Floyd testify.

Since at least Baldwin, writers and politicians alike have figured race in terms of physical health or sickness in the body politic. As Baldwin had it, America is a Plaguestown. In 2020, several officials characterized race as a public health crisis. *Theater and Crisis* argues for a different approach, through myth. I reject the tropes of physical health and sickness, with the language of plague, pandemic, or cancer, which requires poisonous solutions like chemotherapy, an analogy that Antoinette Nwandu used in 2017 in discussing her play, *Pass Over*. Rather, myth, drama, and psychoanalysis provide a better framework for figuring the virulence and stability of race and its long-overdue resolution, talked about publicly in 2020 as a reckoning. Building on this psychological framework, the theoretical tropes of hauntology revealed how and why a specter like that of Emmett Till might remain in the culture for the better part of a century, manifesting again in George Floyd. The haunt is to the culture as memory is to the individual, and vice versa. Storytelling in the form of myth and drama shows how this past, as memories encoded in new ways across time, remains meaningful to groups, but also changes.

My framework shifts the perspective on the significance of the closing of theaters during the early months of 2020 from one of economic and commercial repercussions to questions of what the event revealed in terms of group identity and psychodynamics. I have used psychoanalysis throughout *Theater and Crisis* as a fitting parallel in collective experience to what happens to individuals. As comprised of people who have memories, groups remember, and they do so through stories and images. Groups also change. Group psychodynamic theorists argue that even the slightest shift in the environment, such as the advent of a new member to the community, materially alters the nature of the group.[1] This potential for ongoing change is the final focus of *Theater and Crisis*.

In these concluding reflections, I take the insights gained from the epiphanies of mythic figures in the real world, from Orestes to Dionysus, Oedipus to Moses, as they have served to encode how individuals and groups have experienced Emmett, George Floyd, and others. I explore the resistance to epiphanic encoding evident in the wake of the fateful year of 2020, when a global pandemic distilled group experiences in observable ways. Richard Nelson's Zoom plays during the early months of the pandemic, *What Do We Need to Talk About?* and *And So We Come Forth*, purport to convey the experiences of millions of people in the U.S. responding to these new circumstances (see Soloski 2020). As events developed and protests ensued, before and after the murder of George Floyd, Nelson charts the reactions from his fictional Apple family, who seem to represent a broad swath of the public. Race surfaces indirectly, and as such we can see it as a psychodynamic phenomenon. Characters struggle to understand what is happening to them and in their societies, but they themselves point to stories and their iconic encoding as formative, individually and collectively.

THE MYTH OF UNIVERSAL HUMANITY

COVID-19 was a catalyst that brought about, among other phenomena, the closing of theaters across the U.S., which the March 12, 2020 Broadway shutdown signaled (see Paulson 2020a). On April 30, when playwright Richard Nelson premiered the Zoom pandemic play, *What Do We Need to Talk About?*, featuring the fictional Apple family online in a dramatic work, the performance met immediate critical acclaim, even if writers were unsure how to characterize the experience.[2] Given that the imagined audience for the performance were having their own, daily experiences on Zoom, the search for meaning on each face contained within discrete boxes in the drama would have been directly recognizable. Writing for the *Washington Post* on May 1, 2020, theater critic

Peter Marks called the phenomenon "theater," in quotation marks, describing the experience as follows:

> Quotation marks appear in my preceding paragraph, around the word connoting a performative art that currently is shifting to the Internet—a whole field with a kind of refugee status. Because theater on the Web can never really be "theater."
>
> (Marks 2020)

"Refugee status" is itself a powerful parenthesis, an announcement that in-person, embodied theater would be in a kind of quarantine of its own, rather than being a pastime that had mutated forever. The quotation marks sequester *What Do We Need to Talk About?* to a temporary state, with a definitive or permanent judgment: the genre to which the performance belongs, the phenomenon known as theater, in quotes, was in a state of play known as "theater on the Web." This designation was to be no more permanent than the quarantine people were under, both in real life and in this representation.

It is worth noting that other theater critics concurred with Marks in giving Nelson's theater-on-videoconference this bracketed, "refugee" status. In his review for *The New York Times*, Ben Brantley opens with a bleak emphasis on the crisis, a note that the "world has turned strange and scary." "Theater"—as it was—would be impossible during this time because "making contact with others, even those closest to you" is a "fraught proposition." Brantley muses that "since theater occurs in a shared physical space, 'What Do We Need to Talk About?' doesn't exactly qualify." In such scary times, however, he finds the event to be a necessary salve. Brantley described the play as "infinitely poignant" (Brantley 2020). As Marks puts it, for "first time, for me, that faces in the gallery view on Zoom truly come across as characters, rather than as actors reciting lines." Alexis Soloski opined that Nelson's play "doesn't necessarily point a way forward...but it reflects a shared present." (Soloski 2020).

The fact that *What Do We Need to Talk About?* drew from familiar settings and characters to recreate community in the wake of a quarantine reveals its potentially psychodynamic role. For many, the protagonists in the drama—the Apple family members—were well-known. Nelson is the winner of several theater awards, including an Obie and a Tony.[3] His Apple Family plays were a fixture in American theater since the opening of *That Hopey Changey Thing* on November 2, 2010. Regional repertory theaters were staging the play by the middle of the decade between 2010 and 2020. Even for viewers without a knowledge of the setting and characters, the familiarity of Zoom and the shared experiences of 2020 were part of the appeal of *What Do We Need to Talk About?* A summary and close reading of aspects of the play will serve to demonstrate its appeal. Set within a family, the play reflects a group psychodynamic, and as such we will see how the unrest reveals more about the group and even slightly shifts the group's perspective over time.

In addition to transforming Zoom into a literary and dramatic trope, the play draws from the shared experiences from its very first lines. As the drama opens, the Zoom box of Barbara Apple's face appears first. She looks directly at the camera, the audience. She adjusts her skin and hair, as if putting on a mask. As other faces appear, Barbara tells her sister Jane a joke about a horse walking up to a bar. The bartender asks, "Why the long face?" A throwaway quip, the joke sets the tone of humor and camaraderie, but "long face" also calls attention to what will be the focus for the next hour: faces, masks, or personae. Read literally, COVID-19 is the cause of sadness, the reason for long faces. The characters' experiences are recognizable to anyone who endured the global, novel coronavirus pandemic in 2020, a contemporary miasma. The play's setting is Rhinebeck, New York during COVID-19. Richard works for New York's Governor, Andrew Cuomo, who prior to his tragic fall, gained widespread fame during the pandemic because of his clear, simple, data-driven daily news conferences.[4] It is evident from the banter that many New Yorkers were critics of Governor Cuomo before COVID-19, but they have had a change of heart (Cillizza 2020). Richard says that people are asking, "What have you been complaining about all these years?" More tellingly, the characters bring up issues that will hit home for many viewers.

Tim, an actor who is living with Jane, one of the three Apple sisters on the Zoom call, is sick with all of the symptoms of COVID-19 but has not yet been able to secure a test, a plight easily forgotten with the ubiquity of tests in the years that followed.[5] Though living in the same house as Jane, Tim is on a different screen from her—on a different computer—because he is isolated in a room until his 14-day quarantine window passes. He is an actor but works as a waiter. He tells a story about a restaurant that gives people a free roll of toilet paper with every takeout order. He says of his workplace, "If we only had toilet paper, we would still be in business." The writing in the play is intelligent and evocative of many currents at once. To the supply-side problems that plagued Americans during COVID-19, Richard has a punchy repartee: "The people who buy toilet paper are incredible optimists. They think there'll still be food."

What Do We Need to Talk About? enters a group psychodynamic with its widely known Apple Family and the familiar experiences of the first month of the pandemic. If the play brings a message to the group, it is that togetherness comes through storytelling, myth as riffs on familiar motifs, recurrent and relevant to the circumstance at hand. The idea of storytelling is an underlying theme of the play. The meta-stories of *What Do We Need to Talk About?*—some of the answers to the play's titular question—include Anton Chekhov's 1903 play, *The Cherry Orchard*, in which a Russian landowner clings to the past and aristocratic status. Other stories that we need to talk about, in the form of theater, include Thornton Wilder's *The Skin of Our Teeth*, a 1942 parable in the aftermath of the Great Depression. In that play, the character Sabina is a

Cassandra-like presence framing the performance, delivering the fateful lines: "That's all we do—always beginning again! Over and over again. Always beginning again ... Don't forget that a few years ago we came through the depression by the skin of our teeth!" Through storytelling, the group recalls the past and finds guidance to "begin again." Implicitly, the characters in *What Do We Need to Talk About?* are cognizant of epiphanic encoding, that figures from the past, like Anya (*The Cherry Orchard*) or Sabina, guide us toward the recognition that "a few years ago" we came through a similar crisis.

Because Tim is an actor, he can help guide the group through these stories that need to be talked about. In a metatheatrical moment, he tells the story of the death of his friend Mark Blum, a real-life actor who succumbed to COVID-19 on March 25, 2020, at Presbyterian Hospital in New York City, less than two months before his seventieth birthday (Pineda 2020). Tim's touching story involves Mark's first performance decades earlier, when his parents visited the theater and saw no one in the audience. Tim imitates Mark's mother, telling his father in a heavy New York accent that if he cares about his boy—"Marty, if you love your son"—he will go and round up an audience to watch Mark's show. The segment serves as an homage to theater through Blum, who like so many had a preexisting condition (asthma in this case) that complicated his experience with COVID-19. The story echoes the commonness of experiences, at all times, but especially with the poignancy of the moment. The fictional Richard Apple is himself 67, and unlike Blum, will make it through, if only by the skin of his teeth. In addition to the crisis of the pandemic, Barbara spent time in the hospital during quarantine for a severe sickness. The seriousness of this illness emerges in conversation. Late in the play, the activity of the hour-long conversation has drained Barbara. She remarks that it might be time to wrap up the call, stating wistfully, "I thought I was going to die. I need to say that." Her brother, Richard, who is in the same house because he has been taking care of her, responds,

"So did we. And I needed to say that." To Barbara's time in the hospital during such a circumstance, Marian quips, "You must have stories." Of all of these tales, the story of Blum centers theater as a site of poignant symbolism during the pandemic, as a community wondered when, if ever, they would gather again as a group, and whether "theater" would ever return without the protective barrier of the quotation marks. As one character puts it in a very valid commentary, "the first cough from the audience and no one will be watching the play."

It is worth saying a bit more about the storytelling dimension of *What Do We Need to Talk About?* In the play, the question of whether theater will ever return culminates in the characters themselves telling stories. Fittingly, Barbara, who almost died and comes back from an abyss, initiates the cycle. A schoolteacher, Barbara had assigned to her students the exercise of each participant telling a story. She drew them into Giovanni Boccaccio's 1353 *Decameron*, a series of stories that seven fictional girls tell while in quarantine from the Black Plague.[6] In *What Do We Need to Talk About?*, as with *Decameron*, each story brings unexpected twists and turns. Barbara luxuriates that she likes the surprise of stories. Borrowing from Barbara's assignment, each character tells a short story. Her sister Jane, for example, tells of Gladys Huntington's 1956 novel, *Madame Solario*, which Jane proposes was in fact written by someone else. Richard's narrative of President Franklin Pierce tells of "a totally failed presidency," from another time, 1853–1859, the irony of which Marian punctuates with a sarcastic jab, "I can't imagine." This joke jabs at the presidency of Donald J. Trump, a hint at the politics of the community Nelson expects to watch his play—or at least a suggestion of Marian's politics. As the storytelling ends, the narratives move closer to home. Barbara plays a staticky recording of a family patriarch, Benjamin, and Marian tells a juicy tidbit about a family member, Paul, who was written out of a forebear's will, all but expunged from family lore. Like the stories in Boccaccio's *Decameron*, kinship and collective desire link these individual narratives, themselves self-contained novellas, not bound by time or space.

Through its trope of storytelling, *What Do We Need to Talk About?* shows how myth can mask as universal. The jab at the Trump presidency, however, is one of many clues about the type of community for which these stories have grounding and significance. On a superficial level, telling stories, bearing witness to one another's experiences, is a pleasurable pastime, as Jane acknowledges: "While you were telling that story I never once thought of a pandemic." More uncomfortably, storytelling brings the community back from the abyss, preventing its annihilation. Reflecting on her own near-death experience and the passing of family members, Barbara asks, "Do you think we just vanish?" Myth is precisely the un-vanishing of the dead, their epiphanic return. It is worth noting that the Apple Family's only respite from quarantine, like so many people, was a walk, in their case a trip to the family gravesite.[7] It is no wonder, then, that the dead talk to them through family stories. Through storytelling, even the exiled family member, Paul, still exists. Another inadvertent sign of possible uses of story, *What Do We Need to Talk About?* concludes in song: Chet Baker's "Alone Together," words that quickly became catchphrase used by many corporations, which turned to storytelling to foster belonging through commerce. They too seemed to understand on a visceral level the power of tropes and figures to ground communities.

The stories in *What Do We Need to Talk About?*, and the play itself, present as universally humanistic, but upon scrutiny it becomes clear that they ground people like the Apple Family and those who identify with them in particular experiences. Prima facie, this is a white, middle- to upper-middle-class family living in suburban America. The play was, as Brantley saw, "human" and "infinitely poignant." He opines that "Nelson and his team have given me hope that the real thing [theater] is still there, nurturing its singular strength and agility, eager to come out of quarantine and meet us face to face" (Brantley 2020). Lurking behind the critics' nostalgia, however, is a possibility, that *being together*, for those to whom that togetherness pertained, had been forever altered if even by the slightest shifts in group psychodynamics. The Apple Family shelter in place, yet they will see that they are not safe from the psychological intrusion of others. These outsiders are often different from them, have different experiences, opinions, and grounding epiphanies and stories.

The differences between groups become salient in *And So We Come Forth*, but a signal of alterity is already present in *What Do We Need to Talk About?* In this case, the immediate sign is not race but rather that of a generation gap. For example, the audience has heard from Jane that older people are packing the grocery stores during quarantine. More directly, as a schoolteacher, Barbara has access to a group of young people whose experience of the pandemic is different from hers. Tim muses about why young people like these students and his own children (who are their age) would be upset with the assurance that "everything is going to be alright." He reflects on their vantage point, giving this group a first-person voice: "You don't see it from our perspective ... it feels like the world is ending just as we are arriving'." The perspective of young people, that the world is, as they might put it, *literally* ending, is a window into social unrest that ensued in the month of June, which exposed race as another alterity that needs to be talked about.

By keeping the existential crisis of COVID-19 central to the drama but not artificially so, Nelson reaches for a sublimity to which critics reacted favorably. In one way or another, everyone encountered the novel coronavirus, and in both similar and dissimilar ways, the ordeal changed every character, altered every face. Nelson brings the Apple family through the same, common crisis. By July 2020, theater itself was in a full-fledged crisis. It was unclear exactly when and how it would come out of quarantine, and a Nelson Apple Family play on Zoom was not the best measure of where things were going. Rather, the "BIPOC Demands" on theater brought the youth protests in the streets front-and-center, giving them a face and a name without even mentioning George Floyd. By July 2020, Rousseau's treatment of drama (discussed in Chapter 4) would be relevant again, as the autonomous, theatrical experience came face to face with the morals of its viewership. To successfully emerge from quarantine, theater could not escape to high-minded art and aesthetics, isolated from the social drama of the moment, namely the protests and demonstrations across the country. Although the "BIPOC Demands" was an intervention that signaled a shift in circumstances, the shift caught some theater practitioners like Nelson flatfooted. Through his Apple Family dramas, Nelson had initially been the most responsive to theater in quarantine. As we have seen, *What Do We Need to Talk About?* was hailed as innovative and daring, breathing life into fictive personalities that stood in for a broad array of people across the country and world.[8] By July, however, the protests and demonstrations across the country had captured the nation's attention. Nelson released *And So We Come Forth* at the end of July 2020 to less fanfare. This was his second Zoom play featuring the Apple family. Only two months had passed since the celebrated *What Do We Need To Talk About?*, but much had happened in those two months, including the murder of George Floyd and the nightly protests that ensued.[9]

GROUNDING EPIPHANIES: MEMORY, MONUMENTS, AND CANCELATION

In its framing and content, *And So We Come Forth* purports to be an artifact of autonomous theater, a realm unto itself with little bearing on social and political issues even when it has a contemporary setting. Nevertheless, the play betrays shifts in the psychodynamics of the group, even a community of primarily white theatergoers. Before the play begins, Mike Nussbaum, the actor who played Benjamin Apple across the Public Theater's stagings of the Apple Family plays, appeals to viewers to donate to the Actor's Fund, the charity introduced as recipients of any contributions from this free Zoom event. As we will recall, *What Do We Need to Talk About?* hinted at the impact of the pandemic on actors like Mark Blum, who lost his life. Tim gave voice to the struggling, out-of-work actors, who relied on theater's stability for their livelihood. This framing has relevance to what viewers will witness, as *And So We Come Forth* continues. With its contemporary setting, the Apple Family plays already break the wall between real life and make believe. For the actors and the characters they play, life does go on, as Barbara quipped in *What Do We Need to Talk About?*. In *And So We Come Forth*, she looks much recuperated from her time in the hospital (before the opening of *What Do We Need To Talk About?*). Richard is looking to purchase a house and is still contemplating retirement. Marian, not previously a gardener, pulls weeds wearing shorts and a halter top in her front yard to entertain any potential "gentleman caller" (which they joke will be either a serious prospect or stalker for this widow of advanced years). Jane, their sister, continues to nurture her relationship with divorcee Tim, who joins the family on Zoom from the Brooklyn, New York City home of his ex-wife, Diane. The group seems caught up in their everyday, domestic affairs, where they draw from significant stories to ground them, but from a psychodynamic perspective, life does not go on unaltered.

There are hints throughout *And So We Come Forth* that characters—and the writers who invent them—are grappling with the social and political toll of the foregoing months. Race looms for them, and yet it is spoken about only in figurative terms in the play. That race is of significance, even if unspoken, is clear in a story that Richard tells about the family's grandmother some time ago walking on 125th Street in Harlem, New York City, an area world-renowned as a Black mecca. Richard begins in a cold, flat delivery that could be attributed the medium of Zoom, although the potential gasps from a live audience could have been a show-stopper. From the moment the tale begins, the transplantation of these white suburbanites to the Black urban landscape is jarring. Grandma, the story goes, believes that she hears the voice of someone calling out, "Whitey, you ought to go home." The white woman's fear while walking in Harlem by herself and being welcomed in this way is palpable. As is seen so often, the phantasy of the racial figure incites fear. Richard has set up a racial conflict between "whitey" and the unidentified Black Harlemite. Richard's story of "whitey" shifts, however, when he reveals what the presumably Black speaker is really saying: "Lady, you dropped your comb." The story is one of misapprehension between white and Black people. It poignantly speaks to the various ways that we misrepresent and mis-see each other, owing to a lifetime of bias, stereotypes, and time spent without truly being together—or being together, but apart, to borrow from a trope used often of the 2020 quarantine.

Through Richard's story, race has significance to the group, in this case, the white American family living in Rhinebeck, a hundred miles north of New York City. Race, though sublimated, surfaces in conscious or semi-conscious ways. The story, however, does not bring Richard or his listeners to a recognition that extends beyond knowable misperception. Moving from the microcosm of family to the macrocosm of society, Richard struggles to see what the protests, the real-life conflict in Black and white, might really be about. Characters in *And So We Come Forth* seem to recognize that groups project significance onto stories and icons, that meaning is somehow encoded epiphanically. In the real world outside of the drama, icons were shifting in the form of the toppling of symbols of racial memory. Protestors were attempting to expiate ghosts. After George Floyd's murder in March 2020, several cities in the U.S. saw some form of protest, in many cases sustained for several weeks. There were at least 25 deaths owing directly to widespread civil unrest by the beginning of October (Beckett 2020). Over ten thousand people had been arrested by June (Snow 2020). The toppling of monuments was not confined to Richmond, Virginia, formerly the capital of the Confederacy that went to war against the

U.S. Union Army in 1861–1865 (Figure 5). The activity of monument toppling was happening across the country and signaled a group psychodynamic shift. Richard's story of grandma, though it moves toward a recognition of misperception, is feeble in the face of the monumental shifts that were occurring.

Understandably, not all agreed with the purpose, desired outcomes, or tactics of the protestors. Nevertheless, race was evidently one of the things the country needed to talk about, but Richard's story of racial misrecognition is fleeting. The family ostensibly moves on to other topics. Indirectly, however, the discussion does not shift. In *And So We Come Forth*, the tearing-down of monuments, presented in terms of a preoccupation with "cancel culture,"[10] purports to be about something other than race. Over the course of June and July 2020, the demonstrators protesting George Floyd's death defaced or removed monuments, making race an inescapable subtext to the discussion. In *And So We Come Forth*,

Figure 5: Base of Confederate Statue, Richmond, VA, Summer 2020.

Richard and Barbara relate the tearing-down of monuments across the globe to their own backyard of Rhinebeck, where a statue of American Vice President Levi Morton (1824–1920) stands. Moving from family matters to apparently impersonal ones, Richard reports a tale of a person having passed away, whose "entire life" is "tossed in a dumpster." The person is deleted, cancelled, as if never having existed. Richard speculates as to whether this is what should happen to Morton. Under the cover of cancel culture, people are afraid to speak out and express their true position because if they do, someone might cancel them. Richard draws the analogy between the potential cancellation of a person and the social question that the tearing-down of monuments poses: "What do we knock down? What do we spare? Who gets a pass?" He passes on answering his own prompts, but he raises the play's—and the society's—existential question.

The question of "who gets a pass" echoes the "pass[ing] over" of the characters in Antoinette Nwandu's play *Pass Over* (discussed in the last chapter), set on the purgatorial South Side of Chicago reminiscent of Samuel Beckett's *Waiting for Godot*. These two Black men also do not want society to discard *them*. These men and Richard Apple face the same existential crisis of annihilation. Richard's suffering is psychological because he has all that he needs materially. His young Black counterparts endure lives of active neglect and even vilification. Like so many others, Richard fears that the tables might be turning. Whereas he was safe before, he is now being cast in the role of the villain. The toppling of monuments signifies something more than performative, the possibility that the icon stood in for something else, an epiphany that prevents one's own obliteration. Despite Richard's concern about who gets a pass, he inadvertently passes over the grounding stories and images of fellow citizens, evidence that racial designations divide this public into discrete groups that separately identify with their own stories and icons. Rather than a sickness in the body politic, the separation is psychological, a product of memory and encoding.

Richard's observations, the presentation of this character's reactions to the protests, astutely conveys the underlying sentiments and structures of thought that pertain to racial reconciliation. Richard would not be convinced to think differently, or even that he is part of a pandemic, one of racism, or at least a psychological separation of races that continues its work even after legal integration. Rather, Richard needs monuments he can revere, at best ones that his BIPOC counterparts also revere. For a moment in 2020, George Floyd seemed to be that figure, as across the U.S. his makeshift effigies on cardboard and plywood were replacing the toppled statues to Christopher Columbus, Robert E. Lee, and others. Alternatively, his words became immortalized in murals, as the photograph of the façade of a restaurant in Washington, D.C., conveyed (Figure 6).

And So We Come Forth represents some of the challenges to crossing a psychological divide, which was being talked about in

Figure 6: "I Can't Breathe," Washington, DC, June 13, 2020.

terms of racial reckoning. These challenges, which manifest as political, economic, or even generational issues, have to do with how communities encode experiences into memory. Richard can recognize his grandmother's misrecognition across a racial divide as a problem of language. Apart from the moniker of "whitey," he never even names race as a challenge. What is more, *And So We Come Forth* sublimates racial misrecognition into a generational divide, as *What Do We Need to Talk About?* did. In *And So We Come Forth*, Barbara's students echo a grievance widely discussed in 2020 in the aftermath of George Floyd's murder. During this period, white people were reaching out to Black people they knew expressing concern and emotional support (Sanders 2020). Public and private intuitions, from corporations to universities, joined the chorus. In the play, Barbara tells of her text messages to her students and their responses when they plead with her to stop. As one student puts it, "Let's just pause this for now, Barbara." Barbara says that she does not "think" she has "ever felt so old." Barbara elides race with age. Jane and Tim, who both belong to Generation X, each have college-aged kids from other relationships. Keeping to this generational motif, the possibility emerges during the play that, much to Jane's dismay, Tim's son might move from Brooklyn to Rhinebeck to live with them because ex-wife Diane "really needs a break." In addition to this, Tim's daughter Karen and her classmate Maggie are also potential squatters; each may also move to Rhinebeck, picking up on a theme (outside of this drama) of the widespread flight from New York City because of COVID-19. In light of a failure of public community, the effort toward togetherness shifts back to the imagined kinship ties of family.

THE BACKLASH: THE GOSPEL ACCORDING TO KYLE RITTENHOUSE

Challenges to identity take an emotional toll on everyone involved. In *And So We Come Forth*, Richard and Barbara show the protests and discussions around monuments to be personally affronting. Barbara is exasperated in a way consistent with the frustrations of many living through the pandemic: "There now is such a great sense of urgency. But for what?" She asks, "Is it wrong to shut off?" The response that "sometimes we have to, Barbara" arrives as a psychological mechanism for coping with a world in unprecedented flux. Sometimes people must shut off for their own psychological well-being and self-preservation, the integrity of their identity. Worse than shutting off, however, by autumn of 2020, a slow but steady backlash, an idea with its own resonances as it pertains to history, time, and memory, could be felt.[11] This backlash had strong racial overtones. Exasperation had manifested itself as early as the first months of the pandemic. Various groups found the mandatory lockdowns excessive, and some of the earliest protests had to do with resistance to government, even before the murder of George Floyd. When energy, attention, and public and private funds moved toward a nebulous idea of racial reconciliation, especially in the form of reparations of the rhetoric of "Defund the Police," some groups had come to their wit's end (Levin 2020). The backlash landed on its own epiphany, further evidence of the role of narratives, or myths, in contemporary society.

Kyle Rittenhouse is the last dramatis persona of *Theater and Crisis*, the epiphany of a return to normalcy, or a new normal. Rittenhouse came to be figured through an ancient narrative, the outrage that Jesus had, for example, with the money changers in the temple. Rittenhouse's story is worth recounting. After a Black man named Jacob Blake was shot several times by police officers in Kenosha, Wisconsin on August 25, 2020, protests flared up in that city (Morales 2021). As in other cities across the U.S., demonstrations had persisted there for the better part of three months. Along with others, some as members of militia like the Proud Boys, Rittenhouse descended on the city that night, armed with an AR-15 assault rifle. His ostensible aim was to serve as a standby paramedic.[12] By his account, he was training to be a nurse and wanted to help anyone in distress. The surrounding violence would be his reason for bringing a weapon of war to a medical intervention. By the end of the night, Rittenhouse would have killed two men and critically wounded a third. In the chaos of protestors and counter-protestors across the country at the time, Rittenhouse claimed self-defense. On November 18, 2021, he was acquitted of criminal charges that the public defendants brought against him in Kenosha, Wisconsin.

The issue of Rittenhouse's guilt or innocence is a juridical matter, separate from the way that he almost immediately became a mythic figure, an epiphany encoded as grounding for a group of people within the U.S. For many, Rittenhouse was as much an epiphanic embodiment as George Floyd was for others. His example underscores the idea that racial reconciliation will be psychodynamic, narrative work within community. It will require shared stories, and the public should be aware of recurrence, or backlash, the reality that groups will project fantasies from the past onto their present circumstances. Conflict will be dramatized, and as such the dramatic stage can be a place to work through the issues that communities face. Although laws and favorable (or unfavorable, depending on the perspective) verdicts influence the direction of public sentiment, psychological healing—racial reconciliation—belongs to the realm of myth and memory. Theater is, once again, an important site for the process.

In the public or social drama, Rittenhouse was a notable counter to George Floyd, and each came to be encoded epiphanically. For some groups, Rittenhouse was as much a Christ figure as Floyd was for others. In an online article, titled "What's in a Meme? The Rise of 'Saint Kyle'," Hampton Stall, David Foran and Hari Prasad show that within two months after Kenosha, memes had proliferated across social media that glorified him. As they put it, "Kyle Rittenhouse represents a type of real-world incident that groups appropriate into their narratives through pre-existing mimetic and aesthetic templates" (Stall et al. 2020). The language that Stall,

Foran, and Prasad use recalls arguments I have deployed throughout *Theater and Crisis*. Myth, as I have argued, is the grounding of groups in significant narratives. Groups assimilate new figures, such as Rittenhouse, into "pre-existing" phantasies, or "mimetic and aesthetic templates." These templates, as we saw with George Floyd, can include stories and ideas from Greek myth, literature, and drama. They might even be symbols drawn from a Judeo-Islamo-Christian stock of settings, characters, and themes, as we saw in the last chapter with the Hebrew leader Moses figured as Black youth surrounded by urban decay.

The internet immortalized Rittenhouse as Christ. Contemporary figures as epiphanies of Christ has been a ready phantasy, as we have seen with Emmett Till or Matthew Shepard. As one online acolyte puts Rittenhouse's case: "guys, I'm not even religious, but how can this be anything other than divine intervention." Finding religious symbolism in Rittenhouse's actions, another writes that Kyle took down "the guy who tried to kill him," who "is named Grosskreutz, literally 'big cross.' Kyle literally defended the cross, like Jesus did."[13] Rittenhouse's sanctification online is prolific. As shocking as this truth may be to some groups, the apotheosis of Georgy Floyd incensed others. When Catholic University in Washington, D.C., displayed an image of Floyd as Christ, returning to the bosom of his mother, reminiscent of Mary collecting the body of her son at the tomb to find an empty container, some people were quite upset. A Tweet from November 22, 2021 reads, "What is this?" Matt Rooney of New Jersey posted the headline "Painting of George Floyd as Jesus on Display at Catholic University," with the caption "It is just another symptom of the liberalization and secularization of our campus."[14] The epiphany, as we have seen, demarcates the group, clearly designating who is inside and who is outside.

I am not suggesting that the type of people the Apple family represent in Nelson's plays would cling to either epiphany, whether Rittenhouse as Christ or Floyd's assimilation to the same. Neither figure seems to be particularly grounding for the fictional upper-middle-class family. Rittenhouse is an extreme embodiment of the backlash, even if the Apple family expresses a corresponding frustration with the protests. Though not through a symbol as extreme as Rittenhouse, the Apple family reaches for figures who convey their sense of a colorless, universal humanity. They find their symbols in stories of old, from Bocaccio's pandemic tales to families in Chekhov's plays whose plight resembles their own. Throughout *Theater and Crisis*, examples across time have included not only Christ, but also the Biblical leader Moses, Aeschylean and Shakespearean ghosts from the *Oresteia* and *Macbeth*, the Greek god Dionysus, and Oedipus. These examples are by no means exhaustive but have served to demonstrate a model of classicizing beyond the literary, narratological, or other existing modes of tradition or reception. Rather, the phantasy projections of figures from the past into the present are part of a process of memory, an encoding that can happen even unconsciously. Although writers and artists might have some control over their use of these phantasies, associations can also be spontaneous because they are deep-seeded, such as in the case of Rittenhouse or Floyd as Christ.

The model of myth and memory that I have presented in *Theater and Crisis* upsets conceptions of time because the phantasy is not confined to the past. It is ever present. The chronological organization that I have offered conveys some sense of momentum and forward progress toward racial reconciliation, such as with the passage of laws. Chronology, however, also reveals the cyclical nature of myth and memory, and even cultural backlash against specific phantasies. Because of recurrence and repetition consistent with psychological processes, there can sometimes be a sense of stagnancy. George Floyd's murder resembles that of Emmett Till or the scores of other people who have died because of outright hatred or more subtle misapprehension.

The pandemic of 2020, moreover, disrupted a collective sense of time. The interruption of daily happenings of work and leisure was welcome for some people. They changed their jobs, retired, or left their marriages, seizing on a realization that the order of things does not have to be as it was. For others, the disruption was too jarring. The isolation of quarantine, the stress on care providers and emergency workers, and the economic impact were shifts with long-term repercussions.[15] Time is a feature of memory, both individually and in communities. Given that monuments mark common or public time, it is no wonder that as sites of contestation they were prominent during the pandemic.

Theater and Crisis can be galvanizing in one last way. The normative political frames of analysis prove unhelpful when we consider Floyd and Rittenhouse both as figures for Christ, i.e., the reality that groups find meaning in narratives, or myths, that bring a sense of significance and grounding. Christ is not a far-right figure any more than he is one of Civil Rights and social justice. The same can be said of Moses or any narrative or mythological figure from classical antiquity. The *molon labe*, "come and take it" Spartan slogan of states' rights is as much a white power mantra as it can be deployed otherwise.

Nelson's Apple family might for the most part be liberal, but they struggle to reconcile themselves to a shifting social landscape to the same extent as those right-wing groups who embraced Kyle Rittenhouse. A path to racial reconciliation is not treating it as a cancer—and therefore our opponents as tumors to be excised—but rather understanding it as a psychological process of myth and memory, which manifests in narrative form. As such, a society coming to terms with conflict, be it interracial or otherwise, needs new narratives to chart its way forward, but these narratives will imbue old symbols with new significance and grounding. Theater can be a primary site of this creative process, a place where communities project and reimagine phantasies, or ghosts, from the past. These phantasies, or ghosts that haunt the present, urge the communities that reckon with them toward the "something to be done," a promised end.

Figure 7: Photo by Miles Wilson taken at a protest in Richmond, VA, during the summer of 2020.

Notes

PREFACE

1 The term "racial reckoning" proliferated in 2020, meriting an entire section in *The Washington Post*. A quick Google search yields several illuminating results. In particular, George Mason University established a site to collect stories of racial reckoning, asserting that "today, unarmed BIPOC encounter individual, institutional, and systemic racism in their everyday lives, and compared to white people, are disproportionately likely to be stopped, falsely arrested, and killed by the police." See https://legacies.gmu.edu/research/racial-reckoning. For an international perspective, see Quarcoo and Husaković 2021.

2 Benedict Anderson popularized the phrase "imagined community" to designate the nation, and more recent scholarship has revisited his work considering the Internet as a new space for the creation and challenging of national identity. See Anderson 2016 and Brønholt 2020.

3 I use this date, rather than 1619, to acknowledge the presence of enslaved people as early as the Spanish presence in areas of what came to be known as the United States, such as Florida. In this case as well, a quick Google search reveals the presence of enslaved people in this territory prior to the sixteenth century as a point of contention with The 1619 Project, which can be found at https://www.nytimes.com/interactive/2019/08/14/magazine/1619-america-slavery.html.

4 See Gurley 2022 for a report that is almost a year earlier than the many others searchable on Google.

5 On the exodus and return, see Hong and Haag 2022. On New York City as the epicenter, see Levenson 2020.

6 See previous note.

7 The image of the place where three roads meet is from Sophocles' *Oedipus*, and it recurs in such contexts as Ralph Ellison's *Invisible Man*.

8 See Feuer et al. 2020. By May 2021, *The Washington Post* would report that hundreds of bodies were still in this condition. See https://www.washingtonpost.com/nation/2021/05/09/coronavirus-bodies-trucks-new-york/.

9 See Paulson 2020a. The move, Paulson wrote, "will likely trigger the collapse of some plays and musicals that will be unable to survive the delays and losses."

10 I am careful in my use of the term "ritual" because as Bottici 2007 argues, rightly, I believe, people confuse myth and ritual, but ritual is a separate matter, requiring precise enactment, failure of which results in an interrupted ritual. From this I would argue that the procession into the theater is ritualized.

11 A Carnegie Endowment report from December 2020 shows that demonstrations were already higher in January as opposed to 2019, although down in February 2020 from February 2019. The surge the report charts in March 2020 is dramatic. The worldwide causes preceding the pandemic include the increasing authoritarianism of governments, such as that of Bulgaria, and backlash among the citizenry. The report can be found at https://carnegieendowment.org/2020/12/21/worldwide-protests-in-2020-year-in-review-pub-83445. The Armed Conflict Location & Event Data Project (ACLED), funded by the Princeton School of Public and International Affairs' Liechtenstein Institute on Self-Determination, also released a report, in September 2020, with data on the protests within the U.S. See https://acleddata.com/2020/09/03/demonstrations-political-violence-in-america-new-data-for-summer-2020/.

12 See Wilson 2020 and Vogel et al. 2020.

13 See the May 30 video https://www.youtube.com/watch?v=FMGUAHBFmjk&t=112s and June 1 video https://www.youtube.com/watch?v=VDd5GlrgvsE.

14 The video can be viewed at "Minneapolis City Council Official Calls for Racism to be Declared a Public Health Emergency," *Axios*, May 28, 2020, https://www.axios.com/minneapolis-george-floyd-racism-public-health-568de687-8d57-411f-96c1-2420114f2327.html, last accessed 00/00/00.

15 See, for example, Clayton 2023, on Florida Governor Ron DeSantis' block on Advance Placement (AP) African American Studies for public schools.

16 The speech can be viewed at "Virginia Governor Discusses his Decision to Remove Confederate Monuments," on WKSU, June 5, 2020, https://www.wksu.org/post/virginia-governor-discusses-his-decision-remove-confederate-monument#stream/0

17 The Pharos website, which collects far-right deployments of classical Greek and Roman symbols, has documented this usage: https://pharos.vassarspaces.net/2021/01/14/capitol-terrorists-take-inspiration-from-ancient-world/. The Battle of Thermopylae has been a feature of a Confederate defense tied to the idea of states rights versus federal ones. Thomas Dew, President of William & Mary College, deployed it in his inauguration address to encourage students to defend slaveholding, and Basil Gildersleeve was also enamored of the association. At the Society for Classical Studies annual conference in 2023, Craig Williams presented a case of a Native American reappropriation of the symbolism, namely that of Ely Parker. At the time of this publication, Williams was working on a volume on broader Native American deployments of classical symbols and tropes.

18 See, for example, Georgetown's President John J. DeGioia's remarks on the discovery that in 1838, the university's Jesuit leadership sold 272 enslaved people to raise funds for the institution, at https://www.georgetown.edu/news/georgetown-apologizes-for-1838-sale-of-272-slaves-dedicates-buildings/.

19 My approach builds on Goldsby 2006 in its treatment of the lynching of Emmett Till as a "spectacular secret," acknowledging the profound human toll and painfulness of the experience while also recognizing the broader significance of the event in establishing norms, even if these are hidden, unspoken, or secret.

20 The approach that myths can be reduced to a set of deeper truths about the human condition was that taken by Joseph Campbell, which is useful to consider but not my ultimate landing place. For this approach, influential to film and literature since its initial articulation, see Campbell 1973.

21 Fukuyama 2019 might help to define "identity politics" as a process whereby "individuals demand public recognition of their worth" (10), which is "driven by the quest for equal recognition by groups that have been marginalized by their societies" (22). He sees identity as a hindrance to the "end of history," the "chief threat" that modern democracies face (xvi). He presents the argument in much the same way as Foley and others can conceive of an apolitical public space. Bottici's treatment of the period prior to Foley's designated 1960s, a rejection of Fukuyama's identity politics and the end of history, might help get at what has always been political about Greek drama

in the U.S.: "The rise of identity politics and the revival of nationalism in recent decades have, perhaps, rendered manifest that, to paraphrase Geertz, the extraordinary has not gone out of modern politics, however much of the banal may have entered it (Geertz 1983: 143)," Bottici 2007: 256, citing Geertz's *Local Knowledge*, New York, Basic Books.

22 As William W. Batstone puts the case in his treatment of classical reception, "if reading like the self is always open, if it is always an act of self-understanding (which cannot *not* be a mirage) and of world construction (which cannot *not* be political), we may ask, 'Why stop here?' It would seem that every reading is, as Nietzsche said in 1880, a will to power" (Batstone 2006: 19).

23 Throughout the book, she will take on Geertz's idea that myth brings meaning, arguing that beyond the meaning that organizes the word, a sense of purpose comes from something other than simple meaning, and she uses the term "significance" to designate this higher, almost religious, calling.

24 She uses the example of Moses as a *figura Christi* (2007: 57).

25 As Bottici puts it, "the passage from the concept of imagination to that of imaginary reflects a change from a subject-oriented approach to a context-oriented one" (Bottici 2007: 224).

26 Bottici continues as follows: "The reason why imagination came to be associated with the idea of fictitiousness is that it creates ex nihilo—not in nihilo or cum nihilo—and the Western ensemble logic, which starts with the identity assumption ex nihilo nihil, as a consequence, could not but conceive of imagination as essentially non-existence" (Bottici 2007: 223).

27 I like Bottici's coinage of "imaginal," as wresting from "imaginary" the sense of make-believe it has acquired, but I am careful not to add too many extraneous definitions. We will have enough with which to grapple.

28 In political philosophy, Bottici cites the idea of the savage as a grounding myth, "recognised as a very powerful source of significance" (Bottici 2007: 194). Charles Mills (2022) elaborates on how this myth was particularly a racial one. For the American origins of Nazism, see Wilkerson 2020.

29 Bottici is citing Flood 1996.

30 Appiah 2018 is another approach to the same.

CHAPTER ONE

1 Videos were posted to YouTube as early as May 30, 2020, with security video from Cubs Foods accessible as early as June 1, 2020. Some videos are included in this bibliography, including body cam footage from officers Thomas Lane and J. Alexander Kueng, who also responded to the call.

2 See Chappell 2021.

3 I use the term "spectacular" in a way that follows Goldsby 2006, who "refer[s] to lynching as 'spectacular': the violence made certain cultural developments and tensions visible. She follows Debord's 1994 analysis of the spectacle as "NOT a collection of images; rather, it is a social relationship between people that is mediated by images" (12).

4 I am cautious here about the voyeurism of the spectacle, the process whereby Floyd's meaningless killing becomes something other than the painful loss of life, and his presence, for his family. An in-depth treatment of his life and personal struggles is Olorunnipa and Witte 2020. See also the announcement of the newspaper's publication of a biography of George Floyd through Viking Press, printed on November 10, 2021 (WashPostPR Blog 2021).

5 As Goldsby puts it, "using the term 'cultural logic' allows me to investigate lynching's connections to the past and present in order to distinguish between its causes and contexts more readily" (Goldsby 2006: 26).

6 I use "encoding" throughout to denote the process whereby memory is made. See, for example, Shimamura 2014. Processes of individual memory function within social contexts; memories are made and reinforced in community. See also Payette 2012, a collection interested in "how individual cognition is influenced (improved, increased or impaired) by social interactions" (viii).

7 Of several modern approaches to theater and ritual within theories of performance, Turner 2001 remains foundational. See also Turner 1979.

8 Lear 2005 is useful in extending Freudian psychology beyond psychoanalysis into, for example, its relationship to Western classical philosophy. My usages here owe something to my reading of Lear.

9 For object relations, see Greenberg and Mitchell 1983.

10 Black killings garner this attention even though the broader problem of state-sanctioned violence affects white people living in poor, rural communities.

11 See Goldsby 2006 on the use of "spectacular" here.

12 See Claycomb 2013 on the relationship between text and performance, as it pertains to written plays or scripts.

13 See Shlien 1959, for a treatment of Santa Claus as a kind of folk hero. Olson 1991 makes a case for beginning any teaching of how myth functions in the world with Santa Claus because a tale such as this "offer[s] intriguing insights into contemporary American society and thus helps to make the case that myth is not a series of silly stories told by 'primitive' societies long ago but an important way in which cultures (including our own) talk to themselves" (295). On change over time and the potential pernicious impact of Santa Claus as role model, see Grills and Halyday 2009.

14 This definition is only 3a (3) from Merriam-Webster.

15 This is, in fact, the first definition in Merriam-Webster.

16 Instructive here is the classical idea of *theoria*, which connects mental image, object or external spectacle, and truth or epiphany. See, for example, Nightingale 2004.

17 This definition is ubiquitously quoted from Freud, as in, for example, Evans 2006, Guy 2014, and Papanikolaou 2017.

18 Melanie Klein is as a good a place as any to start on studies of object relation. See Klein 2002.

19 I follow Appiah 2016 in recognizing "Western" as a relatively new category rooted in the nineteenth century, and yet the term is ubiquitously recognized for what it represents. Consider, for example, Said 1979 and its legacy.

20 For a discussion of this formulation and why "all lives matter" has been problematic, see Yancy and Butler 2015.

21 On Saint Nicholas, see English 2012.

22 Although in the West these narratives are relied upon, a similar case could be made about Confucius and Chinese antiquity, or Muhammad and Islam, more strongly outside of Western countries.

23 The quote is from Smithsonian Magazine: "Emmett Till's Open Casket Funeral Reignited the Civil Rights Movement," September 2, 2015, https://www.smithsonianmag.com/smithsonian-institution/emmett-tills-open-casket-funeral-reignited-the-civil-rights-movement-180956483/. Compare the imagery of Bunch's quote to sonnets from the early part of the twentieth century, like Claude McKay's "The Lynching," which also parallels the lynch victim to the Christ figure.

24 Martindale 1993 is widely considered the beginning of this subdiscipline.

25 See, for example, Hall and Macintosh 2005, Hall and Harrop 2010, Macintosh 2010, Macintosh and McConnell 2020, to name only a few of the most compendious examples. Dorf 2018 is helpful in thinking about the ephemerality of performance as reception, especially in such instances as the performance of music. For a poignant debate on whether Martindale's theory of reception can apply to performance, see his debate with Simon Goldhill in Hall and Harrop 2010.

26 These categories of classical and modern can be a helpful framework to consider along with James Baldwin's formulation of the "Western," but they are also contested terms. See Parker and Mathews 2011.

27 For Kerr 1973, the classic is the thing, and Soyinka's *Bacchae* "is evidence of the continuing ability of Greek drama and Greek myths to help us pose and answer questions about our existence and to inspire fresh works of art."

A classic among classics, Euripides' play is the object of the critic's longest-standing fantasies: "Having been chilled and finally overpowered by it in the reading, I've been waiting half my life to hear and feel its harrowing rhythms on stage, now conclude I'm not going to."

28 See Lecznar 2020 for a treatment that resonates with what I will discuss in Chapter 3.

29 See Rankine 2006 for a reading of the novel as deeply allusive to Homer's *Odyssey*; and Roynon 2014 on broader classical allusions in this novel and across Morrison's oeuvre.

30 On naming in *Song of Solomon*, see Rankine 2006. Morrison 1988 herself points to the significance of Guitar's rejection of this framework, his "mercy."

31 See Rankine 2006 for a discussion of some of Morrison's interviews and statements about classical influence.

32 See the introduction to Bosher et al. 2015.

33 See also Shields 2001.

34 Some of the American founders, such as Alexander Hamilton, certainly read Plutarch and Demosthenes (Richard 1994: 26). His contemporaries compared him to Julius Caesar (92), and his pseudonym was Phocion. Reading for ancient influences on law and justice, therefore, when we come to Federalist #75 is not a leap, although there are not copious, overt references to Plato or later classical jurisprudence in that document. Alongside the deliberate classicism of Hamilton and Thomas Jefferson, however, there were other, more inadvertent exemplars. These were writers not necessarily steeped in the classical texts but certainly aware of their value. Richard demonstrates that there was already a gap between the training of Hamilton and that of Jefferson. Writers recognized the cultural cache of the classics, even when they themselves were not necessarily fully immersed in its tools.

35 On the potential elusiveness of the classical within modern and contemporary works as "fuzzy connection," see Hardwick 2011.

36 In addition to the notion of "fuzzy connection," Hardwick 2011 also uses the metaphor of the rhizome, the classical as subterranean, everywhere and nowhere, ever-present but difficult to trace.

37 Later published in *Notes of a Native Son* (Baldwin 2012), *Harper's Magazine* first published the essay in 1953.

38 In his rejoinder to Baldwin, Teju Cole (2014) would write that by 2014, for these villagers in Switzerland, "maybe some xenophobia or racism are part of their lives, but part of their lives, too, are Beyoncé, Drake, and Meek Mill, the music I hear pulsing from Swiss clubs on Friday nights."

39 On Ralph Ellison, for example, see Rankine 2006. Cook and Tatum 2012 make a strong argument for classicism in the work of other authors in the U.S., such as Frederick Douglass, Fran Ross, and Richard Wright.

40 These traumatic experiences repeat for others, generations later, as we hear in the reverberation half a century later in the rap lyrics of Common, when "corners leave souls opened and closed, hopin' for mo'."

41 See Kim 2017, who reads Baldwin's interest in Freud in the context of Franz Fanon.

42 "The Artist's Struggle for Integrity," which appears in the volume, *The Cross of Redemption: Uncollected Writings* (Baldwin 2010). Baldwin asserts that "the poets (by which I mean all artists) are finally the only people who know the truth about us" (51).

43 See Miller 2004.

44 See Miller 2004.

45 For real ghosts, consider Harold Bloom's discussion of his experience in Edinburgh, in his book on Macbeth, where actual spirits appear onstage: "In Edinburgh, during the summer I turned twenty-one, I distinctly saw a ghost wandering the mazelike garden of the Carlyle Hostel, at 3:00 a.m. in the murky fog. Two-thirds of a century later, I can still see that uncanny bundle of rags coming by me as I turned in the labyrinth. The grand Scottish lady who administered the hostel told me the next morning of a seventeenth-century cleaning woman who had been murdered there" (Bloom 2019: 25).

46 The full quote is as follows: "To believe or not believe in ghosts no longer involves a determination about the empirical (im)possibility of the supernatural, but indicates contrasting validated attitudes—a welcoming seen as ethical and enabling, and a rejection considered unethical and dispossessing—towards the uncertainty, heterogeneity, multiplicity, and indeterminacy that characterizes language and Being because of their inevitable entanglement with alterity and difference" (Blanco and Peeren 2013: 9).

47 Cited by Blanco and Peeren 2013: 13.

48 King used the phrase often, notably in his 1957 "Birth of a New Nation" speech at Dexter Avenue Baptist Church. See Calloway-Thomas and Lucaites 1993.

49 As Blight puts it, "history is what historians do." Maurantonio 2019, which is a study of Confederate memory in the U.S., has been instrumental to my understanding of these matters.

50 See also Rhodes-Pitts 2011.

51 On queer and Black responses to chronological time and notions of progress, see Rao 2020.

52 As is often the case with performance, anyone interested in knowing how a particular work impacted audiences is in the realm of mixed- or cross-viewing and responses. Because performance is a one-time event, researchers will never know how each member of the audience responded, but we can gather a sense of the performance's impact. Critics are important to this question of impact and success of a theatrical work. Reviews and awards can convey the meaningfulness to their audiences of specific dramatic works.

CHAPTER TWO

1 To view the document, go to https://www.archives.gov/milestone-documents/civil-rights-act.

2 See https://www.archives.gov/milestone-documents/brown-v-board-of-education.

3 Go to https://www.archives.gov/milestone-documents/plessy-v-ferguson.

4 From the standpoint of distant reading and meta-analysis, the word "legend" recurs in at least six different places on *Notes of a Native Son*, "myth" at least five times; "legend" appears at least five times in *The Devil Finds Work*. To put this in modern psychological terms rather than ancient, ritual ones, "fantasy" occurs several times as well in *Devil* (three times); the word "fantasy" occurs five times in *Notes*, "fantastic" five times as well. These denote places where Baldwin is either delving into ideas of myth, legend, or fantasy, or taking these ideas as givens.

5 Other writing, such as the novel *Giovanni's Room*, were workshopped. See Mullen 2019.

6 Among other parallels, see Leeming 2015 on Baldwin's relationship to Beuford Delaney, the painter who was "trying to rework Greek tragedy" in his painting (195).

7 Turning again to distant reading and metatext, "West" as a concept of American and European life recurs in at least five different places in *Notes of a Native Son*, and "Western" also occurs, i.e., "the Western world." In *The Fire Next Time*, "West" recurs in at least six different passages, "Western," i.e., "world," "civilization," "culture," "idea," or "populations." There are at least three significant passages of the recurrence of "Western" in some of these formulations in *The Devil Finds Work*.

8 This is an unforgettable phrase that figures prominently in Mitchell 2012 as well.

9 See Baldwin 2011 [1976]: 29, 33, and 59.

10 See "Stranger in the Village" in *Notes of a Native Son* (Baldwin 2012), first published in 1955. See also Teju Cole's 2014 significant redaction of this vision, where the important Western references are no longer Aeschylus, Shakespeare, or Michelangelo, but rather Jay-Z and Beyoncé.

11 I will explore the postcolonial potentiality in the United States in the next chapter.

12 Baldwin first published *The Fire Next Time* in 1963, a year before the staging of *Blues*.

13 This phrase becomes the title of Ta-Nehisi Coates' 2015 Baldwinian memoir, which won a National Book Award.

14 He seldom cites his references, preferring a mode of riffing proposed in Henry Louis Gates, Jr.'s *The Signifying Monkey* (2014). For a look at how the trope of the Signifying Monkey might operate in other authors of Baldwin's period, see Rankine 2019.

15 One can imagine that Baldwin might have plays like Jack Kirkland's *Mandingo* in mind, when he thinks of American theater of the 1950s and 1960s. This escapist fantasy graced the American stage in 1961, from May 22–27. The plot summary in the playbill reads as follows: "An African slave is trained to fight other slaves on an antebellum Southern plantation, and is ultimately seduced by his mistress after her husband rejects her for a female slave on their wedding night." Kirkland adapted of Kyle Onstott's 1957 novel of the same name, which trades in stereotyped slave figures and uses ritual for optics and pageantry rather than the powerful, dreadful reality of the violence of slavery and its aftermath. In the preface to *Blues*, Baldwin finds theater to be "a series, merely, of commercial speculations, stale, repetitious, and timid" (Baldwin 1995a: 4). He does not give any examples, but Kirkland's or any number of others could easily make his point.

16 Tyson 2017. A Grand Jury investigation to bring charges against Carolyn Bryant was dismissed in 2022. See Rojas 2022.

17 The image graced the cover of *Jet Magazine*. For this and other stories in the *Jet* archive on Till, go to the Emmett Till Project, http://www.emmetttillproject.com/jetmagazine.

18 For a review of the experience, see Thompson 2016.

19 See Nodjimbaden 2015. Compare the imagery of Bunch's quote to sonnets from the early part of the twentieth century, like Claude McKay's "The Lynching," which also parallels the lynch victim to the Christ figure.

20 Till's body is a painful memento that perhaps fits into neither of Wolin 2017's categories of "relic," sacred object upheld but not wholly interacted with, or "archaism," emblem from the past that is brought into the present whole and

that motivates us toward action. It is closer to the latter, but it has no official, state-sanctioned authority, which Wolin's archaisms, such as the Bible and the Constitution, have.

21 Here I am judiciously avoiding the idea of the "origin" of theater in ancient Greece, notwithstanding the lore of the innovation of the first actor, Thespis, in Aristotle's recounting. For theater as a ritual practice outside of—and perhaps previous to—Athenian drama, see Soyinka 1990. Soyinka is an important subject in the next chapter.

22 I do not want to overemphasize Gates 2014 as a mode of reading in this context, but the provocation of the Signifying Monkey is the closest analog to what I see Baldwin doing throughout the play.

23 Baldwin could have easily been referring to the early Church fathers, who hailed from what is currently known as North Africa and the Middle East, before any construct of "the West." See Appiah 2016, whose point on the lateness of this moniker of "the West" I take, although I would refine some of his details.

24 Outside of his reference to Aeschylus in "Stranger in the Village," I have not found any direct evidence that Baldwin read or saw the *Oresteia*, although a kind of secondary reception through Shakespeare is certainly possible. Because of the lack of any direct or clear line of reception or allusion, I use the idea of haunting throughout this chapter. Hardwick's "fuzzy connections" (2011) also applies.

25 See Vellacott 1962. This would likely be the translation most close at hand for Baldwin. I use Vellacott's language in juxtaposition to Baldwin's, but all other translations are my own.

26 The text of Du Bois' 1903 *The Souls of Black Folk* is available through open access at the Gutenberg Project, https://www.gutenberg.org/files/408/408-h/408-h.htm.

27 Characters beyond the protagonists might include Lorenzo who, like the other black characters, makes the case for consideration as fully human. "I don't want to be better than they are," when in fact "I got as much right to be bad as anybody else."

28 Richard believes that "some white man pushed her down those steps," whereas the character Mother Henry reports that his mother slipped on a staircase and fell.

29 See Mitchell 2012. Anecdotally, a Southern white writer I invited to a production of *Blues* in 2019 walked out of the play early in the first act, disgusted by the caricature he saw on stage in the portrayal of Lyle and others in the white part of Plaguestown. I believe this disgust was more a function of the acting and directing than of Baldwin's play or writing.

30 J. Peter Euben puts the case as follows: "Without his inheritance Orestes is a nonentity. Yet with it he is cursed" (1982: 27).

31 Baldwin writes these words in his description of Ava Gardner, a white actress and a "buddy" who expresses a desire to play Billie Holiday on film, notwithstanding the fact the Billie "had been widely rumored to be black" (2011 [1976]: 100).

32 I will take up gender more fully in Chapter 5, but it is worthwhile here to note that Baldwin, himself an out queer man during an era hostile to the public acceptance of homosexuality within and across racial lines, could be extremely sophisticated in addressing gender and sexuality. He was ahead of his time, although the subtle ways that he discussed gender and sexuality are not necessarily evident in *Blues*, where male characters of *Blues*, Black and white alike, are at the forefront. The example of his treatment of Billie Holiday in *Devil* should serve to convey Baldwin's sensitivity to dynamics of gender and power. Discussing Holiday's portrayal by Diana Ross in the 1972 film, *Lady Sings the Blues*, Baldwin reminds his reader of the horrific violence she encountered at the hands of men of every hue. These foundational terrors included young Billie's loss of her father to a lynching, an event that she describes as engendering the song "Strange Fruit." Baldwin calls upon Billie's autobiography as critique of the film, since in the latter "we do not know that she was raped at ten, sentenced, as a result, to a 'Catholic institution' where she beat her hands to 'a bloody damn pulp' when she was locked in with the body of a dead girl" (Baldwin 2011 [1976]: 103). Baldwin adds dimension and background to a flattening of Holiday's life in film, which focuses in on the "fix" that she would later find in drugs, but characterizes her without the deeper context.

33 The North/South distinction is one such distortion, wherein for Lyle, Richard's problem is that he is a "northern nigger." Of Black people, Lyle "just doesn't think they're human." "These people are sick," Juanita is probably pregnant, etc.

34 Baldwin's Meridian hangs his hope on Parnell, the "only white man in this town who's ever *really* stuck his neck out in order to do—to do right."

35 This is the case with Sophocles' *Oedipus* play, where the body politic is corrupted, and miasma confounds all action.

36 In *Eumenides*, Apollo is his "wise teacher" (279). Apollo is, alongside Orestes, "answerable" (*epaitios*, 464, from Orestes, and 579–80, from Apollo himself).

37 There are echoes here of Oedipus' need to leave Thebes and return purified.

38 This is not to accept the revenge versus punishment dichotomy between the *Agamemnon* and the *Libation Bearers*, on the one hand, and the third play in

the trilogy, on the other. Allen has already done well to complicate any simplistic reading of the plays (Allen 2002: 21). Legal punishment exists before 458 BCE, and retribution and vengeance continue after the trilogy.

39 The Christian register of forgiveness is operative in the question of Blacks being the "equal" to their murderers. Instead, Blacks are "equal to" themselves, drawing from another fount of strength and wisdom, perhaps the ancient traditions that Baldwin intimates exist in Black Christianity.

40 "Without his inheritance Orestes is a nonentity. Yet with it he is cursed" (Euben 1982: 27).

41 The inexact role of the mother in ties of blood, *Eumenides* 213ff. The slaying of the mother, *metroktonein* recurring in the text, is central and recurrent, thematically. See, for example, *Eumenides* 427ff., where the chorus is extremely wrought.

42 As Allen puts it of the power to judge, "authority is created by acquiescence" (Allen 2002: 24).

43 Peck 2016 puts these three murders together in the most compelling, filmic representation, based on Baldwin's unpublished reflections.

44 For a deeper analysis of the connection between the American South and broader actions within the United States as late as 2020, see Richardson 2020.

45 See Menard 2021. More on Brustein in Chapter 4.

46 For Mitchell, the "black actor" is the focal point of Baldwin's theorizing about theater, "not the audience" (Mitchell 2012: 34).

47 Go to https://time.com/longform/beale-street-could-talk-true-story/, for the story.

48 For an analysis of the United States as a colonial power, see Gilroy 2006.

CHAPTER THREE

1 I credit Allannah Karas for bringing this piece to my attention in her 2022 lecture on Black art and the classics at Baylor University, which can be read in her chapter for the 2024 publication, *Radical Formalism* (eds. Sarah Nooter and Mario Telò).

2 Go to https://whitney.org/collection/works/11712.

3 Lecznar 2020 does inscribe Soyinka's as a racial treatment of Euripides' *Bacchae*, but he does not transport the analysis to the United States.

4 On the problematic non-humanness of Black women in biology and European philosophy, see Jackson 2020.

5 Segments of the actual interview can be found on YouTube, although the crucial portion discussed below is missing from the sequence. Comparison

of selected scenes between the play, later a Ron Howard-directed film (2008), and the actual interviews can be accessed here: https://www.youtube.com/watch?v=rVaKJlE4Tqk.

6 On the debate, see Gellman 2022.

7 Semele is the daughter of Cadmus, the founder of the city, whose grandson Pentheus is currently ruling the land. As I have already indicated, racial miscegenation (i.e., incorporating the god Dionysus) would be one of the phantasmas of the period, as such promiscuity, to cite the Penthean projection, can unravel a social order. See Gantz 1993.

8 Dionysus presides over wine and sexual liberation, and Pentheus, who is also the god's cousin, will have none of his revolutionary potentiality in his city. In his article on the play, Schechner (1961) makes Dionysus, not Pentheus, the real villain of the play.

9 On the racial dimensions—broadly, European and African, see Lecznar 2020. Thompson's "Triumph of Bacchus" returns us to the epiphanic possibilities of Dionysus during this period, one that Baraka and Soyinka also sense.

10 Indeed, Pentheus is concerned about the women's sexual activity on the mountain side, but their militaristic revolt, including their sack of the rural community, is the actual site of interest reported back. In fact, the play repeatedly refers to the women's lack of sexual activity or drunkenness.

11 King had escaped many previous attempts on his life, and Barack Obama became the most protected president in U.S. history because he was the most threatened.

12 My reading in some ways picks up on John Levi Barnard's idea of an anti-imperial strand in Black American letters. See Barnard 2018.

13 For Hinton's death, see Malcolm X 1992; for Stokes, Malcolm X's words at his murder on May 5, 1962 can be found here: https://www.youtube.com/watch?v=D-Da4b1HF6k.

14 The spending in dollars since 1961, according to *The New York Times*, May 1, 1975, was $141 billion.

15 For a sense of the ongoing struggle to extend rights to include voting, housing, and other inalienable rights, see Johnson 1968.

16 Baldwin shows a sensitivity to the question of language as something the subaltern can possess—perhaps even master and reform. For example, in his discussion of how he came to appreciate William Shakespeare (cited in the previous chapter), he reveals that his previous resistance to Shakespeare owed to the fact that he did not recognize the English language as his own. He later realized, however, that English might be "made to bear the burden of my experience if I could find the stamina to challenge it, and me, to such a

test" (Baldwin 2010: 67) A witness to the appropriation of language for which Baldwin strives were "my black ancestors, who evolved the sorrow song, the blues, and jazz, and created an entirely new idiom in an overwhelmingly hostile place." Beginning with language, Baldwin would enter an anticolonial process, that of coming to understand the degree to which Black Americans were from one perspective not so much a minority within the United States, but more a people unto themselves, with separate cultural norms to be upheld as part of the resistance to colonial power.

17 The term Global South seems to have picked up in usage later than the period with which I am concerned in this chapter, but there is precedent for its use at the end of the 1960s. See Oglesby 1969.

18 "Possibility" or some form of it is repeated over a dozen times in the essay.

19 From a national perspective, the Black population constituted a "subjugated" people, in Baldwin's language. It would be a "terrible" thing for Americans to think that one-ninth of its population was beneath them, and yet this was precisely the situation.

20 See the Introduction of this book.

21 King (1967b) famously spoke at Riverside Church in April of 1967. In addition to the transcript at the digital archive, the speech can also be heard online.

22 As King put it in his speech "Why I am Opposed to the War in Vietnam" (1967a), "The greatest irony and tragedy of all is that our nation, which initiated so much of the revolutionary spirit of the modern world, is now cast in the mold of being an arch anti-revolutionary."

23 His appearance on the *Merv Griffin Show* in 1967 is an example of this. His response to a questioner who asked if those opposed to the war were traitors to the country amplifies his position on Vietnam, conscientious object to war, and communism.

24 The term is one that recurs throughout Blanco and Peeren 2013 and is from Derrida, as his figure for what a ghost means within culture. As he puts it, "undecidability is always a determinate oscillation between possibilities (for example, of meaning but also of acts)" (Blanco and Peeren 2013: 175).

25 See, for example, Euripides' *Bacchae* 216–225, where he indicts the Maenads for using Bacchic worship as an excuse for promiscuous sex.

26 See, for example, Duong 2019, although it pertains to a different period.

27 Lecznar calls Schechner's deployment of Dionysus "racial" because the playwright turns to Euripides' *Bacchae* for a sense of European, cultural authenticity. Asmat ceremonies are not European, but "to define the Greek theatre that he wants to align with Western 'traditional' theatre, he invokes

Nietzsche and *The Birth of Tragedy*" (Lecznar 2020: 157). Transported from ancient Greece to some degree through Nietzsche, Dionysus, as Schechner saw, "is present in today's America—showing himself in the hippies, in the 'carnival spirit' of black insurrectionists, on campuses; and even, in disguise, on the patios and in the living-rooms of suburbia" (Zeitlin 2004: 53), although he did not incorporate these Black insurrectionists into his fictional, dramatic epiphanies.

28 In *Dionysus after Nietzsche: The Birth of Tragedy in Twentieth-Century Literature and Thought*, Adam Lecznar traces Schechner's own development of his approach to performance to interactions with "luminaries like Paul de Man, Tzvetan Todorov, René Girard, Jacques Derrida, Roland Barthes and Jacque Lacan" (Lecznar 2020: 142). Already a Ph.D. in 1962, Schechner encountered these scholars at the 1966 conference in Baltimore, Maryland. Lecznar methodically builds his case for the connection between Schechner and these intellectuals, demonstrating Schechner's own groping toward a performative or ritual theory of drama. At the 1966 conference, in response to Barthes' sense that "drama requires a specific critical lexicon," Schechner seeks instead a "language of gesture" (Lecznar 2020: 144). He is interested in how the experience of performance can lead to cultural revolution, and spiritual revelation. He turns to ritual to enliven his sense of drama.

29 Victor Turner defined Experimental Theatre, perhaps a precursor to Environmental Theatre, as follows: "'Experimental' theatre is nothing less than 'performed,' in other words, 'restored' experience, that moment in the experimental process – that often prolonged and internally segmented 'moment' – in which meaning emerges through 'reliving' the original experience (often a social drama subjectively perceived), and is given an appropriate aesthetic form" (Turner 2001: 18). It is worth noting that this movement was felt from as far afield as London, England, to Lagos, Nigeria. See Fischer-Lichte in Hall et al. 2004.

30 The *New York Times* reviewer of *There Was A Country*, Achebe's memoir of the war, finds the famous author's nostalgia "jarring and misplaced" (Nossiter 2012). From Achebe's perspective at the time, Biafra's secession from Nigeria was "simply politically and military unwise," although he expresses this from the perspective of an Igbo writer. As late as 2020, proponents of Biafra secession remain wistful for an independent African state autonomous from Nigeria.

31 Characterizing the conflict in *Half of a Yellow Sun* (titled for the planet emblazoned on the Biafra flag), Nigerian novelist Chimamanda Ngozi Adichie

captures the revolutionary zeal in Nigeria through the character Edna, a black woman from Montgomery, Alabama. In the novel, American soldiers dismissively see Biafra as "under Britain's sphere of influence." The Igbo secessionists, however, see their struggle as akin to that of Black liberation in the U.S. The alignment I am suggesting overly reduces a war that was fought over power and control of a burgeoning country, but it demonstrates the power of culture, so impactful as to serve as grounds for armed conflict. See Adichie 2006: 324.

32 Soyinka voiced an overall skepticism about the postcolonial project of negritude that had captured the imagination of his contemporaries across the African continent (Lecznar 2020), the same ideas Baldwin had encountered in 1956. Nevertheless, he wanted to repossess theater as an African phenomenon, especially as it pertained to ritual and performance. The play is a "black racial" document (Lecznar 2020: 163), one that challenges Schechner's equally racial proposition. Soyinka "uses the conjunction of race and tragedy to reflect on the revolutionary hopes of earlier anticolonial thinkers, and to reconsider them at the dawn of the postcolonial age" (164).

33 In Yoruba cosmology, a slave shatters the original unity, Atunda, to create a new order. See Bishop 1983.

34 In the translation of Euripides' *Bacchae* on which Soyinka relied, the word "slave" occurs five times, reflecting the limited role of that character in the play. In Euripides' play, slaves are called upon to put out the fire to the royal palace that Dionysus sets, and they are mentioned only a few other times. In Soyinka's adaptation, however, there are over fifty references to "slave."

35 The character of the Old Slave, at the beginning of the play, absent from the Greek source, articulates Christianity's ultimate sacrificial ritual, the death of Christ on behalf of his followers: "We know full well that some must die ... lest we die" (Soyinka 2004: 18). The slaves are washing the courthouse, ritually preparing for the New Year. See also Wright 1990.

36 Ogun as first actor is a revision of the European genealogy of theater, where Thespis breaks from the dancers, who represent the collective, to perform an independent role.

37 It is worth noting that in *Myth, Literature, and the African World*, Soyinka (1990) turns to actual, New World cultures of enslaved people, such as Brazil, as sites of "a significant piece in the fabric of Yoruba metaphysics." Any number of practices across the New World testify to the role of the suppressed subaltern in anticolonial efforts, the slave being the ultimate subaltern, socially dead. In Salvador, Brazil, for example, the *lavagem* or "ritual washing" of the church of Bom Fim is a New Year's ritual that draws 2½ million people annually.

Lecznar sees that the slave leader in the play, whom Soyinka's stage directions say should be "fully negroid," allows the playwright "to create complex links between the Nietzschean tradition of ancient Greece and the ideology of négritude" (Lecznar 2020: 180). As with the "double edged" cultural realities described in *Aké* (Soyinka 1989) and about which Baldwin reported in 1956, the washing is a syncretic experience, a Christian tradition that masks deeper African ties—or perhaps an African ritual disguised in European clothing. This is not the assimilation that replaces "habits of feeling ... and thinking" but rather evidence of how memory returns in unexpected ways.

38 The fourth stage is indeed, as Lecznar sees it, an "enforced individuality and exclusion from the connectivity that underpins the world" (2020: 173), and it is within this space that the participants in the ritual drama that Soyinka creates experience ecstasy.

39 As Astrid van Weyenberg argues, "Soyinka does not ignore history" (75), any more than did his American counterparts. Rather, having served time as a political prisoner, Soyinka well recognized the limits of his power, whereas by waging war on the cultural battlefield, he "displays a mythopoetic attitude to history, in which all experience is transformed into trans-historical dimensions" (van Weyenberg 2013: 75).

40 See Manning 2006: 10. Susan Manning discusses the idea of cross-viewing across the 2006 book on modern dance.

41 See the previous chapter on Baldwin's discussion of theater from *The Devil Finds Work*.

42 The references are too many to mention, but even before the bloody dismemberment of Pentheus at the end of the play, the audience hears of the substitute, the blood of a sacrificial goat, from the chorus' first ode. As it pertains to fire, the symbol extends the figuration of Dionysus throughout the play as Bromius, who thunders with the fiery bolts of his father. The celestial fire touches down on Semele's tomb and is persistently connected to Dionysus.

43 Baraka was formerly LeRoi Jones, a beatnik poet in New York City who was married to the poet Hettie Cohen and moved in circles with Allen Ginsberg and Jack Kerouac.

44 See Dieke 1990 for a fuller argument of Dionysus in the work. See, again, Lecznar 2020 on Dionysus after Nietzsche. The hero of Baraka's novella, Roi, is "Baraka's black prototype of the Dionysian hero, a hero born out of primal instincts and urges, orgiastic rites and drunken frenzy," all of which Dionysus represents (108). He is "molded out of the Dionysian myth of suffering and death, of being constantly sundered from himself" (109).

45 Heron's poem appears on the album, *Flying Dutchman*, which is also resonant with Baraka's play, *The Dutchman* (Baraka 2002 [1964].

46 In addition to race, class consciousness is also an important feature of the treatise. "The Revolutionary Theatre" hears "the mad cries of the poor" (Baraka 1965).

47 See Gantz 1993 for background on the idea of Dionysus being twice-born, having first been dismembered as Zagreus.

48 Papp's sentiment echoed what Brustein wrote about Baldwin, for which, see the previous chapter. Brustein will figure in conversation with August Wilson, in the next chapter.

49 Papp, of course, was a king- and queen-maker on the New York theater scene, understanding well the tastes of the theatergoing audience in the city. At the same time, as the child of Jewish immigrants who had grown up extremely poor, Papp was eager to expand that audience, within reasonable measure. Having founded Shakespeare in the Park in 1954, he was able to secure funds to open the Delacorte Theater on June 18, 1962 (Turan and Papp 2009). His idea of having theater that would be "free for all" led to exhilarating episodes of "collective effervescence" (Best 2021), such as the performance of Shakespeare's *Romeo and Juliet* where Puerto Rican kids screamed out to Romeo, who believes Juliet to be dead and will now take his own life, "Don't do it, Romeo! Don't do it! She ain't dead!" (Turan and Papp 2009: 102). When it came to theater that pushed audiences' tastes through its characters, however, Papp was much more conservative. He recognized that even the musical *Hair*, which brought the free-love, gender, and racial revolution to the stage in 1967, "was really a white man's show" (Turan and Papp 2009: 195).

50 It is worth a summary of Gordone's play (2019 [1969]). On its surface, *No Place to Be Somebody* would seem jarring for audiences, absorbing and reflecting some of the revolutionary energy of 1969. After King's assassination in 1968, social unrest had ensued in cities across the country. There were uprisings across over a hundred cities, which bled into national politics, owing to protests over the ongoing war in Vietnam, by the time of the Democratic National Convention in Chicago, in August. These protests included anti-war, Women's Rights, and various Black organizations. Premièring on May 2, *No Place* is set in "Johnny's Bar," where "the napalm of hurt has seared each man's skin," as the *Time* review had it, echoing the language of war, napalm being the incendiary chemical blend that the United States military used against Vietnamese. As bar proprietor Johnny "Cakes" Williams, who is Black and a pimp, puts it, "We at war.

Black against white." Johnny is a foil to Gabe Gabriel, "the nearly white actor and playwright who finds himself becoming blacker than black in his search for identity." In one scene, Gabe is angelically singing the Christian hymn, "Whiter Than Snow." The singer's plea to God to "wash me, and I shall be whiter than snow" shifts from an assertion of existential sin to the curse of being black. Throughout the play, Gordone indulges the audience in Johnny's get-rich and anti-establishment (read antiwhite) schemes, both as a pimp and a gangster, while Gabe pursues a higher calling of personal artistry, as a writer, which another Black character mirrors in his desire to be a ballet dancer. In its setting and characters, *No Place* to some extent borrows from Eugene O'Neill's *Iceman Cometh*, Johnny's criminal mentor Sweets Crane returning to the scene after years in prison but now professing to be reformed. Reviews of *No Place* identified with the human struggles of these black figures, seeing in them a kind of roundedness of character, even in Johnny's ambitious but sordid aims. Gabe is "the spokesman for black moderation," who in contrast to Johnny "eventually realizes that he will achieve nothing by making himself into a pretend-black out of guilt." In *No Place*, there is certainly, for the audience, a good deal of "sad sentimental groping for a warmth" in the despair. This is the case both with the Black characters and with the young, innocent white girl, Mary Lou Bolton, on whom Johnny is a corrupting influence. Stopping into Johnny's Bar en route to a civil rights protest, she asserts that social justice is "everyone's responsibility," before the audience witnesses her slippage due to wayward admiration for Johnny White; audiences, however, could remain viewers or voyeurs of whom nothing is asked, no moral or ethical response required.

51 Her comments can be seen and heard at Shange and McIntyre 2013.

52 Compellingly, when asked in 2012 if she would add anything to the play's original production, she answers that she would add a piece linking women to theaters of combat, by they serving in the armed forces, or "girls in Afghanistan" contending with their martial surroundings (Shange and McIntyre 2013).

53 Go to https://www.merriam-webster.com/dictionary/shaman.

54 The diversity to which I am referring is encoded in the 1978 U.S. Supreme Court decision, *Regents of the University of California v. Bakke*.

55 There is an ongoing association of Bacchic figures, like Orpheus, to Christ and the eucharist, which, as we have seen, is discernable in Soyinka's *Bacchae*.

CHAPTER FOUR

1 See Dowland 2018, who directly places "family values" as a political slogan and agenda after the 1960s cultural revolution and into the 1970s, the interval between these last two chapters.

2 On kinship as a fiction, see Butler 2017.

3 See Schanberg 1984 for early coverage; see also LaBouvier et al. 2019 for a comprehensive set of articles on the case and the Basquiat work emanating from it, "Defacement."

4 Basquiat's "Charles the First," which links Charlie Parker in mythological lineage to King Charles I and Thor, is an example. See Mitter 2019 for image and review of the 2019 Guggenheim exhibition. For an extensive look at "Defacement," through the exhibition's catalogue, see LaBouvier et al. 2019.

5 See Hinojosa 1997, Fried 1999, and Toobin 2002, which profiles Charles Schwarz, a police officer who was convicted in 1999 for taking part in the brutality. Because it is so unthinkable, it is worth recounting what Justin Volpe, the officer who was the main assailant, did to Abner: "The 'driver' [of the police car, which was a role ascribed to Schwarz] then lifted Louima by his handcuffs and Volpe rammed the broom handle into Louima's rectum, rupturing his bladder and rectum. (The attack led to massive internal injuries, causing Louima to be given a colostomy bag to let him defecate and a cystostomy tube to help him urinate.) Volpe put the broom handle in front of Louima's face. 'That's your shit,' he said. His pants still around his knees, Louima was then taken to a holding cell" (Toobin 2002).

6 See Smith 2019 and Alexander 2020.

7 More on Baldwin and queerness in the next chapter, but Mullen 2019 contextualizes Baldwin as a queer theorist even before the coming of its complex theorization by the early twenty-first century.

8 Barnard 2018 explores this claim, particularly as it pertains to Charles Chestnutt's 1889 "The Origins of the Hatchet Story," and the hagiography of Washington's honesty, having cut down the cherry tree. In Chestnutt's story, the Washingtonian hagiography is found to have originated with the Egyptian son of Ramses III, whose hatchet kills an enslaved person: "The violation and destruction of enslaved human bodies instead of trees make apparent the real historical violence that is hidden in such hagiographic and nationalistic accounts of the country's founding" (Barnard 2018: 131).

9 The reference is to the title character of Richard Wright's 1940 novel, *Native Son*, who is condemned after the predictable fate of murdering two women, one white, the other Black.

10 Beyond tragic, in American society the lynched Black figure, the "Boy Breaking Glass" of Gwendolyn Brooks' poem, which I discuss in the previous chapter, does not mature. This is the strange fruit that rots on trees before it ripens. If mature, the Black male figure is emasculated. Such a symbol as Oedipus, moreover, is already problematic from the standpoint of whether Oedipus could represent anything other than the heteronormative family based on kinship.

11 As evidence, consider the birther claims against Obama, the idea that he was born outside of the United States and—somehow an equivalent scandal—was only pretending to be Christian. See the previous chapter.

12 The 1988 incident was revisited when George H.W. Bush died in 2018. See, for example, Baker 2018 and Scott 2018.

13 The Report's influence on the sociology of the Black family is unquestionable. For the ongoing return to it, see, for example, Patterson 2016.

14 This strand of thought extends into the twenty-first century, with the idea of a complete disintegration of values. See Deneen 2016, who argues that liberalism went too far in dismantling shared values and ideals. Deneen's arguments are well-encapsulated on his Podcast with Ezra Klein, available at https://www.nytimes.com/2022/05/13/opinion/ezra-klein-podcast-patrick-deneen.html.

15 For an overview of Richard Nixon's creation of the War on Crime mantra and its failure, see Vorenberg 1972.

16 It is worth comparing this iteration of schizophrenia to Baldwin's idea of white desire as it pertains to Black people. See Chapter 2.

17 Bottici 2014 replaces words like "fantasy" and "imaginary" with "imaginal," arguing that "in contrast to imagination and imaginary, the concept of imaginal emphasizes the centrality of images, rather than the faculty or the context that produces them; therefore, it does not make any assumptions about the individual or social character of such a faculty" (5).

18 See, for example, the *60 Minutes* episode that aired in 2020, for an overview of the idea ("Examining Excited Delirium" 2020).

19 See Redden 2021, and Kartik-Narayan 2018 for the arguments in favor of trauma-informed responses.

20 See https://www.cdc.gov/mmwr/preview/mmwrhtml/mm5021a2.htm#tab1.

21 Klonoff and Landrine 1999. The statement in question was "HIV/AIDS is a man-made virus that the federal government made to kill and wipe out black people." This theory persisted well into the 2000s. See Nattrass 2013.

22 For the Nixon-aide John Ehrlichman's late confession that the War on Drugs was racially motivated, go to https://www.govinfo.gov/content/pkg/

BILLS-115hres933ih/html/BILLS-115hres933ih.htm. For the Reagan resumption of the rhetoric after President Jimmy Carter's term in office, see https://www.reaganfoundation.org/ronald-reagan/nancy-reagan/her-causes/.

23 The story of the Central Park Five has now been retold in the 2019 film *When They See Us*, which Ava DuVernay co-wrote and directed.

24 For Trump's continued commitment to this position, even after the exoneration of the five accused men, go to https://www.bbc.com/news/world-us-canada-48687356.

25 The insidiousness of this myth cannot be overstated. In a January 21, 1983 question-and-answer session with high schoolers, President Reagan responded to such questions as whether he was more concerned with the military than "the problems of the, say, middle class, unfortunate, and the poor and their welfare beings." To another such question, the president responded, citing "one case in Chicago when a woman finally was tried who was collecting welfare under 123 different names." He offers that the case "hasn't been matched far and wide," but he created and perpetuated the fantasy: https://www.nytimes.com/1976/02/15/archives/welfare-queen-becomes-issue-in-reagan-campaign-hitting-a-nerve-now.html. See Reagan 1983.

26 For a female-centered, "reparative" response to Freud, see Klein 2002.

27 The previous chapter on the Dionysus paradigm amplifies this position.

28 The trope of fugitivity proliferated by the 2010s, so much so that in 2018, a white woman, Jessica A. Krug, posing as Black, published a book on the subject and had a successful academic career, attending conferences that could be viewed on YouTube, until she was uncovered. The George Washington University Department of History, where she worked, released a statement that her conduct "has raised questions about the veracity of her own research and teaching," cited in *The New Yorker* profile published on September 12, 2020 (Jackson 2020). For a more earnest perspective on fugitivity, see Moten and Harney 2004.

29 See McConnell in Bosher et al. 2015 for an analysis.

30 Macintosh 2004 raises the chief example of Laurence Olivier playing Oedipus in 1945.

31 In 2018, BAM revived the play. Its executive director Joseph V. Melillo was in his last year overseeing the Next Wave Festival, which Harvey Lichtenstein founded in 1983 and where *Gospel* debuted. BAM was a struggling venue when Melillo became its director.

32 Peter Libbey (2018), writing for *The New York Times*, put it as follows: "The story of Oedipus is supposed to be timeless, for better or worse. In Mark-Anthony

Turnage's 'Greek,' Sophocles' tragedy plays out on the troubled streets of 1980s London, where the renamed Eddy tries to avoid fulfilling a fortune teller's prediction but winds up in the arms of a curiously familiar cafe manager."

33 See Woolfe 2018. In *The New York Times* review, he continues by noting that Eddy "longs for a life fancier than that of his pub-going parents," consistent with the individualism of the "me" era. The play's staging and its denouement, however, the "slow, frieze-like procession that leads the blinded Eddy offstage," is "an image of love and community, as well as sadness" (Woolfe 2018). Reviewing the play for *The New York Times* as well, Roslyn Sulcas describes the "trash strewn streets of contemporary London" that *Greek* inhabits, where the plagues are "unemployment, poverty, police brutality and consumerism" (Sulcas 2018).

34 See the Introduction of this book for the language of haunting.

35 The Next Wave Festival, patterned after its namesake in Melbourne, Australia, brought exciting new work that revitalized the venue, which in 2021 boasted three performance spaces, an opera house, and is a vibrant hub for film. For a catalogue of images and productions, see Serafin and Yung 2018.

36 Freud 2017; translation by H. W. Chase.

37 Fundamental to understanding the classical sources of Freud's use of the idea of phantasy, the "visual impression" from Stoic philosophy (21), is Gregory A. Staley's *Seneca and the Idea of Tragedy* (2010). *Phantasia*, as Staley clarifies, is to the Stoics the mental image and its "vivid recreation" in poetry or onstage (Staley 2010: 32).

38 As Gregory A. Staley puts it of Freud's use of the image of Juno from the *Aeneid* for his epigraph in the 1900 *The Interpretation of Dreams*, "Freud turns to Vergil to thematize his discussion of the soul because poetry offers an image of what even science, with its methods and measurements, cannot see" (Staley 2010: 101).

39 Freud speculates that the story would have played better in Euripides' "critical" hands, but Sophocles "the believer" steers his character down the blind path of religion.

40 The religious portents of the play are something akin to what Staley defines as Senecan *monstra*, the "shocking, unnatural events that offered warnings from the gods" (Staley 2010: 22).

41 Such *monstra* challenge the rational order that Freud imagined.

42 Ricardo Khan directed the play, which premiered at Crossroads Theatre in New Jersey in 1997 and the Kennedy Center in Washington, D.C., during the same year.

43 The quote is from the company's mission statement, which can be found at https://www.crossroadstheatrecompany.org/about#mission.

44 For religion during the Haitian Revolution, see Dubois 2005; in *Darker Face*, Rankine 2013.

45 Staging the drama at the University of Georgia in 2012, Director Freda Scott Giles, who was also Associate Professor, notes the play's "resonance in our present" as Americans and our need to encounter the past "as we step into our collective future." This gesture toward a collective future is consonant with one other goal of the Crossroads Theatre Company, that of "promot[ing] a deeper, more informed cross-cultural conversation on community, our interconnectedness, the histories we share and don't share." See Canup 2012.

46 For the argument pertaining to narrative form and classical reception through the play, see Rankine 2013.

47 The director of a Washington University production in 2001, Andrea Urice, puts it as follows: "For slaves, the white power structure must have been as capricious and unyielding as the will of the Greek gods" (Otten 2001).

48 The is reminiscent of the self-fathering which the protagonist of Ralph Ellison's *Invisible Man* pointed: "Be your own father, young man." (1980 [1952]).

49 A review of *Closing* from ten years after its initial publication notes the book's "anti-democratic" thesis (Green 1998: 29), stating that from Bloom's perspective, "the academic body must necessarily detach itself from democracy."

50 It is worth clarifying that by "political" Bloom here is specifically referring to something like a separation between church and state. Like the state, the university was a space to be pure from contact with its counterpart, in this case the political realm (like the corrupting church in the analogy). Bloom recognized and reveled in the placement of his students in political spheres. Bellow 2002 indulges in these associations.

51 Ravelstein encounters Michael Jackson in a restaurant in Paris and rails even more revealingly. See Bellow 2002.

52 For LORT (League of Resident Theaters) membership of 77 theaters in 2021, see http://lort.org.

53 As Osipovich (2004) argues, critics have enlisted Rousseau into each of two camps, on the one side, the moralists who believe theater directly interacts with and impacts social and political life, and the autonomists, on the other.

54 IQ is the *g* factor in James J. Heckman's review for the *Journal of Political Economy* (Heckman 1995: 1091).

55 A longer quote from Kaye might be worthwhile: "That *The Bell Curve* has 'struck a chord' or 'touches an open nerve' (depending on one's point of view) is clear. That it can serve as 'an ideological marker for the period'" (Duster 1995) or a "mirror for our morally exhausted Times (*Newsweek*), in which

much is also revealed "about the intellectual temper of our era" (Murray 1995a) may well be true. But which "chords," whose "nerves" and what "ideologies?" What precisely does this "mirror" reveal to us about the state of our nation, and, incidentally, the state of our discipline as well" (Kaye 1996: 79)?

56 I mean this term here not quite as Blackface, although casting Oedipus as Black, as I have demonstrated, leads to significations that are consonant with such performances, as Moses 1993 helped to illuminate. Rather, by Black[ened] I mean more generally the processes by which human beings are made within culture into racial embodiments. On Black[ened], see, for example, Wilderson 2020 and Jackson 2020.

57 Go to https://web.archive.org/web/20090827084308/http://www.arts.gov/resources/Accessibility/NTCP.html.

58 Same as above.

59 This is the *megalothumos* or "great-souled" personality. See Rankine 2013 and Rankine in Bosher et al. 2015.

60 As Rousseau writes, autonomists believe that theater takes its cues from the society rather than influencing it. Osipovich convincingly argues that Rousseau parses theater's processes not only on this first level, but also on two others.

61 Highlights from the debate are available on Terry Gross' National Public Radio show "Fresh Air," here, https://www.youtube.com/watch?v=Dfc_u3Xdyf8.

62 See previous note.

63 The author was, incidentally, born into this neighborhood at an institution called the Brooklyn Jewish Hospital, which has since shut down operation.

64 I was able to watch a recording of the play at the New York Public Library's Theatre on Film and Tape Archive (TOFT).

CHAPTER FIVE

1 See Introduction for discussion of the spectacular. Cf. Goldsby 2006.

2 Go to https://www.matthewshepard.org/about-us/our-story/.

3 Go to https://buffalonews.com/news/killing-of-gay-stirs-concern-poll-shows/article_2a4f8686-0489-51e5-bb71-5f095a6b2682.html.

4 Go to https://www.justice.gov/crt/matthew-shepard-and-james-byrd-jr-hate-crimes-prevention-act-2009-0.

5 In some portion of the collective conscience, there would be a connection between Matt's death and that of Emmett Till, and the federal legislation affirms this. Along with gender, sexual orientation, gender identity, or disability, the indices of race, color, religion, and national origin in the 2009

legislation continued the legacies of the 1964 and 1965 Civil Rights Act and Voting Rights Act, in language and intention.

6 For the full poem, go to https://www.poetryfoundation.org/poems/56983/the-lynching.

7 For the Tectonic Theater Project's assent in 2000, we might take as a precursor the documentary theater of Anna Deavere Smith, whose 1993 *Fires in the Mirror* embodied and relived the lives of members of the Brooklyn community involved in the killing of Gavin Cato, the 7-year-old Black boy whom a Jewish man stuck with his car (see Smith 1993).

8 These descriptions are taken from the project's website, at https://www.tectonictheaterproject.org.

9 The play is part of *The Laramie Project*'s framework. The University of Wyoming acting student Jedediah Schultz hears his mother telling him this supposed truth when he reports that he will audition for the university production of *Angels in America*, the 1991 foundational theatrical text of HIV/AIDs and its impact, written by Tony Kushner.

10 See Rao 2020: 2.

11 Broadly speaking, *Head Over Heels* itself was notable for its queering of at least two noteworthy phenomena from the European stage: Greek classical drama, with the shamanistic character Pythio, a nonbinary oracle; and the Elizabethan stage, as the musical is an adaptation of Sir Philip Sidney's pastoral poem, *The Countess of Pembroke's Arcadia*. the story of the daughters of Basilius, the king of Arcadia, Pamela and Piloclea, his daughters, and ending with the authority (if not actual rule) of the queen, Gynecia. In the hand of Tony Award-winning author Jeff Daniel Whitty, Arcadia becomes a liberatory queer space. Gender reversal and disguise-and-recognition scenes that audiences have come to know from the most famous Elizabethan, Shakespeare, are premises for trans- and nonbinary identity, as well as the revelation of true love as opposed to the normative male suitor. Pamela's female handmaiden Mopsa is her romantic partner, the culminating, comic outcome being their happy union. Pamela's sister Piloclea has long been in love with Musidorus, who is gendered as a man but who attracts both Basilius and Gynecia when he cross-dresses as a woman, Cleophila. In addition to the fluid role of Musidorus, the audience learns that Pythio, who identifies as they, are Mopsa's mother. Miss Peppermint, who had been a runner-up on the television show "RuPaul's Drag Race," plays the role of Pythio.

12 Rao's case in point is India, not a Western nation, but his observations apply as a matter of a study of the nation view from the perspective of international relations.

13 In 2017, in fact, when Public Theater staged a production of Shakespeare's *Julius Caesar* "that depicted a Donald Trump lookalike character being assassinated," which Eustis directed, his wife Laurie received threats. See Gray 2017.

14 In her book, *Reclaiming Greek Drama for Diverse Audiences* (2020), Melinda Powers enlists the discourse of diversity and inclusion in the progressive cause. The book ranges widely across classical reception frameworks and audiences for performance: African American reception and bodies, Latinx performance, gendered receptions among women and LGBTQI groups, and disability studies and performance. There are risks but tangible payoffs in the range of subjects Powers covers. Consistent with Eustis' observations, these productions want to push their audiences to hear other viewpoints, and they sometimes do so by trading in stereotypes in order to overcome them, what Powers calls "'executing the stereotype', i.e. playing up a stereotype with the intention of eliminating it" (53). Such an approach, however, "can work against the playwright's intentions and inadvertently reinforce the very stereotypes it aims to overturn" (54).

15 For a broad application of queer theory across the Euripidean corpus, see Olsen and Telò 2022. In that volume, Patrice Rankine writes on *Helen* but primarily from the perspective of the othering—or queering—of the Egyptian character, Theoclymenus. Helen herself is not a focal point of this essay.

16 Isherwood was not yet at *The New York Times*, where he would move in 2004.

17 See Rankine 2013 and Rankine in Bosher et al. 2015.

18 See, for example, Pierce 2002. The presence of Io recalls a play with another hero at the margins of society, where she encounters him on her travels: Aeschylus' *Prometheus Bound*. Helen as Prometheus underscores McLaughlin's move to further lionize her feminist character, but Helen's whiteness is regressive, too second-wave feminist in its normativity to speak for broader democratic constituencies.

19 Brantley places it "in a postmodern tradition that is starting to feel threadbare."

20 Brantley concludes that McLaughlin has not given the director Tony Kushner much to work with.

21 Aspects of the interview are incorporated in *Ten Years Later* (2014). See also Lee 2004.

22 Susan Muska and Gréta Olafsdóttir's 1998 documentary, *The Brandon Teena Story*, preceded *Boys Don't Cry* and conveys some of the crucial events, such as Sheriff Charles Laux's interrogation of Brandon. See also Jones 2016 for a detailed account of the events around Teena's murder.

23 Laux falls into a Foucauldian trap, wherein sex—both the organs of its performance, and the acts of sex themselves—is the *telos*, the thing to see and know. Rather than a focus on sex, both the organs and how they appear and perform, a focus on sexuality, which is a discourse or cultural phenomenon, allows for a deeper understanding of what occurred.

24 Brendix 2018 conveys some of the lingering controversies of the film *Boys Don't Cry*, twenty years later, and in particular the struggle of trans* representation.

25 The 1996 Defense of Marriage Act begins as follows: "H.R. 3396, the Defense of Marriage Act, has two primary purposes. The first is to defend the institution of traditional heterosexual marriage. The second is to protect the right of the States to formulate their own public policy regarding the legal recognition of same-sex unions, free from any federal constitutional implications that might attend the recognition by one State of the right for homosexual couples to acquire marriage licenses." The act, which separates a federal "defense" from states' rights to craft their own approaches, can be found at https://www.congress.gov/104/crpt/hrpt664/CRPT-104 hrpt664.pdf.

26 I have been unable to verify this claim beyond the two newspaper articles of *The Chicago Tribune*, https://archive.ph/20071016104201/http://findarticles.com/p/articles/mi_qn4155/is_20000311/ai_n13848099, and specifically to the white trash comment, *The Age*, https://www.theage.com.au/entertainment/movies/seeing-doubles-20020301-gduoft.html.

27 This is a word that would be used in the Brandon Teena case as well as that of Matthew Shepard.

28 Kaufman et al. 2014: 56. Fluty "lost ten pounds and lost my hair" because AZT is "a mean, nasty medicine. Mean."

29 Whether deliberate or inadvertent, the reference in the film version calls to mind the 1938 Thornton Wilder play, *Our Town*.

30 The film version of the play features a restaurant with the sign, "Put Yourself in Our Place."

31 At the time of Matt's murder, the population of Laramie, Wyoming was approximately 27,000.

32 On myth as grounding groups in significant narratives, see Chapter 1.

33 The making of the setting is reminiscent of "Plaguestown" in James Baldwin's *Blues for Mister Charlie*, and Ralph Ellison's essay "Harlem is Nowhere" also established the quintessential American "racial" setting. See Chapter 3.

34 Kaufman et al. 2014: 89. This is an argument regarding "diminished capacity" that Dan White, who killed Harvey Milk, used, and a noted aspect of

the argument is that certain incidents, such as the panic resulting from the advances of a gay person, can lead to diminished capacity.

35 Stageman names a number of these people throughout his essay, including Marsha P. Johnson, another "gay Puerto Rican named Gino," and another unnamed gay Puerto Rican man. Kaufman does also mention Johnson in his article.

36 On the idea of seeing like a state, see Scott 2020.

37 See "Diagnoses of HIV/AIDS—32 States, 2000–2003," Center for Disease Control, https://www.cdc.gov/mmwr/preview/mmwrhtml/mm5347a3.htm.

38 See "Crime Rates and Conviction Rates Broken Down By Race," January 18, 2008, https://www.cga.ct.gov/2008/rpt/2008-R-0008.htm.

CHAPTER SIX

1 See Chapter 1 and especially Bottici 2007 for her analysis of Blumenberg 1988.

2 See the foregoing Chapters 5 and 2, respectively.

3 See Rankine 2013 for a treatment of Parks' essay and its potential applications.

4 See Nightingale 2004 for a discussion of the ancient pilgrimage capture in the concept of *theoria*.

5 Candace Owens (2022) best exemplifies the counternarrative on George Floyd in her brief YouTube videos. A simple Google search yields enough content from Owens on this topic to serve as an introduction to the controversy. See, for example, this commentary titled "Candace Owens The Greatest Lie Ever Told: George Floyd & the Rise of BLM" https://www.youtube.com/watch?v=qR6qILl7NnY.

6 See Jones 2017 and Akbar 2020b for reviews (the latter upon the film's release on Amazon Prime).

7 Chicago theater critic Heidi Weiss had this very reaction in 2017. I discuss Weiss' treatment below. For a response, see Tran 2017.

8 For example, the American Shakespeare Center staged the play, with its original ending, from August 11–28, 2022. My Zoom interview with the Center's newly appointed Artistic Director at the time Brandon Carter, solidified my view of the impact of Nwandu's second ending as an instance of epiphanic encoding.

9 See Fukuyama 2006 on the end of history.

10 See Nwandu's artist profile for the Steppenwolf Theater, https://www.steppenwolf.org/artists/antoinette--nwandu/.

11 See the Kiln Theatre's site at https://kilntheatre.com/whats-on/pass-over/. For a review, see Akbar 2020a, who writes that "Pass Over is theatre for the

heart and head, reinventing and complicating old stories to make them newly and fiercely relevant."

12 See Moses 1993 on the American myths that play out in the literature and culture, such as that of America as an Eden. See also Shields 2001 for the interplay of the tropes of an American Adam and American Aeneas.

13 Nwandu's revision of the 2017 play in 2021 is not necessarily the play's final form. For the 2022 production at the American Shakespeare Center Carter chose the 2017 ending, deeming it still necessary and urgent.

14 Along with the picnic basket and stroll through parts unknown, Mister seems a male version of Little Red Riding Hood. Nwandu's mood and imagery are Morrisonian. On Toni Morrison's use of fables, folklore, and classical myth, see Rankine 2006 and 2013.

15 The mythic evocations (that he is going to a picnic, the red tablecloth, the innocence) make Master a kind of Red Riding Hood and Ossifer the wolf. The asymmetrical relationship between both the fantasy white American and Ossifer, on the one side, and Kitch and Moses, on the other, is a schema reminiscent of necropolitics, as Mbembe 2019 defines it. The following much-quoted passage conveys the idea saliently: "The ultimate expression of sovereignty largely resides in the power and capacity to dictate who is able to live and who must die. To kill or to let live thus constitutes sovereignty's limits, its principal attributes. To be sovereign is to exert one's control over mortality and to define life as the deployment and manifestation of power." Mister/Master is sovereign, as is Ossifer.

16 On which, his long-term relationship with an enslaved woman, Sally Hemings, who bore him children, see Gorden-Reed 2009.

17 This much-cited passage is from Jefferson 1784 in Jefferson 2011.

18 For Lincoln's interactions with Frederick Douglass on this matter, see Blight 2020.

19 On the Tuskegee experiment beginning in 1932, where Black men went untreated for syphilis despite readily available treatment, see https://www.cdc.gov/tuskegee/timeline.htm. The study did not end until 1972. On HIV/AIDS, see Chapter 4.

20 See Kenny 2018 on the film's uniqueness.

21 The street signs are specific to the Chicago production but not visible on the drama's Broadway set in 2021. The specific locale could be any similar corner in cities across the United States, which calls us back to Baldwin's image of "sharpies" on street corners. See the Introduction. Stills are available for viewing at https://www.imdb.com/title/tt7768846/mediaviewer/rm1547042049?ref_=ttmi_mi_all_sf_14.

22 On Black life as overdetermined, see Fanon 1994.

23 For a clip of Reagan delivering these words in his 1989 farewell address, see https://www.youtube.com/watch?v=c32G868toro.

24 For a review of the play's opening at the Berkeley Rep, see McNulty 2018.

25 For critic responses to Fairview that trouble notions of racial solidarity on either side of the Black-white divide, see Green and Tillet 2019.

26 See Wheatley's "An Elegy, To Miss Mary Moorhead, On the Death of Her Father, The Rev. Mr. John Moorhead," https://www.masshist.org/database/viewer.php?item_id=782&img_step=1&mode=dual.

27 As early as 1988, the rap group N.W.A. released "Fuck Da Police" on *Straight Outta Compton*. This theme was picked up later in KRS ONE's 1993 rap album *Return of the Boom Bap* included a song called "Sound of da Police" that works through the antagonism.

28 The "house in order" has to do with precisely the issue Weiss raises in her criticism.

29 On the "personal cost" of performance to the actors playing Kitch and Moses in the 2021 Broadway staging, Namir Smallwood and Jon Michael Hill, respectively, see Kumar 2021.

30 See Anderson 2016 on the nation as an imagined community.

CONCLUSION

1 As an active psychological and coaching approach, several texts record and amplify the approach. Group psychodynamic journals can be found at the Tavistock Institute, a leading organization for the method, https://www.tavinstitute.org/our-journals.

2 A handful of factors distinguish Nelson's contribution from what preceded it. First, it was written specifically for the videoconference platform, whereas theater companies had previously offered taped versions of their plays for quarantine consumption—and for their own relevance and survival. This boon, the ongoing release of recorded performances for audience consumption, would continue for months.

3 Nelson had directed Luis Alfaro's *Oedipus el Rey* three years before the Zoom production. Go to https://www.newyorktheatreguide.com/news-features/public-theater-announces-full-cast-of-oedipus-el-rey.

4 On the opinion of Andrew Cuomo's failures, see "Andrew Cuomo is No Hero" in *The Guardian*, May 20, 2020, https://www.theguardian.com/commentisfree/2020/may/20/andrew-cuomo-new-york-coronavirus-catastrophe. The

deification that can came with COVID-19 is evident in earlier treatments, such as Farago 2020.

5 On access to testing, go to https://www.npr.org/sections/health-shots/2020/05/03/849243723/californias-coronavirus-testing-still-a-frustrating-patchwork-of-haves-and-have. The plot details of Jane's underlying insecurity ("Are you talking about me?") and the status of her relationship with Tim ("We are working on a lot of stuff.") are extraneous, but they might add a degree of relatability for some audience members.

6 By June 2020, the *Decameron* itself had become a subject of a videoconference performance. For a review, go to https://www.washingtonpost.com/goingoutguide/theater-dance/the-decameron-at-synetic-theater/2020/06/02/fe467afa-a108-11ea-9590-1858a893bd59_story.html.

7 An article that the National Institute for Health published, with over half a dozen coauthors, concluded there were "dramatic declines in walking, particularly utilitarian walking, while recreational walking has recovered and even surpassed pre-pandemic levels. Our findings also demonstrate important social patterns, widening existing inequalities in walking behavior" (Hunter et al. 2021).

8 By the time of the second play in early July 2020, the applefamilyplays.com website had been boasting that the first play had been viewed more than 80,000 times. This would be beyond the hopes of most single plays.

9 In the city of Richmond, Virginia, all the Confederate monuments that lined a world-renowned thoroughfare, Monument Avenue, had been toppled within a month. The preceding decades of debate and legislation could not accomplish this. By mid-July, however, the statue of Robert E. Lee was the last one standing, and this only because the state rather than city owned it. The world had been changing swiftly, and few could feel secure with where things were going.

10 Cancelation here refers to the deletion of social media accounts, where in some cases even the mere accusation of wrongdoing leads to a person's ostracism. A July 22, 2020 article in *Politico* noted the first official polls on cancel culture: https://www.politico.com/news/2020/07/22/americans-cancel-culture-377412.

11 In a brief study of the word, I have found it used most often prior to 2020 in terms, first, of women's rights, and particularly *Roe v. Wade*. The racial politics of the 1960s is a close parallel, with gender and sexuality approximating the idea of "racial backlash" in the waning days of the 2020 pandemic. See Roe 1998 on backlash and legal policy as it pertains to economics and wealth. Applying an emotional theory of backlash to national and international

security, Rythoven 2018 homes in on the phenomena of "reaction, hostility, emotion, and contagion."

12 See Holmes and Redman 2021. Any ostensible link between Rittenhouse and the Proud Boys or other white supremacist militia groups was inadmissible in his murder trial. See Richmond 2021.

13 See https://br.ifunny.co/picture/kyle-is-literally-a-saint-no-274906820-guys-i-m-RcbIA5i49.

14 See https://marketresearchtelecast.com/a-major-us-catholic-university-exhibits-a-painting-with-george-floyd-depicting-jesus-christ-in-the-arms-of-the-virgin-mary/209763/.

15 See, for example, https://www.psycom.net/covid-19-suicide-rates, on the rise in suicide rates.

Bibliography

Adichie, Chimamanda Ngozi. 2006. *Half of a Yellow Sun*. New York: Alfred A. Knopf.

Akbar, Arifa. 2020a. "Pass Over Review – Fiercely Relevant and Compelling." *The Guardian*, February 20, 2020. https://www.theguardian.com/stage/2020/feb/20/pass-over-review-kiln-london.

Akbar, Arifa. 2020b. "Pass Over Review – Spike Lee Directs Antoinette Nwandu's Masterful Tragedy." *The Guardian*, June 3, 2020, sec. Theater. https://www.theguardian.com/stage/2020/jun/03/pass-over-review-spike-lee-antoinette-nwandu.

Alexander, Michelle. 2020. *The New Jim Crow*. 10th anniversary ed. New York: New Press.

Alfaro, Luis. 2020. *The Greek Trilogy of Luis Alfaro: Electricidad; Oedipus El Rey; Mojada*. Edited by Rosa Andújar. Grantham: Methuen Drama.

Allen, Daneille S. 2002. *The World of Prometheus: The Politics of Punishing in Democratic Athens*. Second. Princeton, NJ: Princeton University Press.

Anderlini, Serena. 1991. "Drama or Performance Art? An Interview with Ntozake Shange." *Journal of Dramatic Theory and Criticism* 6. https://journals.ku.edu/jdtc/article/view/1820.

Anderson, Benedict. 2016. *Imagined Communities: Reflections on the Origin and Spread of Nationalism*. Revised. New York: Verso.

Appiah, Kwame Anthony. 1988. "An Evening with Wole Soyinka." *American Literature Forum* 22: 777–85.

Appiah, Kwame Anthony. 2016. "There Is No Such Thing As Western Civilization." *The Guardian*, November 9, 2016.

———. 2018. *The Lies That Bind: Rethinking Identity*. New York: Liveright.
Baker, Houston Jr., and Merinda Simmons, eds. 2015. *The Trouble with Post-Blackness*. New York: Columbia University Press.
Baker, Peter. 2018. "Bush Made Willie Horton an Issue in 1988, and the Racial Scars Are Still Fresh." *The New York Times*, December 3, 2018. https://www.nytimes.com/2018/12/03/us/politics/bush-willie-horton.html.
Baldwin, James. 1974. *If Beale Street Could Talk*. New York: Dial Press.
Baldwin, James. 1992 [1963]. *The Fire Next Time*. New York: Vintage Press.
Baldwin, James. 1993. "Princes and Powers." In *Nobody Knows My Name*, First Vintage Edition, 13–55. New York: Vintage Press.
Baldwin, James. 1995a [1964]. *Blues for Mister Charlie*. New York: Vintage Press.
Baldwin, James. 1995b [1965]. *Going to Meet the Man*. New York: Dial Press.
Baldwin, James. 2006 [1974]. *If Beale Street Could Talk*. Reprinted edition. New York: Vintage Press.
Baldwin, James. 2007 [1972]. *No Name in the Street*. New York: Dial Press.
Baldwin, James. 2010. *The Cross of Redemption: Uncollected Writings*. New York: Vintage Press (with an introduction by Randall Kenan).
Baldwin, James. 2011 [1976]. *The Devil Finds Work: An Essay*. New York: The Dial Press.
Baldwin, James. 2012 [1955]. *Notes of a Native Son*. New York: Beacon Press.
Baldwin, James. 2021. *The Price of the Ticket: Collected Nonfiction: 1948–1985*. Reprint. New York: Beacon Press.
Barnard, John Levi. 2018. *Empire of Ruin: Black Classicism and American Imperial Culture*. New York: Oxford University Press.
Baraka, Amiri. 1965. "The Revolutionary Theatre." *Liberator*, 5 July 1965: 4–6. https://nationalhumanitiescenter.org/pds/maai3/protest/text12/barakatheatre.pdf.
Baraka, Amiri. 2002 [1964]. Dutchman and the Slave. New York: Faber & Faber.
Baraka, Amiri. 2016 [1966]. The System of Dante's Hell. Reprint edition. Brooklyn, NY: Akashic Books.
Batstone, William W. 2006. "Provocation: The Point of Reception." In *Classics and the Uses of Reception*, 1st ed., 14–20. Hoboken, NJ: Wiley-Blackwell.
Beckett, Lois. 2020. "At Least 25 Americans Were Killed during Protests and Political Unrest in 2020." *The Guardian*, October 31, 2020. https://www.theguardian.com/world/2020/oct/31/americans-killed-protests-political-unrest-acled.
Bellow, Saul. 2002. *Ravelstein*. 1st ed. New York: The Penguin Group.

Best, Stephen. 2018. *None Like Us: Blackness, Belonging, Aesthetic Life*. Durham, NC: Duke University Press.

Best, Susan. 2021. *It's Not Personal: Post 60s Body Art and Performance*. London: Bloomsbury.

"BIPOC Demands for White American Theatre." 2020. July 2020. https://static1.squarespace.com/static/5ede42fd6cb927448d9d0525/t/5f064e63f21dd43ad6ab3162/1594248809279/Tier2.pdf.

Bishop, Norman. 1983. "A Nigerian Version of a Greek Classic: Soyinka's Transformation of "The Bacchae." Research in African Literature. 14: 68–80.

Blanco, María Pilar, and Esther Peeren, eds. 2013. *The Spectralities Reader: Ghosts and Haunting in Contemporary Cultural Theory*. London: Bloomsbury Academic.

Blight, David W. 2002. "If You Don't Tell It Like It Was, It Can Never Be As It Ought to Be." Presented at the Gilder Lehrman Center for the Study of Slavery, Resistance, and Abolition, Keynote talk, Yale McMillan Center University.

Blight, David W. 2020. *Frederick Douglass: Prophet of Freedom*. New York: Simon & Schuster.

Bloom, Allan. 2012 [1987]. *The Closing of the American Mind: How Higher Education Has Failed Democracy and Impoverished the Souls of Today's Students*. New York: Simon & Schuster.

Bloom, Allan, trans. n.d. *The Republic of Plato*. 3rd ed. New York.

Bloom, Allan, Charles Butterworth, and Christopher Kelly, trans. 2004. *Letter to D'Alembert and Writings for the Theater*. The University Press of New England.

Bloom, Harold. 2019. *Macbeth: A Dagger of the Mind*. New York: Scribner.

Blumenberg, Hans. 1988. *Work on Myth*. Translated by Robert M. Wallace. Boston, MA: MIT Press.

Bosher, Katheryn, Fiona Macintosh, Justine McConnell, and Patrice Rankine, eds. 2015. *Oxford Handbook of Greek Drama in the Americas*. Oxford: Oxford University Press.

Bottici, Chiara. 2007. *A Philosophy of Political Myth*. Cambridge: Cambridge University Press.

———. 2014. *Imaginal Politics: Images Beyond Imagination and the Imaginary*. New York: Columbia University Press.

Brantley, Ben. 2000. "A Brutal Act Alters a Town." *The New York Times*, May 19, 2000. https://www.nytimes.com/2000/05/19/movies/theater-review-a-brutal-act-alters-a-town.html.

Brantley, Ben. 2002. "THEATER REVIEW; The Face Again, Still Gorgeous But a Bit Weary." *The New York Times*, 2002. https://www.nytimes.com/2002/04/09/theater/theater-review-the-face-again-still-gorgeous-but-a-bit-weary.html.

Brantley, Ben. 2020. "Review: Same Apple Family, New Kind of Theater." *The New York Times*, April 30, 2020. https://www.nytimes.com/2020/04/30/theater/what-do-we-need-to-talk-about-review.html.

Brendix, Trish. 2019. "'Boys Don't Cry' 20 Years Later: For Trans Men, a Divisive Legacy," October 9, 2019. https://www.nytimes.com/2019/10/09/movies/boys-dont-cry-anniversary.html.

Breuer, Lee. 1993. *The Gospel at Colonus*. First edition. New York: Theatre Communications Group.

Brønholt, Thorsten. 2020. "Gated Communities of the Digitised Mind." In *Big Data and Democracy*, 104–18. Edinburgh: Edinburgh University Press.

Brooks, Gwendolyn. 1994. *Blacks*. Chicago, IL: Third World Press.

Brustein, Robert. 1993. "On Theater: Unity from Diversity." *The New Republic*, July.

Butler, Judith. 2017. "Breaks in the Bond: Reflections on Kinship Trouble." University College London, February 8.

Calloway-Thomas, Carolyn, and John Louis Lucaites, eds. 1993. *Martin Luther King Jr. and the Sermonic Power of Public Discourse*. Tuscaloosa: University of Alabama Press.

Campbell, Joseph. 1973. *The Hero with a Thousand Faces*. 21st ed. Princeton, NJ: Princeton University Press.

Canup, Dina. 2012. "Oedipus Myth Set on a Plantation in University Theatre's 'Darker Face of the Earth.'" *UGAToday*, October 11, 2012. https://news.uga.edu/darker-face-of-the-earth-101112/.

Carlson, Marvin. 2003. *The Haunted Stage: The Theatre as Memory Machine*. Ann Arbor: University of Michigan Press.

Casey, Edward S. 2004. "Public Memory in Place and Time." In *Framing Public Memory*, 17–44. Tuscaloosa: The University of Alabama Press.

Chappell, Bill. 2021. "Derek Chauvin Is Sentenced to 22 1/2 Years for George Floyd's Murder." *National Public Radio*, June 25, 2021. https://www.npr.org/sections/trial-over-killing-of-george-floyd/2021/06/25/1009524284/derek-chauvin-sentencing-george-floyd-murder.

Cillizza, Chris. 2020. "Andrew Cuomo May Be the Single Most Popular Politician in America Right Now." *Cnn.Com* (blog). May 1, 2020. https://www.cnn.com/2020/05/01/politics/andrew-cuomo-coronavirus-poll/index.html.

Cineas, Fabiola. 2022. "What an Anti-Lynching Law Means in 2022." *Vox*, March 29, 2022. https://www.vox.com/22995013/anti-lynching-act-emmett-till.

Claycomb, Ryan. 2013. "Here's How You Produce This Play: Toward a Narratology of Dramatic Texts." *Narrative* 21: 159–79.

Clayton, Abené. 2023. "Ron DeSantis Bans African American Studies Class from Florida High Schools." *The Guardian*, January 19, 2023. https://www.theguardian.com/us-news/2023/jan/19/ron-desantis-bans-african-american-studies-florida-schools.

Coates, Ta-Nehisi. 2012. "Fear of a Black President." *The Atlantic*, September. https://www.theatlantic.com/magazine/archive/2012/09/fear-of-a-black-president/309064/.

Coates, Ta-Nehisi. 2015. *Between the World and Me*. Spiegel & Grau.

"A Conversation with Ntozake Shange and Dianne McIntyre." 2013. Barnard Center for Research on Women. https://www.youtube.com/watch?v=nJmORjVKNys.

Cook, William W., and James Tatum. 2012. *African American Writers and Classical Tradition*. Chicago, IL: University of Chicago Press.

Cullen, Countee. 1935. *Medea and Some Poems*. New York: Harper & Brothers.

Cullors, Patrisse, and asha bandele. 2018. *When They Call You a Terrorist: A Black Lives Matter Memoir*. New York: St. Martin's Press.

De Palma, Brian, and Richard Schechner, dirs. 1970. *Dionysus in '69*.

Debord, Guy. 1994. *The Society of the Spectacle*. New York: Zone Books.

Deleuze, Gilles, and Felix Guattari. 2009 [1972]. *Anti-Oedipus: Capitalism and Schizophrenia*. Translated by Robert Hurley and Mark Seem. New York: Penguin Books.

Deneen, Patrick J. 2016. *Conserving America?: Essays on Present Discontents*. South Bend, IN: St. Augustines Press.

Dieke, Ikenna. 1990. "Tragic Faith and the Dionysian Unconscious: An Interfacing of Novelist Baraka and Friedrich Nietzsche" *Black American Literature Forum* 24 (1): 99–116.

Dorf, Samuel. 2018. Performing Antiquity: Ancient Greek Music and Dance from Paris to Delphi, 1890-1930. Oxford: Oxford University Press.

Dove, Rita. 1994. *The Darker Face of the Earth*. 1st edition. Brownsville, OR: Story Line Press.

Dowland, Seth. 2018. *Family Values and the Rise of the Christian Right*. Reprint edition. Philadelphia: University of Pennsylvania Press.

Drury, Jackie Sibblies. 2019. *Fairview*. New York: Theatre Communications Group.

Dubois, Laurent. 2005. Avengers of the New World: The Story of the Haitian Revolution. Cambridge: The Belknap Press.

Duggan, Joe. 2007. "Nissen: 'I Am the Person Who Shot and Stabbed Teena Brandon.'" *Lincoln Journal Star*, September 19, 2007. https://journalstar.com/news/state-and-regional/govt-and-politics/nissen-i-am-the-person-who-shot-and-stabbed-teena-brandon/article_0b534ed4-60b2-5d84-9529-ac44c989a117.html.

Duong, Kevin. 2019. "No Social Revolution Without Sexual Revolution." *Political Theory* 47: 809–35.

Duster, Troy. 1995. "Review of *The Bell Curve* by Richard J. Herrnstein and Charles Murray." *Contemporary Sociology* 24: 158–161.

Ellison, Ralph. 1980 [1952]. *Invisible Man*. New York: Vintage Press.

Ellison, Ralph. 1995. *Shadow and Act*. Reissue. New York: Vintage Press.

Emmerich, Roland, dir. 2015. Stonewall. Los Angeles, CA: Roadside Attractions.

English, Adam C. 2012. *The Saint Who Would Be Santa Claus: The True Life and Trials of Saint Nicholas of Myrna*. Waco, TX: Baylor University Press.

Euben, J. Peter. 1982. "Justice and the Oresteia." *The American Political Science Review* 76: 22–33.

Eustis, Oskar, dir. 2018. *Why Theater Is Essential to Democracy*. TedTalk. https://www.youtube.com/watch?v=5foou7mlAow.

Evans, Dylan. 2006. *An Introductory Dictionary of Lacanian Psychoanalysis*. Taylor & Francis.

"Examining Excited Delirium." 2020. *60 Minutes*. https://www.cbs.com/shows/video/_kAhNp2JxEP84P4MilnhDKscs_2uSLJA/.

Fahim, Kareem. 2017. "Fleeing Anger in America, James Baldwin Found Solace in 1960s Turkey." *The Washington Post*, February 27, 2017, sec. Middle East. https://www.washingtonpost.com/world/middle_east/james-baldwin-lived-in-turkey-on-and-off-for-a-decade-a-look-at-what-remains-of-his-istanbul/2017/02/26/fb94fa44-ee13-11e6-a100-fdaaf400369a_story.html.

Fanon, Frantz. 1994 [1952]. *Black Skin, White Masks*. Translated by Constance Farrington. New York: Grove Press.

Farago, Jason. 2020. "'Andrew Cuomo Ascends to the Mountaintop with His Pandemic Poster.'" *The New York Times*, July 20, 2020. https://www.nytimes.com/2020/07/14/arts/design/cuomo-covid-poster-new-york.html.

Fields, Karen E., and Barbara J. Fields. 2012. *Racecraft: The Soul of Inequity in American Life*. London: Verso.

Flood, Christopher. 1996. *Political Myth: A Theoretical Introduction*. 1st ed. London: Routledge.

Foley, Helena P. 2012. *Reimagining Greek Tragedy on the American Stage*. Oakland: University of California Press.

Freud, Sigmund. 2017. *The Collected Works of Sigmund Freud*. Translated by H. W. Chase. Musaicum Books.

Fried, Joseph P. 1999. "In Surprise, Witness Says Officer Bragged About Louima Torture." *The New York Times*, May 20, 1999. https://web.archive.org/web/20131214084725/http://www.nytimes.com/1999/05/20/nyregion/in-surprise-witness-says-officer-bragged-about-louima-torture.html.

Fukuyama, Francis. 2006. *The End of History and the Last Man*. New York: Free Press.

Fukuyama, Francis. 2019. *Identity: The Demand for Dignity and the Politics of Resentment*. Reprint ed. London: Picador.

Gantz, Timothy. 1993. *Early Greek Myth*. Baltimore, MD: Johns Hopkins University Press.

Gates, Jr., Henry Louis. 2014. *The Signifying Monkey: A Theory of African American Literary Criticism*. 25th ed. Oxford: Oxford University Press.

Gellman, Irwin F. 2022. *Campaign of the Century: Kennedy, Nixon, and the Election of 1960*. New Haven, CT: Yale University Press.

Getachew, Adom. 2020. *Worldmaking after Empire: The Rise and Fall of Self-Determination*. Princeton, NJ: Princeton University Press.

Gilliam, Franklin D., Jr. 1999. "The 'Welfare Queen' Experiment: How Viewers React to Images of African-American Mothers on Welfare." https://escholarship.org/uc/item/17m7r1rq.

Gilroy, Paul. 1993. *The Black Atlantic: Modernity and Double-Consciousness*. Reissued. Cambridge, MA: Harvard University Press.

Gilroy, Paul. 2006. *Postcolonial Melancholia*. New York: Columbia University Press.

Ginzburg, Ralph. 1996. *100 Years of Lynchings*. Reprint. Maryland: Black Classic Press.

Goldsby, Jacqueline. 2006. *A Spectacular Secret: Lynching in American Life and Literature*. Chicago, IL: The University of Chicago Press.

Gordon, Avery F. 2008. *Ghostly Matters: Haunting and the Sociological Imagination*. Minneapolis: University of Minnesota Press.

Gordone, Charles. 2019 [1969]. No Place to Be Somebody. New York: Broadway Play Publishing.

Gordon-Reed, Annette. 2009. *The Hemingses of Monticello: An American Family*. Reprint. New York: W. W. Norton & Company.

Gray, Channing. 2017. "Police Probe Threats to Wife of Oskar Eustis, Director of Trump-like 'Caesar' Play." *Providence Journal*, June 22, 2017. https://www.providencejournal.com/news/20170622/police-probe-threats-to-wife-of-oskar-eustis-director-of-trump-like-caesar-play.

Green, Jesse, and Salamishah Tillet. 2019. "'Fairview': Watching a Play in Black and White." *The New York Times*, August 7, 2019. https://www.nytimes.com/2019/08/07/theater/fairview-ending-debate.html.

Green, S. J. D. 1998. "'The Closing of the American Mind,' Revisited." *The Antioch Review* 56: 26–36.

Greenberg, Jay R., and Stephen A. Mitchell. 1983. *Object Relations in Psychoanalytic Theory*. Cambridge, MA: Harvard University Press.

Greenspun, Roger. 1970. "De Palma's 'Dionysus in 69.'" *The New York Times*, March 23, 1970. https://www.nytimes.com/1970/03/23/archives/screende-palmas-dionysus-in-69.html.

Grills, Nathan, and Brendan Halyday. 2009. "Santa Claus: A Public Heath Pariah?" *British Medical Journal* 339: 19–26.

Gurley, Lauren Kaori. 2022. "Newly Unionized Starbucks Workers Are on Strike for COVID Protections." *Vice*, January 6, 2022. https://www.vice.com/en/article/m7v7pv/newly-unionized-starbucks-workers-are-on-strike-for-covid-protections.

Guy, Peter. 2014. *As Mirrors Are Lonely: A Lacanian Reading on the Modern Irish Novel*. Cambridge: Cambridge University Press.

Hall, Edith, and Stephe Harrop. 2010. *Theorising Performance: Greek Drama, Cultural History and Critical Practice*. London: Bristol Classical Press.

Hall, Edith, and Fiona Macintosh. 2005. *Greek Tragedy and the British Theatre: 1660–1914*. Oxford: Oxford University Press.

Hall, Edith, Amanda Wrigley, and Fiona Macintosh, eds. 2004. *Dionysus since 69:Greek Tragedy at the Dawn of the Third Millennium*. Oxford: Oxford University Press.

Hardwick, Lorna. 2011. "Fuzzy Connections: Classical Texts and Modern Poetry in English." In *Tradition, Translation, Trauma: The Classic and the Modern*. Oxford: Oxford University Press.

Harris, Elizabeth A. 2018. "Director Quits 'All My Sons' Amid Dispute Over Cast's Racial Makeup." *The New York Times*, December 19, 2018. https://www.nytimes.com/2018/12/19/theater/all-my-sons-director-quits.html.

Harris, Jeremy O. 2020. *Slave Play*. New York: Theatre Communications Group.

Hartman, Saidiya. 2019. *Wayward Lives, Beautiful Experiments: Intimate Histories of Social Upheaval*. New York: W. W. Norton & Company.

Heckman, James J. 1995. "Lessons from the Bell Curve." *Journal of Political Economy* 103: 1091–1120.

Herrnstein, Richard J., and Charles Murray. 1996. *The Bell Curve: Intelligence and Class Structure in American Life*. Free Press.

Hinojosa, Maria. 1997. "NYC Officer Arrested in Alleged Sexual Attack on Suspect." *CNN*, August 14, 1997. http://www.cnn.com/US/9708/14/police.torture/.

Hinton, Elizabeth. 2021. *America on Fire: The Untold History of Police Violence and Black Rebellion Since the 1960s*. New York: Liveright.

Holland, Eugene W. 1999. *Deleuze and Guattari's Anti-Oedipus: Introduction to Schizoanalysis*. London: Routledge.

Holmes, Isiah, and Henry Redman. 2021. "Texts Show Kenosha Officers Called Armed Civilians 'Very Friendly' Hours before Rittenhouse Shooting." *Wisconsin Examiner*, 2021. https://wisconsinexaminer.com/2021/07/07/kenosha-officers-called-armed-civilians-very-friendly/.

Hong, Nicole, and Matthew Haag. 2022. "The Flight of New York City's Wealthy Was a Once-in-a-Century Shock." *The New York Times*, June 28, 2022. https://www.nytimes.com/2022/06/28/nyregion/wealthy-pandemic-nyc.html.

Howard, Ron, dir. 2008. *Frost/Nixon*.

Hunter, Ruth F. et al 2021. "Effect of COVID-19 Response Policies on Walking Behavior in US Cities." *Nature Communications*, June. https://pubmed.ncbi.nlm.nih.gov/34135325/.

Isherwood, Charles. 2002. "Helen, Review." *Variety*, April 8, 2002. https://variety.com/2002/legit/reviews/helen-4-1200550400/.

Isherwood, Charles. 2013. "Laramie's Past Isn't Dead. It's Not Even Past. February 14, 2013. https://www.nytimes.com/2013/02/15/theater/reviews/the-laramie-project-at-bams-harvey-theater.html/.

Jackson, Lauren Michele. 2020. "The Layered Deceptions of Jessica Krug, the Black-Studies Professor Who Hid That She Is White." *The New Yorker*, September 12, 2020. https://www.newyorker.com/culture/cultural-comment/the-layered-deceptions-of-jessica-krug-the-black-studies-professor-who-hid-that-she-is-white.

Jackson, Zakiyyah Iman. 2020. *Becoming Human: Matter and Meaning in an Antiblack World*. New York: NYU Press.

Jacobs-Jenkins, Branden. 2019. *Appropriate/An Octoroon: Plays*. New York: Theatre Communications Group.

Jefferson, Thomas. 2011. *Notes on the State of Virginia*, R. P. Forbes, ed. New Haven, CT: Yale University Press.

Johnson, Lyndon B. 1964. "Remarks at the University of Michigan, Mat 22, 1964." Ann Arbor, Michigan, May 22. https://www.lbjlibrary.org/object/text/remarks-university-michigan-05-22-1964.

Johnson, Lyndon B. 1968. "Remarks upon Signing the Civil Rights Act of 1968." Washington, D.C., April 11. https://www.lbjlibrary.org/object/text/remarks-upon-signing-civil-rights-act-1968.

Jones, Aphrodite. 2016. *All He Wanted: "Brandon Teena" A Transgender Boy Who Paid the Ultimate Price*. CreateSpace Independent Publishing Platform.

Jones, Chris. 2017. "Spike Lee Secretly Filmed 'Pass Over' at Steppenwolf." *The Chicago Tribune*, December 5, 2017. https://www.chicagotribune.com/entertainment/theater/ct-ent-pass-over-spike-lee-1205-story.html.

Jouvenal, Justin. 2015. "'Excited Delirium' Cited in Dozens of Deaths in Police Custody. Is It Real or a Cover for Brutality?" *The Washington Post*, May 6, 2015. https://www.washingtonpost.com/local/crime/existence-of-excited-delirium-ruling-in-va-womans-death-has-experts-split/2015/05/06/b1cc9499-ddaa-474c-9e8a-9ae89a9ae679_story.html.

Kartik-Narayan, Ashvini. 2018. "The Fight Over Chicago's Largest Private Police Force." *South Side Weekly*, July 16, 2018. https://southsideweekly.com/the-fight-over-chicagos-largest-private-police-force-university-of-chicago-ucpd/.

Kaufman, Moises. 2019. "A Dangerous Euphoria." *The New York Times*, June 16, 2019. https://www.nytimes.com/2019/06/16/us/moises-kaufman-stonewall-50.html.

Kaufman, Moises, Leigh Fondakowski, and Tectonic Theater Project. 2014. *The Laramie Project and The Laramie Project: Ten Years Later*. New York: Vintage Press.

Kaye, Howard L. 1996. "Reviewing the Reviewers: The Bell Curve." *The American Sociologist* 27: 79–86.

Kenny, Glenn. 2018. "Spike Lee's 'Pass Over,' An Offbeat Melding of Cinema and Theater." *The New York Times*, May 11, 2018. https://www.nytimes.com/2018/05/11/movies/spike-lees-pass-over-melds-cinema-and-theater.html.

Kerr, Walter. 1973. "Will We Ever See 'The Bacchae' as Euripides Wrote It?" *The New York Times*, August 19, 1973. https://www.nytimes.com/1973/08/19/archives/will-we-ever-see-the-bacchae-as-euripides-wrote-it-will-we-see-the-.html.

Kim, Kwangsoon. 2017. "Oedipus Complex in the South: Castration Anxiety and Lynching Ritual in James Baldwin's 'Going to Meet the Man.'" *CLA Journal* 60: 319–33.

King, Martin Luther, Jr. April 4, 1967a. *Beyond Vietnam*. https://www.youtube.com/watch?v=AJhgXKGldUk.

King, Martin Luther, Jr. April 4, 1967b. "Beyond Vietnam." Riverside Baptist Church. https://web.mit.edu/21h.102/www/Primary%20source%20collections/Civil%20Rights/Beyond_Vietnam.htm.

King, Martin Luther, Jr. 1967c. *Why I Am Opposed to the War in Vietnam*. https://www.youtube.com/watch?v=zyE4eo_leX8.

King, Martin Luther, Jr. 1967d. "Why I Am Opposed to the War in Vietnam." https://www.theatlantic.com/magazine/archive/2018/02/martin-luther-king-jr-vietnam/552521/.

Klein, Melanie. 2002. *Love, Guilt and Reparation: And Other Works 1921–1945*. New York: Free Press.

Klonoff, E. A., and H. Landrine. 1999. "Do Blacks Believe That HIV/AIDS Is a Government Conspiracy against Them?" *Preventive Medicine* 28: 451–57.

Knowles, Hannah. 2019. "Jeremy O. Harris Responds." *The Washington Post*, December 1, 2019. https://www.washingtonpost.com/arts-entertainment/2019/12/01/broadway-goer-shouted-play-was-racist-against-white-people-playwright-responded/.

Kumar, Naveen. 2021. "'There's Still So Much to Unearth' in 'Pass Over.'" *The New York Times*, August 4, 2021. https://www.nytimes.com/2021/08/04/theater/pass-over-broadway-cast.html.

LaBouvier, Chaédria et al. 2019. *Basquiat "Defacement:" The Untold Story*. New York: Guggenheim Museum.

Lear, Jonathan. 2005. *Freud*. 1st ed. London: Routledge.

Lecznar, Adam. 2020. *Dionysus after Nietzsche: The Birth of Tragedy in Twentieth-Century Literature and Thought*. Cambridge: Cambridge University Press.

Lee, Felicia R. 2004. "ABC News Revisits Student's Killing, and Angers Some Gays." *The New York Times*, November 26, 2004. https://www.nytimes.com/2004/11/26/us/abc-news-revisits-students-killing-and-angers-some-gays.html.

Lee, Spike, dir. 2018. *Pass Over*.

Leeming, David. 2015. *James Baldwin: A Biography*. Arcade.

Lester, Neal A. 1988. *Ntozake Shange's Development of the Choreopoem*. Vanderbilt University.

Levenson, Eric. 2020. "Why New York Is the Epicenter of the American Coronavirus Outbreak." *CNN* (blog). March 26, 2020. https://www.cnn.com/2020/03/26/us/new-york-coronavirus-explainer/index.html.

Levin, Sam. 2020. "What Does 'defund the Police' Mean? The Rallying Cry Sweeping the US – Explained." *The Guardian*, June 6, 2020. https://www.theguardian.com/us-news/2020/jun/05/defunding-the-police-us-what-does-it-mean.

Libbey, Peter. 2018. "How Next Wave Is It? Joseph V. Melillo Picks His Kind of Show From His Final Program." *The New York Times*, September 13, 2018. https://www.nytimes.com/2018/09/13/theater/next-wave-festival-joseph-melillo-brooklyn-academy-of-music.html.

Lincoln, Bruce. 2000. *Theorizing Myth: Narrative, Ideology, and Scholarship*. 1st ed. Chicago, IL: The University of Chicago Press.

Macintosh, Fiona. 2004. “Oedipus in the East End: From Freud to Berkoff.” In *Dionysus Since ’69*, Revised, 313–24. Oxford: Oxford University Press.

Macintosh, Fiona. 2010. *The Ancient Dancer in the Modern World: Responses to Greek and Roman Dance*. Oxford: Oxford University Press.

Macintosh, Fiona, and Justine McConnell. 2020. *Performing Epic or Telling Tales*. Oxford: Oxford University Press.

Malcolm X, and Alex Haley. 1992. *The Autobiography of Malcolm X: As Told to Alex Haley*. New York: Ballantine Books.

Manning, Susan. 2006. *Modern Dance, Negro Dance: Race in Motion*. First. Minneapolis: University of Minnesota Press.

Marks, Peter. 2020. “A Play Premières Online—And It Couldn’t Be More Relevant to How We Are Right Now.” *The Washington Post*, May 1, 2020. https://www.washingtonpost.com/entertainment/a-play-premieres-online--and-it-couldnt-be-more-relevant-to-how-we-are-right-now/2020/04/30/515821d2-8aeb-11ea-8ac1-bfb250876b7a_story.html.

Martindale, Charles. 1993. *Redeeming the Text: Latin Poetry and the Hermeneutics of Reception*. Cambridge: Cambridge University Press.

Maurantonio, Nicole. 2019. *Confederate Exceptionalism: Civil War Myth and Memory in the Twenty-First Century*. Lawrence: University Press of Kansas.

Mbembe, Achille. 2019. *Necropolitics*. Durham, NC: Duke University Press.

McIntosh, Peggy. 1989. “White Privilege: Unpacking the Invisible Knapsack.” *Peace and Freedom* (blog). 1989. https://psychology.umbc.edu/wp-content/uploads/sites/57/2016/10/White-Privilege_McIntosh-1989.pdf.

McLaughlin, Ellen. 2004. *The Greek Plays*. New York: Theatre Communications Group.

McMurray, Peter. 2019. “Witnessing Race in the New Digital Cinema.” *The Librarian-Seeley Historical Library*, 124–29.

McNulty, Charles. 2018. “Review: Playwright Jackie Sibblies Drury Daringly Deconstructs the Theater of Black Identity in ‘Fairview’ at Berkeley Rep.” *The Los Angeles Times*, October 15, 2018. https://www.latimes.com/entertainment/arts/theater/reviews/la-et-cm-fairview-20181015-story.html.

Menand, Louis. 2021. *The Free World: Art and Thought in the Cold War*. New York: Farrar, Straus and Giroux.

Miller, Elise. 2004. “The ‘Maw of Western Culture:’ James Baldwin and the Anxieties of Influence.” *African American Review* 38: 625–636.

Mills, Charles. 2022. The Racial Contract. 25th Anniversary Edition. Ithaca, NY: Cornell University Press.

Mitchell, Koritha. 2012. “James Baldwin, Performance Theorist, Sings the ‘Blues for Mister Charlie.’” *American Quarterly* 64: 33–60.

Mitter, Siddhartha. 2019. "Behind Basquiat's 'Defacement': Reframing a Tragedy." *The New York Times*, July 30, 2019. https://www.nytimes.com/2019/07/30/arts/design/behind-basquiats-defacement-reframing-a-tragedy.html.

Morrison, Toni. 1988. "Unspeakable Things Unspoken: The Afro-American Presence in American Literature" (presented at the The Tanner Lectures on Human Values, Ann Arbor: The University of Michigan) https://tannerlectures.utah.edu/_resources/documents/a-to-z/m/morrison90.pdf.

Morrison, Toni. 2004 [1977]. Song of Solomon. Reprint edition. New York: Vintage.

Morrison, Toni. 2022 [1987]. Beloved. New York: Vintage Classics.

Morgan, Peter. 2007. *Frost/Nixon: A Play*. London: Faber and Faber.

Morrison, Toni. 1988. "Unspeakable Things Unspoken: The Afro-American Presence in American Literature." In. Ann Arbor: The University of Michigan.

Morrison, Toni. 1992. *Playing in the Dark: Whiteness and the Literary Imagination*. Cambridge: Harvard University Press.

Morrison, Toni, and Claudia Brodsky Lacour, eds. 1997. *Birth of a Nation'hood*. Pantheon.

Moses, Wilson Jeremiah. 1993. *Black Messiahs and Uncle Toms: Social and Literary Manipulations of a Religious Myth*. Revised ed. edition. University Park: Pennsylvania State University Press.

Moten, Fred. 2003. *In the Break: The Aesthetics of the Black Radical Tradition*. Minneapolis: University of Minnesota Press.

Moten, Fred, and Stefano Harney. 2004. "The University and the Undercommons: Seven Theses." *Social Text* 22: 101–15.

Moynihan, Daniel Patrick. 1965. *The Negro Family: The Case for National Action*. US Department of Labor. https://web.stanford.edu/~mrosenfe/Moynihan%27s%20The%20Negro%20Family.pdf.

Mullen, Bill V. 2019. *James Baldwin: Living in Fire*. Pluto Press.

Murray, Charles. 1995a. "'The Bell Curve' and Its Critics." *Commentary* 99: 23–30.

Muska, Susan, and Gréta Olafsdóttir, dirs. 1998. *The Brandon Teena Story*.

Nattrass, Nicoli. 2013. *The AIDS Conspiracy: Science Fights Back*. New York: Columbia University Press.

Nightingale, Andrea Wilson. 2004. *Spectacles of Truth in Classical Greek Philosophy: Theoria in Its Cultural Context*. Cambridge: Cambridge University Press.

Nodjimbaden, Katie. 2015. "Emmett Till's Open Casket Funeral Reignited the Civil Rights Movement." *Smithsonian Magazine*, September 2, 2015. https://www.smithsonianmag.com/smithsonian-institution/emmett-tills-open-casket-funeral-reignited-the-civil-rights-movement-180956483/.

Nossiter, Adam. 2012. "Remembering Biafra." *The New York Times*, November 1, 2012. https://www.nytimes.com/2012/11/04/books/review/there-was-a-country-by-chinua-achebe.html.

Nottage, Lynn. 2017. *Sweat*. New York. Theatre Communications Group.

Ntozake Shange on Stage and Screen. 2012. Barnard College. https://www.youtube.com/watch?v=nB5wbtXS6-Q.

Nwandu, Antoinette. *Pass Over*. 2019. New York: Grove Press.

Odets, Clifford. 1994. *Waiting for Lefty and Other Plays*. Reissue edition. New York: Grove Press.

Oglesby, Carl. 1969. "Vietnamism Has Failed…The Revolution Can Only Be Mauled, Not Defeated." *Journal of Commonweal* 90: 199–200.

Olorunnipa, Toluse, and Griff Witte. 2020. "Born with Two Strikes: How Systemic Racism Shaped Floyd's Life and Hobbled His Ambition." *The Washington Post*, October 8, 2020. https://www.washingtonpost.com/graphics/2020/national/george-floyd-america/systemic-racism/.

Olsen, Sarah, and Mario Telò, eds. 2022. *Queer Euripides: Re-Readings in Greek Tragedy*. London: Bloomsbury Publishing.

Olson, Douglas S. 1991. "Classical Mythology, Day 1: The Pilgrims, George Washington and Santa Claus." *The Classical World* 84: 295–301.

Osipovich, David. 2004. "What Rousseau Teaches Us about Live Theatrical Performance." *Journal of Aesthetics and Art Criticism* 62: 355–62.

Otten, Liam. 2001. "'The Darker Face of the Earth,' a St. Louis Premiere, at Edison." *Washington University Publications*, March 23, 2001, Digital Commons@Becker edition. https://digitalcommons.wustl.edu/cgi/viewcontent.cgi?article=1891&context=record.

Owens, Candace, dir. 2022. *George Floyd Didn't Deserve It, But He Also Wasn't a Saint*. https://www.youtube.com/watch?v=BlRgAN7yoJs.

Page, Clarence. 1991. "Thomas' Sister's Life Gives Lie to His Welfare Fable." *The Chicago Tribune*, July 24, 1991. https://www.chicagotribune.com/news/ct-xpm-1991-07-24-9103220246-story.html.

Papanikolaou, Dimitris. 2017. *Singing Poets: Literature and Popular Music in France and Greece*. New York: Taylor & Francis.

Pareles, Jon. 1983. "Pop/Jazz; Gospel Choir Goes Greek for Next Wave Festival." *The New York Times*, November 11, 1983. https://www.nytimes.com/1983/11/11/arts/pop-jazz-gospel-choir-goes-greek-for-next-wave-festival.html.

Parker, Jan, and Timothy Mathews, eds. 2011. *Tradition, Translation, Trauma: The Classic and the Modern*. Oxford: Oxford University Press.

Parks, Suzan-Lori. 2005. "New Black Math." *Theatre Journal* 57: 576–583.

Patterson, Orlando. 1999. *Rituals of Blood: The Consequences of Slavery in Two American Centuries*. Revised. New York: Civitas.

Patterson, Orlando, ed. 2016. *The Cultural Matrix: Understanding Black Youth*. Cambridge, MA: Harvard University Press.

Patterson, Orlando. 2018. *Slavery and Social Death: A Comparative Study*. 2nd edition. Cambridge, MA: Harvard University Press.

Paulson, Michael. 2020a. "Broadway, Symbol of New York Resilience, Shuts Down Amid Virus." *The New York Times*, March 12, 2020. https://www.nytimes.com/2020/03/12/theater/coronavirus-broadway-shutdown.html.

Paulson, Michael. 2020b. "Theater Artists of Color Enumerate Demands for Change." *The New York Times*, July 10, 2020.

Payette, Nicolas, ed. 2012. *Connected Minds: Cognition and Interaction in the Social World*. Cambridge: Cambridge Scholars Publishing.

Peck, Raoul, dir. 2016. *I Am Not Your Negro*. Magnolia Pictures, Amazon Studios.

Peirce, Kimberly, dir. 1999. *Boys Don't Cry*.

Pérez-Peña, Richard. 2017. "Woman Linked to 1955 Emmett Till Murder Tells Historian Her Claims Were False." *The New York Times*, January 27, 2017, sec. U.S. https://www.nytimes.com/2017/01/27/us/emmett-till-lynching-carolyn-bryant-donham.html.

Pierce, Brooke. 2002. "Helen, Review." *Theater Mania*, April 10, 2002. https://www.theatermania.com/new-york-city-theater/reviews/helen_2074.html.

Pilger, Lori. 2021. "Nebraska Supreme Court Justices Grapple with Latest Challenge to Condemned Killer's Death Sentence." *Lincoln Journal Star*, February. https://journalstar.com/news/state-and-regional/govt-and-politics/nebraska-supreme-court-justices-grapple-with-latest-challenge-to-condemned-killers-death-sentence/article_ee684b65-f856-544f-bd31-57a6d25d1c0e.html.

Pineda, Dorany. 2020. "Mark Blum Actor Dead FromComplications of COVID-19." *The Los Angeles Times*, March 25, 2020. https://www.latimes.com/obituaries/story/2020-03-26/mark-blum-actor-dead-coronavirus.

Pinsky, Robert. 2005. "A Recurrent American Nightmare ... " *The Washington Post*, September 11, 2005. https://www.washingtonpost.com/archive/entertainment/books/2005/09/11/a-recurrent-american-nightmare/63f3ebf7-e694-4b9f-a40e-b3233ede5fc3/.

Pollard, Sam, dir. 2020. *MLK/FBI*.

Powers, Melinda. 2018. *Diversifying Greek Tragedy on the Contemporary US Stage*. Oxford: Oxford University Press.

Quarcoo, Ashley, and Medina Husakovic'. 2021. "Racial Reckoning in the United States: Expanding and Innovating on the Global Transitional Justice Experience."

Carnegie Endowment for International Peace (blog). October 26, 2021. https://carnegieendowment.org/2021/10/26/racial-reckoning-in-united-states-expanding-and-innovating-on-global-transitional-justice-experience-pub-85638.

Rankine, Patrice. 2005. "Passing as Tragedy: Philip Roth's The Human Stain, the Oedipus Myth, and the Self-Made Man." *Critique: Studies in Contemporary Fiction* 47: 101–12.

———. 2006. *Ulysses in Black: Ralph Ellison, Classicism, and African American Literature*. Madison: University of Wisconsin Press.

———. 2013. *Aristotle and Black Drama: A Theater of Civil Disobedience*. Waco, TX: Baylor University Press.

———. 2019. "Aftermath: Du Bois, Classical Humanism and the Matter of Black Lives." *International Journal of the Classical Tradition* 26: 86–96.

Rao, Rahul. 2020. *Out of Time: The Queer Politics of Postcoloniality*. Oxford: Oxford University Press.

Rathje, Steve, Lear Hackel, and Jami Zaki. 2021. "Attending Live Theatre Improves Empathy, Changes Attitudes, and Leads to pro-Social Behavior." *Journal of Experimental Social Psychology* 95.

Reagan, Ronald. 1980a. "1980 Presidential Forum." *Ronald Reagan Presidential Library & Museum* (blog). April 23, 1980. https://www.reaganlibrary.gov/archives/speech/1980-presidential-forum.

———. 1980b. "Ronald Reagan and John Anderson Presidential Debate." *Ronald Reagan Presidential Library & Museum* (blog). September 21, 1980. https://www.reaganlibrary.gov/archives/speech/ronald-reagan-and-john-anderson-presidential-debate.

———. 1980c. "1980 Ronald Reagan and Jimmy Carter Presidential Debate." *Ronald Reagan Presidential Library & Museum* (blog). October 28, 1980. https://www.reaganlibrary.gov/archives/speech/1980-ronald-reagan-and-jimmy-carter-presidential-debate.

———. 1980d. "Election Eve Address: 'A Vision for America'." (blog). November 3, 1980. https://www.reaganlibrary.gov/archives/speech/election-eve-address-vision-america.

———. 1983. "Question-and-Answer Session with High School Students on Domestic and Foreign Policy Issues." *Ronald Reagan Presidential Library & Museum* (blog). January 21, 1983. https://www.reaganlibrary.gov/archives/speech/question-and-answer-session-high-school-students-domestic-and-foreign-policy-2.

Redden, Elizabeth. 2021. "Increasing Police." *Inside Higher Education*, December 15, 2021. https://www.insidehighered.com/news/2021/12/15/u-chicago-confronts-increase-violent-crime-around-campus.

Reilly, Charles. 1994. *Conversations with Amiri Baraka*. Jackson: University Press of Mississippi.

Reinhold, Meyer. 1984. *Classica Americana: The Greek and Roman Heritage in the United States*. Detroit, MI: Wayne State University Press.

Reuben, Anthony. 2020. "Coronavirus: Why Have There Been so Many Outbreaks in Meat Processing Plants?" *The British Broadcasting Company*, June 23, 2020. https://www.bbc.com/news/53137613.

Rhodes-Pitts, Sharifa. 2011. *Harlem Is Nowhere: A Journey to the Mecca of Black America*. Reprint. New York: Black Bay Books.

Richard, Carl J. 1994. *The Founders and the Classics: Greece, Rome, and the American Enlightenment*. Cambridge, MA: Harvard University Press.

Richardson, Heather Cox. 2020. *How the South Won the Civil War: Oligarchy, Democracy, and the Continuing Fight for the Soul of America*. Oxford: Oxford University Press.

Richmond, Todd. 2021. "Judge: Prosecutors Can't Show Rittenhouse Link to Proud Boys." *Associated Press*, September 17, 2021. https://apnews.com/article/wisconsin-police-trials-gun-politics-kenosha-8cd887f731ace320bf945f9524ceb252.

Rodriquez, Tessie J. 2009. *Understanding Human Behavior*. Rex.

Roe, Mark J. 1998. "Backlash." *Columbia Law Review* 98: 217–41.

Rojas, Rick. 2022. "Mississippi Grand Jury Declines to Indict Woman in Emmett Till Murder Case." *The New York Times*, August 9, 2022.

Rousseau, Jean-Jacques. 1968 [1758]. *Politics and the Arts:* Letter to d'Alembert on Theater. Translated, with notes and introduction by Allan Bloom. Agora Editions.

Roynon, Tessa. 2014. *Toni Morrison and the Classical Tradition: Transforming American Culture*. Oxford: Oxford University Press.

Roynon, Tessa. 2021. *The Classical Tradition in Modern American Fiction*. Edinburgh: Edinburgh University Press.

Rythoven, Eric Van. 2018. "On Backlash: Emotion and the Politicisation of Security." *European Review of International Studies* 5: 139–60.

Said, Edward W. 1979. *Orientalism*. New York: Vintage Press.

Sanders, Chad. 2020. "I Don't Need 'Love' Texts from My White Friends: I Need Them to Fight Anti-Blackness." *The New York Times*, June 5, 2020. https://www.nytimes.com/2020/06/05/opinion/whites-anti-blackness-protests.html.

Schanberg, Sydney H. 1984. "The Stewart Case." *The New York Times*, January 14, 1984. https://www.nytimes.com/1984/01/14/opinion/new-york-the-stewart-case.html.

Schechner, Richard. 1970. *Dionysus in '69*. First edition. New York: Farrar, Straus, & Giroux.

Schechner, Richard. 2000. *Environmental Theater*. Expanded, Subsequent. New York: Applause.

Scott, Eugene. 2018. "How the Willie Horton Story Factors into George H.W. Bush's Legacy." *The Washington Post*, December 3, 2018. https://www.washingtonpost.com/politics/2018/12/03/how-willie-horton-ad-factors-into-george-hw-bushs-legacy/.

Scott, James C. 2020. *Seeing Like a State: How Certain Schemes to Improve the Human Condition Have Failed*. New Haven, CT: Yale University Press.

Sedano, Michael. 2008. "Oedipus the Pinto," *La Bloga*, February 19. https://labloga.blogspot.com/2008/02/oedipus-pinto.html.

Senghor, Léopold Sédar. 1998. *The Collected Poems*. Trans. Melvin Dixon. Charlottesville: University of Virginia Press.

Serafin, Steven, and Susan Yung, eds. 2018. *BAM: Next Wave Festival*. New York: Print Matters Productions, Inc.

Shange, Ntozake. 1997. for colored girls who have considered suicide / when the rainbow is enuf. Reprint edition. New York: Scribner.

Shange, Ntozake, and Brenda Lyons. 1987. "Interview with Ntozake Shange." *The Massachusetts Review* 28: 687–96.

Shange, Ntozake, and Marlon B. Ross. 2014. "An Interview with Ntozake Shange." *Callaloo* 37: 486–89.

Shenk, Joshua Wolf. 2002. "Beyond a Black-and-White Lincoln." *The New York Times*. April 7, 2002. https://www.nytimes.com/2002/04/07/theater/theater-beyond-a-black-and-white-lincoln.html.

Shields, John C. 2001. *The American Aeneas: Classical Origins of the American Self*. Knoxville: University of Tennessee Press.

Shimamura, Arthur P. 2014. "Remembering the Past: Neural Substrates Underlying Episodic Encoding and Retrieval." *Current Directions in Psychological Science* 23: 257–63.

Shlien, John. 1959. "Santa Claus: The Myth in America." *ETC: A Review of General Semantics* 16: 389–400.

Smith, Anna Deavere. 1993. *Fires in the Mirror*. First edition. New York; Anchor.

Smith, Anna Deavere. 2019. *Notes from the Field: Doing Time in Education*. New York: Anchor.

Snow, Anita. 2020. "AP Tally: Arrests at Widespread US Protests Hit 10,000." *Associated Press*, June 4, 2020. https://apnews.com/article/american-protests-us-news-arrests-minnesota-burglary-bb2404f9b13c8b53b94c73f818f6a0b7.

Soloski, Alexis. 2020. "The Apple Family's Check-in on Zoom." *The New York Times*, April 25, 2020. https://www.nytimes.com/2020/04/25/theater/richard-nelson-apple-play-zoom-coronavirus.html?action=click&module=RelatedLinks&pgtype=Article.

Soyinka, Wole. 1989. *Aké: The Years of Childhood*. New York: Vintage Press.

Soyinka, Wole. 1990. *Myth, Literature and the African World*. Reprint. Cambridge: Cambridge University Press.

Soyinka, Wole. 2004. *The Bacchae of Euripides: A Communion Rite*. New York: W.W. Norton & Company.

Spivak, Gayatri Chakravorty. 2013. "Ghostwriting." In *The Spectralities Reader: Ghosts and Haunting in Contemporary Cultural Theory*, 317ff. London: Bloomsbury Academy.

Stageman, Sam. 2017. "Whitewashing of the Stonewall Riots." *Digital Commons@ WOU*. https://digitalcommons.wou.edu/cgi/viewcontent.cgi?article=1137&context=honors_theses.

Staley, Gregory A. 2010. Seneca and the Idea of Tragedy. New York: Oxford University Press.

Stall, Hampton, David Foran, and Hari Prasad. 2020. "What's in a Meme? The Rise of 'Saint Kyle.'" *Global Network on Extremism & Technology* (blog). October 29, 2020. https://gnet-research.org/2020/10/29/whats-in-a-meme-the-rise-of-saint-kyle/.

Steinmetz, Katy. 2015. "See Obama's 20-Year Evolution on LGBT Rights." *Time*, April 10, 2015. https://time.com/3816952/obama-gay-lesbian-transgender-lgbt-rights/.

Sulcas, Roslyn. 2018. "In an Oedipal Opera, Londoners Chant, Curse and Brawl." *The New York Times*, December 1, 2018. https://www.nytimes.com/2018/11/30/arts/music/turnage-greek-bam-opera.html.

Taubman, Howard. 1964. "Theater: 'Blues for Mister Charlie.'" *The New York Times*, April 24, 1964. https://archive.nytimes.com/www.nytimes.com/books/98/03/29/specials/baldwin-charlie.html?module=inline.

The JBHE Foundation, ed. 2000. "The Bell Curve Goes Belly Up." *The Journal of Blacks in Higher Education* 30: 32.

"The Washington Post's Biography of George Floyd to Be Published by Viking." 2021. *WashPost PR Blog* (blog). November 10, 2021. https://www.washingtonpost.com/pr/2021/11/10/washington-posts-biography-george-floyd-be-published-by-viking/.

The New York Times. 1976. "'Welfare Queen' Becomes Issue in Reagan Campaign," February 15, 1976. https://www.nytimes.com/1976/02/15/archives/welfare-queen-becomes-issue-in-reagan-campaign-hitting-a-nerve-now.html.

Thompson, Krissah. 2016. "Painful but Crucial: Why You'll See Emmett Till's Casket at the African American Museum." *The Washington Post*, August 18, 2016, sec. Style. https://www.washingtonpost.com/lifestyle/style/painful-but-crucial-why-youll-see-emmett-tills-casket-at-the-african-american-museum/2016/08/18/66d1dc2e-484b-11e6-acbc-4d4870a079da_story.html.

Thompson, Robert Farris. 1984. *Flash of the Spirit: African & Afro-American Art & Philosophy*. First edition. New York: Vintage Press.

Tillet, Salamishah. 2021. "Finding Redemption and Rebirth on the Road to Broadway." *The New York Times*, September 23, 2021. https://www.nytimes.com/2021/09/23/theater/pass-over-broadway.html.

Toobin, Jeffrey. 2002. "The Driver: Did the Prosecutors in the Louima Case Have the Right Man All Along?" *The New Yorker*, June 2, 2002. https://www.newyorker.com/magazine/2002/06/10/the-driver-2.

Tran, Diep. 2017. "The Review That Shook Chicago." *American Theatre*, June 27, 2017. https://www.americantheatre.org/2017/06/27/the-review-that-shook-chicago/.

Turan, Kenneth, and Joseph Papp. 2009. *Free for All: Joe Papp, The Public, and the Greatest Theater Story Ever Told*. New York: Anchor.

Turner, Victor. 1979. "Dramatic Ritual/Ritual Drama: Performative and Reflexive Anthropology." *The Kenyon Review* 1: 80–93.

Turner, Victor. 2001. *From Ritual to Theatre: The Human Seriousness of Play*. Later print edition. PAJ Publications.

Tyson, Timothy. 2017. *The Blood of Emmett Till*. New York: Simon & Schuster.

Van Weyenberg, Astrid. 2013. *The Politics of Adaptation: Contemporary African Drama and Greek Tragedy*. New York: Rodopi.

Vellacott, Phillip, trans. 1962. *The Oresteian Trilogy*. 4th Printing edition. Penguin Books.

Vogel, Kenneth P., Jim Rutenberg, and Lisa Lerer. 2020. "The Quiet Hand of Conservative Groups in the Anti-Lockdown Protests." *The New York Times*, April 21, 2020. https://www.nytimes.com/2020/04/21/us/politics/coronavirus-protests-trump.html.

Vorenberg, James. 1972. "The War on Crime: The First Five Years." *The Atlantic*, May 1972. https://www.theatlantic.com/past/docs/politics/crime/crimewar.htm.

Weiss, Heidi. 2017. "'Pass Over' Envisions a Godot-like Endgame for Young Black Men." *Chicago Sun Times*, June 13, 2017. https://chicago.suntimes.com/2017/6/13/18440050/pass-over-envisions-a-godot-like-endgame-for-young-black-men.

Wilderson, Frank B. III. 2020. *Afropessimism*. New York: Liveright.

Wilkerson, Isabel. 2020. *Caste: The Origins of Our Discontent*. New York: Random House.

Wilson, August. 1997. "The Ground on Which I Stand." *Callaloo* 20: 493–503.

Wilson, Jason. 2020. "The Rightwing Groups behind Wave of Protests against Covid-19 Restrictions." *The Guardian*, April 17, 2020. https://www.theguardian.com/world/2020/apr/17/far-right-coronavirus-protests-restrictions.

Wilson, Jonathan, dir. 2001. *Oedipus the King*. Videotape. Hartford, CT.

Winterer, Caroline. 2004. *The Culture of Classicism: Ancient Greece and Rome in American Intellectual Life: 1780–1910*. Baltimore, MD: Johns Hopkins Press.

Wolin, Sheldon S. 2017. *Democracy Incorporated: Managed Democracy and the Specter of Inverted Totalitarianism*. New Edition. Princeton, NJ: Princeton University Press.

Woolfe, Zachary. 2018. "Review: An Opera Updates Oedipus, with Peroxide-Blond Hair." *The New York Times*, December 6, 2018. https://www.nytimes.com/2018/12/06/arts/music/review-greek-bam.html.

Wright, David. 1990. "The Festive Year: Wole Soyinka's Annus Mirabilis." *The Journal of Modern African Studies* 28: 511–19.

Yancy, George, and Judith Butler. 2015. "What's Wrong with 'All Lives Matter?'" *The New York Times*, January 12, 2015. https://archive.nytimes.com/opinionator.blogs.nytimes.com/2015/01/12/whats-wrong-with-all-lives-matter/.

Zaborowska, Magdalena J. 2009. *James Baldwin's Turkish Decade: Erotics of Exile*. Durham, NC: Duke University Press.

Zeitlin, Froma I. 2004. "Dionysus in 69." In *Dionysus Since 69: Greek Tragedy at the Dawn of the Third Millennium*, Revised. Oxford: Oxford University Press.